ENFORCING EC LAW

Josephine Steiner, BA, LLB

BLACKSTONE
PRESS LIMITED

First published in Great Britain 1995 by Blackstone Press Limited,
9-15 Aldine Street, London W12 8AW. Telephone: 0181-740 1173

© J. Steiner, 1995

ISBN: 1 85431 320 7

British Library Cataloguing in Publication Data
A CIP catalogue record for this book is available from the British Library.

Typeset by Montage Studios Ltd, Tonbridge, Kent
Printed by Livesey Ltd, Shrewsbury, Shropshire

ONE WEEK LOAN

Renew Books on PHONE-it: 01443 654456

Books are to be returned on or before the last date below

Contents

The scope of Community law — The EC institutions and their role in the legislative process — EC legislation — General principles of law — The problems of enforcement

The principle of direct effects — The principle of indirect effect — The principle of state liability for breach of Community law — The principle of supremacy of EC law — Application of Community law in the UK

Preface

In the member states of the European Union few areas of domestic law are now untouched by EC law. Where Community law exists, whether in the form of Treaty provisions, Regulations, Directives or Decisions, it is capable of giving rise to rights and obligations for individuals. These rights may be invoked, and obligations challenged, in actions before domestic courts, as well as, indeed, to a greater extent than, before Community courts. As the body of Community law increases, and public awareness of its potential, grows, questions of enforcement of Community law have rightly become an area of major concern for lawyers.

Although national courts are not required in principle to provide special remedies and procedures in actions before them based on EC law, they are obliged, both by their general obligation under the EC treaty and by rulings of the European Court, to ensure effective judicial protection for individuals' Community rights. The application of that principle has resulted in significant modifications of national law in all member states. *Francovich* v *Italian State* introduced a new principle of state liability in damages for breaches of Community law: *Emmott* v *Minister for Social Welfare* has affected the application of national limitation rules; *Marshall* v *Southampton AHA (No. 2)* has laid down a principle of full compensation for damage resulting from infringements of EC sex discrimination rules. The full implications of these decisions have yet to be explored.

The purpose of this book is to examine the principles and problems relating to the provision of remedies for breaches of EC law, whether by member states, Community institutions or individuals. It will consider the ways in which domestic law, particularly, but by no means exclusively, in the United Kingdom, has been changed, and may be required further to change, to meet the demands of EC law. Its principal focus will be on the protection of the rights of individuals, 'natural or legal persons', in actions before domestic courts.

Whilst many books examine the remedies provided under the EC Treaty before the European Courts, no book has so far comprehensively addressed the many problems, academic and practical, arising from the enforcement of Community law by national courts, which now play a major role in enforcing Community law. Nevertheless, since any assessment of the effectiveness of the system of judicial protection of individuals under Community law requires an examination of the full range of remedies, both before the Court of Justice and before national courts, the remedies available before the European courts will also be considered, as well as other informal methods of enforcement.

My thanks go to all those who helped in the preparation of this book: to my many colleagues, for providing insights into the problems in their particular field; to my fellow EC lawyers, particularly Clare Campbell in Sheffield and John Tillotson in Manchester: to Julia Dagg, for her assistance in the library: to my ever willing and efficient secretary Shirley Peacock; and finally to my family, for their unfailing interest and support.

Table of cases

Court of Justice of the European Communities

Cases have been arranged in chronological order by case number and year. See page xvii for alphabetical list of European Communities Court of Justice cases.

Court of Justice of the European Communities

Cases have been arranged in alphabetical order. See page xi for numerical list of European Communities Court of Justice cases.

French Courts

United Kingdom Courts

United States Courts

European Court of Human Rights

Table of UK statutes

Table of UK secondary legislation

Table of European Community Treaties

Table of European Community secondary legislation

PART ONE

Introduction

ONE

The need for enforcement

As the Court of Justice said in 1963, in the landmark case of *Van Gend en Loos Nederlandse Administratie der Belastingen* (case 26/62), the European Community

constitutes a new legal order in international law, for whose benefit the states have limited their sovereign rights . . . and the subjects of which comprise not only the member states but also their nationals.

Whilst some may dispute the unique nature of this new legal order (see Wyatt, D., 'New Legal Order or Old?' (1982) 7 EL Rev 147) there is no doubt that the law stemming from the three EC treaties comprising the European Coal and Steel Community (ECSC) Treaty 1951, the Euratom Treaty 1957 and the European Economic Community (EEC) Treaty 1957, renamed the Economic Community (EC) by the Treaty on European Union 1992, differs from traditional international law in a number of important respects. First, the Treaties, particularly the EC Treaty, are much more extensive in their scope than most international agreements, embracing many areas of activity normally reserved to national law alone; secondly they created a strong framework of institutions, endowed with the power to make laws, binding on states and individuals, on all matters within their scope; and thirdly, and as a result of the first two factors, EC law is exceptional in the extent to which it penetrates domestic law, creating rights and obligations enforceable by and even against individuals before their national courts. These characteristics, taken together, have resulted in an immense and ever-growing body of Community law, existing alongside and often conflicting with domestic law, and enforceable, directly or indirectly, within domestic legal systems.

Because of its 'special' nature the enforcement of EC law raises particular problems for English lawyers. It requires a new approach to interpretation; the application of new techniques and principles; the modification of national remedies and procedures, sometimes the introduction of new remedies and procedures. If EC rights are to be effectively protected, and EC obligations challenged, it is necessary for domestic lawyers to be aware both of the scope, nature and effect of Community law, and of the principles relevant to its enforcement, whether before the Court of Justice, or, more importantly, before the courts of member states. These problems and principles will form the subject matter of this book. Since the ECSC and Euratom Treaties create separate régimes, subject to special rules, and are confined to the specific and limited areas of coal and steel and atomic energy, the focus of this book will be on the enforcement of the law arising from the European Community Treaty. Although most of the principles relevant to the enforcement of EC law will apply to all three Community treaties, the ECSC and Euratom Treaties are more limited in scope, and tend to be interpreted by the Court restrictively (e.g., *HJ Banks & Co.* v *British Coal Corporation* (case C 128/92)).

THE SCOPE OF COMMUNITY LAW

If the goals of the original EEC Treaty were, as its name implied, primarily economic, they were so in the widest sense. The treaty was from the beginning much more than a free trade agreement. The Community's activities, outlined in Article 3 EEC, were to include the elimination of all internal barriers to the free movement of goods, persons, services and capital (the common or single 'internal market', see now Article 7a EC); the approximation of the laws of member states to the extent required for the proper functioning of the common market (Article 100 EEC); the harmonisation of indirect taxation (Articles 95–99); the establishment of common policies in the spheres of agriculture and transport and the creation of a Community competition policy. States were to co-ordinate their economic policies 'in order that disequilibria in their balances of payments might be remedied'. In the field of external affairs the Community was to establish a common customs tariff and a common commercial policy towards countries outside the EEC ('third countries') and to 'associate with overseas countries in order to increase trade and to promote jointly economic and social development'. The Community thus had extensive internal and external competence in economic matters.

But even at the outset the goals of the EEC were not purely economic. The preamble of the EEC Treaty expressed the resolve of member states 'to ensure the economic and social progress of their countries'; their essential objective being the 'constant improvement of the living and working conditions of their peoples'. Articles 117–128 provided for action in the field of social policy, requiring states to promote improved working conditions and improved living standards for workers. Article 119 provided a principle of equal pay for equal work for men and women, the purpose of which, according to the European Court, was both economic, to remove the competitive advantage of a (normally) cheaper workforce in states which failed to provide for equal pay, and social (*Defrenne* v *Sabena (No. 2)*, case 43/75)).

If the sphere of Community competence was large even at the Community's inception, it has been greatly extended since then, either by action by the EC institutions under Article 235, which allows the institutions to 'take the appropriate measures' if action by the Community 'should prove necessary to attain ... one of the objectives of the Community and this Treaty has not provided the necessary powers', or by amendments to the EEC Treaty provided by subsequent treaties, the Single European Act (1986) and the Treaty on European Union (the Maastricht Treaty (1992)). Article 235 formed the basis for the Community's regional policy in the 1970s and for measures in the sphere of consumer and environmental protection, as well as for legislation to promote the health and safety of workers and research and technological development. Community competence in all these areas was expressly recognised in the Single European Act 1986. The Single European Act also provided for the first time for co-operation (as opposed to 'co-ordination') in the field of economic and monetary policy and for co-operation in matters of security and foreign policy.

The Treaty on European Union (TEU) took matters a stage further by providing for a gradual progression towards full economic and monetary union including the creation of a common currency by 1 January 1999 (with permission to opt out for Britain and Denmark). It introduced the concept of citizenship of the Union, and provided for the creation of a floor of rights for Union citizens (Article 8 EC). A Protocol on Social Policy attached to the treaty, from which Britain opted out, declared as its objectives

the promotion of employment, improved living and working conditions, proper social protection, dialogue between management and labour, the development of human resources with a view to lasting high employment and the combating of exclusion (Article 1).

The Community was required to develop trans-European networks (Article 129b EC) and to contribute to the development of education and vocational training and the flowering of European culture (Articles 126, 127, 128 EC), albeit in these latter cases in a supporting role, 'supplementing' and 'encouraging' the actions of member states, pursuant to the principle of subsidiarity.

As well as amending the EC Treaty the treaty on European Union provided for co-operation with a view to the framing of common policies in the fields of foreign and security policy, and eventually defence (Title V TEU, Article J), and in justice and home affairs (Title VI TEU, Article K). These matters remain strictly intergovernmental, in the nature of a 'normal' international agreement and outside the institutional framework of the EC treaty; as such they will not be subject to the jurisdiction of the European Court, nor will they be the concern of the British courts. When member states are acting under these provisions of the TEU they are acting as members of the European Union. The term 'European Community' will continue to apply to matters pertaining specifically to the EC treaty.

It is clear from the above brief outline that the scope of the law stemming from the EC treaty, and of Community competence, is now extremely wide.

Within this area of competence the Community institutions have power, subject only to the limitations provided by the treaty, to pass laws, binding on states and individuals. As well as provisions of the EC Treaty which may be enforced by national courts, there now exists a substantial body of EC secondary legislation in all the areas of activity outlined above, fleshing out the basic principles of the treaty. Much of this law is directly enforceable within national legal systems. Where it is not it may be necessary for national courts to take it into account in interpreting national law. The Index of Community Activities listed in the Directory of Community Legislation in force, Official Journal (OJ) of the European Communities, which is set out in Table I in the Appendix, indicates the range of Community law. All EC secondary legislation is published in the Official Journal (L) series; it is listed, analytically (Volume I) and chronologically (Volume II), with the appropriate OJ reference, in the Directory itself.

THE EC INSTITUTIONS AND THEIR ROLE IN THE LEGISLATIVE PROCESS

The four principal Community Institutions, set up by the EEC treaty, and, since the passing of the Merger Treaty 1965, common to all three EC communities, are the Commission, the Council of Ministers, the European Parliament and the European Court, the Court of Justice. The first three are concerned, inter alia, in the enactment of Community secondary legislation in the form of Regulations, Directives and Decisions. The Court's duty is to see 'that the law is observed' (Article 164). Since 1989 it has been assisted by the Court of First Instance.

The Commission

The Commission is the executive of the Community, a wholly impartial body ('it shall neither seek nor take instructions from any . . . other body' (Article 10, Merger Treaty)). It is divided into a number of Directorates-General, each headed by a Director-General, responsible for different areas of community policy (the 'portfolio') (see Table 2 in the Appendix). One of the Commission's principal functions is to introduce proposals for legislation, either under the general provision of Article 235, or under more specific provisions governing particular areas (e.g., Article 87, competition law, Article 100a, internal market). Most major legislation originates from the Commission following wide-ranging consultation with government representatives and interested bodies from the member states, many of which maintain a permanent presence in Brussels. It also has its own power to issue Decisions (Article 155). In its executive capacity it plays a major role in the implementation of Community policy acting under authorising Regulations approved by the Council of Ministers. It also has an important watchdog role, monitoring the implementation of Community law by member states and even by individuals. It has primary responsibility for enforcing EC competition policy.

The Council of Ministers

The Council of Ministers consists of representatives of the member states. They are members of national governments, normally government ministers, chosen to represent their state according to their expertise in the particular subject under discussion. It is thus not a permanent body and it is a political body, although it is required 'to ensure that the objectives set out in [the] Treaty are attained' (Article 145). It is the Council which is generally required under the treaty to approve EC legislation, either unanimously, or (rarely) by a majority of its members, or, increasingly, by qualified majority. The qualified majority system is a system of weighted voting, under which the bigger states have a larger number of votes, ranging from ten (France, Germany, Italy, the UK, i.e., the 'big four'), to two (Luxembourg). Since 1 January 1995, with the accession of the three new member states, Austria, Sweden and Finland the required number for a qualified majority is 62 out of a total of 87 votes, with a 'blocking minority' vote of 26. Thus it is possible for two big states or up to six small states to be outvoted. The Treaty prescribes the majority required for the particular measure, depending on its nature. For example Article 235, the 'blanket' law-making provision and Article 100, which provides for the approximation of such provisions of domestic law as directly affect the common market, require unanimity. Article 100a, which was introduced by the Single European Act 1986, allowed (with exception in Article 100a(2) for fiscal provisions, or measures relating to the free movement of persons or to the rights and interests of employed persons) for legislation by qualified majority 'by way of derogation from Article 100' for measures designed to achieve the internal market. In order to speed up the decision-making process the Single European Act and now the TEU have increased the number of measures which may be passed by qualified majority. This clearly has an impact on national sovereignty.

The European Parliament

Although it is the only institution of the EC which is democratically elected, direct elections having been introduced in 1979, the European Parliament is not a parliament in the real sense. It is not itself a law-making body, although its role in the law-making process has been steadily increasing over the last ten years. Originally it was required by the Treaty to be *consulted* by the Council on proposals for legislation in a number of specific (and important) areas (e.g., Articles 54, 87, 235). However, whilst the Council was obliged to consider Parliament's opinion in these areas it was not obliged to follow it. In 1977 conciliation procedures were introduced, extending the consultation process and in 1986 the Single European Act introduced new *co-operation* procedures, which further increased Parliament's powers. Whilst it could not block legislation its opposition could impose on the Council a requirement of unanimous approval where a qualified majority would have sufficed under the treaty. Finally, with the Maastricht Treaty, Parliament has been given powers of *co-decision* with the Council in certain defined areas (e.g., Article 100a).

Under the co-decision procedures Parliament may, ultimately, veto legislation by an absolute majority of its component members. The co-operation and co-decision procedures are now laid down in Articles 189(c) and 189(b) respectively.

In addition to these four institutions another EC institution, the *Economic and Social Committee*, may also be required by the Treaty to be consulted in the law-making process. A new body, the *Committee of the Regions*, was created at Maastricht, also with a consultative role.

The procedures prescribed in the Treaty as to consultation and voting requirements must be followed. Legislation adopted in breach of these procedures may be annulled (see Chapters 8 and 9). Since different provisions of the Treaty impose different requirements, some more onerous than others, and since there may be an element of flexibility in the institutions' choice of legal base, there being some overlap between different treaty provisions, that choice may need to be scrutinised to ensure its correctness. It has on occasions been successfully challenged (see *European Parliament* v *Council* (case C 295/90): Students' Rights of Residence Directive annulled).

The European Courts

The Court of Justice, the principal court of the European Communities, has jurisdiction to act on cases brought directly before it or on reference from national courts or tribunals under the preliminary rulings procedure of Article 177 (see Chapters 4 and 8). The Court of First Instance has no jurisdiction under Article 177. Its principal jurisdiction is in respect of actions against the Community by 'natural or legal persons' under Article 173 (action for annulment), Article 175 (action for failure to act), and Article 215(2) (action for damages) (see Chapters 9 and 10) and 'staff cases', disputes between the Community and its servants under Article 179 EC.

The Court of Justice is the supreme arbiter on all matters of Community law. Since the EC treaty is a 'framework' treaty, many of its provisions being expressed in broad general principles, and even EC secondary legislation, unlike UK law, can be imprecise in its terms, much of the Court's work consists in adding flesh to the bones of Community law, filling in the legislative gaps according to the 'spirit and purpose' of the legislation in question. In this respect 'its law-making function cannot be overestimated' (Schwartze J, 1992). It is not afraid to interpret against the prima facie meaning of a provision in order to achieve a result which is more consistent with its purpose. In assessing its purpose it draws heavily on the preambles to legislation (see Table 3 in the Appendix); where relevant it will also consider its legislative history. In interpreting Community law, and particularly domestic law designed to give effect to Community law, national courts are required to adopt the same teleological approach (see e.g., Lord Diplock in *R* v *Henn and Darby* [1981] AC 850), although they do not have the same freedom to develop Community law. Faced with a lacuna or ambiguity in EC law they are advised, sometimes obliged, to apply to the Court of Justice for interpretation under Article 177 (see Chapter 4).

EC LEGISLATION

The EC institutions have power under Article 189 EC to make Regulations, issue Directives, take Decisions, make Recommendations or deliver Opinions. Regulations, Directives and Decisions are all described as 'binding'. Recommendations and Opinions have 'no binding force', although they may be invoked as an aid to interpretation (*Grimaldi* v *Fonds des Maladies Professionelles* (case C 322/88)).

Regulations

'A Regulation shall have general application. It shall be binding in its entirety and directly applicable in all member states' (Article 189(2)).

Thus it has two distinguishing features. It is of 'general application', that is, it is *normative*, designed to apply to situations in the abstract and as a whole; and it is '*directly applicable* in all member states'; it is intended to take effect immediately, as it stands, within member states; it does not require implementation by national authorities (although it may occasionally do so).

Regulations are the most widely used of all Community instruments, being the principal vehicle employed in the detailed implementation of Community policies, most notably the Common Agricultural Policy.

Directives

A Directive is 'binding, as to the result to be achieved, upon each member state to which it is addressed, but shall leave to the national authorities the choice of form and methods' (Article 189(3)).

Thus Directives are addressed to member states and, unlike Regulations, they require implementation by national authorities, normally within a deadline specified in the Directive. They allow member states some discretion as to the form and method of implementation, but none as to the result to be achieved. They are not intended to be 'directly applicable'. They are designed to achieve the harmonisation or approximation of national legislation. They have been the principal instrument employed in the creation of the internal market.

Decisions

A Decision is 'binding in its entirety upon those to whom it is addressed' (Article 189(4)).

By contrast with a Regulation, a Decision is an *individual* act, with a particular addressee. It may be addressed to a state, or a number of states, or to individuals, natural or legal persons. It is widely used by the Commission against individuals in the enforcement of EC competition policy.

Regulations, Directives and Decisions must 'state the reasons on which they are based and shall refer to any proposals or opinions which were required to be obtained pursuant to [the] Treaty' (Article 190). This will be done in the preamble to legislation (see Table 3 in the Appendix for an example of a preamble). Legislation which fails to comply with these requirements can be annulled (see Chapters 8 and 9).

Originally only Regulations were required under Article 191 to be published in the Official Journal of the Community (L Series), although most Directives and many Decisions were in fact published. Following the TEU 1992, which amended Article 191, Regulations, Directives and Decisions passed under the co-decision procedure of Article 189(b) must be published in the Official Journal, as must Directives which are addressed to all member states. Other Directives and Decisions must be notified to those to whom they are addressed and take effect upon such notification.

GENERAL PRINCIPLES OF LAW

In addition to the law derived from the EC Treaty and EC secondary legislation, the Court of Justice has introduced a further source of EC law in the form of general principles of law. The purpose of introducing general principles as part of the 'unwritten' law of the Community was to ensure that EC law did not conflict with law which states might regard as having special protected status, such as (in some states) obligations of international law or the law laid down in a written Constitution. Only if Community law could be guaranteed not to infringe these rights could its full application by national courts be secured.

The general principles held by the ECJ to be recognised and protected under Community law are those drawn from the 'constitutional traditions common to the member states' or from 'international treaties for the protection of human rights on which the member states have collaborated or of which they are signatories' (*J. Nold KG* v *Commission* (case 4/73)).

Whilst it is not necessary for the right or principle to be identical in all member states, the Court does appear to require evidence of the observance by all states of some common core of principle for it to be respected as part of Community law. Thus in *Hoechst* v *Commission* (cases 46/87 and 227/88) the Court distinguished between the right to the inviolability of the home, the 'private dwelling of physical persons', which was universally protected throughout the Community, and the protection against public intrusion offered to commercial premises, which was not. Only the former would be guaranteed as a general principle of Community law.

The principal treaty for the protection of human rights from which EC general principles may be derived is the European Convention on Human Rights and Fundamental Freedoms (ECHR 1953). A number of rights expressed in this treaty have already been adopted as principles of Community law. In *R* v *Kirk* (case 63/83) the principle of non-retroactivity of penal measures enshrined in Article 7 ECHR was applied. The right to judicial process guaranteed under Articles 6 and 13 ECHR was invoked by the Court in *Johnston* v *Royal Ulster Constabulary* (case 222/84). Here the Court found the Secretary of State's decision, described under the Northern Ireland (Sex Discrimination) Order as 'conclusive evidence' that the plaintiff's claim of sex discrimination was unfounded, to be in breach of this right. Adherence to the rights protected in the ECHR has now been made explicit in the Maastricht Treaty (Article F), although this was not incorporated into the EC Treaty. Other treaties suggested as possible sources of rights are the European Social Charter (1971) and Convention 111 of the International Labour Organisation (1958).

The category of general principles accepted as part of Community law is not closed. Principles so far adopted by the Court include the principles of equality (e.g., *Royal Scholten-Honig Holdings Ltd* v *Intervention Board for Agricultural Produce* (cases 103 and 145/77), proportionality (e.g., *Werner A. Bock KG* v *Commission* (case 62/70)) certainty, (which embraces the principles of non-retroactivity and the protection of legitimate expectations (e.g., *Defrenne* v *Sabena (No. 2)* (case 43/75)), the principle of unjust enrichment (*Amministrazione delle Finanze dello Stato* v *SpA San Giorgio* (case 199/82)), and procedural rights in the form of a right to a fair hearing (e.g., *Transocean Marine Paint Association* v *Commission* (case 17/74)), the duty to give reasons (e.g., *UNECTEF* v *Heylens* (case 222/86)) and the right of individuals to 'pursue their claims by judicial process after possible recourse to the competent authorities' ('due process', see *Johnston* v *RUC* (case 222/84)). The Court has also recognised a principle of legal professional privilege for independent (but not in-house) lawyers (*Australian Mining & Smelting Europe Ltd* v *Commission* (case 155/79)) and a limited privilege against self incrimination in criminal, and even punitive administrative proceedings (*Otto BV* v *Postbank NV* (case C 60/92) (see also *Funke* v *France* (case SA 256A) ECHR). These principles and their relevance will be discussed in more detail in further chapters of the book (Chapters 6, 8, 9 and 10). Whilst these principles are not absolute, and like all constitutional rights may have to give way to other, overriding rights, or pressing considerations of public or Community policy, they have proved valuable as a means of judicial control of acts or omissions of both the EC institutions and, albeit to a lesser extent, of the authorities of member states when acting (or failing to act) in a public capacity pursuant to obligations of Community law. General principles of law thus play an important role in the judicial review not only of Community action but of domestic measures adopted pursuant to obligations of Community law (see further chapters 6, 8 and 9)

THE PROBLEMS OF ENFORCEMENT

The wide scope of EC law, and the range and volume of EC secondary legislation, inevitably led to problems of enforcement. Both the EC treaty and secondary legislation impose extensive obligations on member states requiring, expressly or impliedly, the enactment or amendment or repeal of domestic laws in order to achieve Community objectives. Under Article 5 EEC states are obliged to

> take all appropriate measures, whether general or particular, to ensure
> fulfilment of the obligations arising out of this Treaty or resulting from

actions taken by the institutions of the Community. They shall facilitate the achievement of the Community's tasks.

They shall abstain from any measure which could jeopardise the attainment of the objectives of this Treaty.

Despite Article 5, states, sometimes deliberately, sometimes inadvertently, not infrequently failed to fulfil their Community obligations. Whilst procedures were provided under the Treaty for action by the Commission or by member states before the Court of Justice against states which had 'failed to fulfil their obligations' under Community law (Articles 169 and 170, see Chapter 11), these provisions proved insufficient on their own to secure the effective enforcement of EC law, for a number of reasons.

First, the Commission (or member state) may simply be unaware of breaches of Community law by member states. In a Community of twelve it is not possible for the Commission, with limited resources, effectively to monitor the laws and practices of all member states.

Secondly, although any person may complain to the Commission of suspected infringements of EC law by member states and request the Commission to act under Article 169, and the majority of Article 169 proceedings have been found to result from such complaints, an individual has no power to compel the Commission to act under Article 169. The Commission has a complete discretion in this matter (see *Alfons Lütticke GmbH* v *Commission* (case 48/65)). The enforcement of EC law against member states by Community institutions is a sensitive matter. The Commission may choose not to proceed against insignificant failures. Where the breach is clear, and significant, the Commission can, and often does, achieve compliance-by-negotiation at the preliminary stages of the Article 169 procedure; it will not then be necessary to proceed to the final stage before the Court. Yet Individuals may have suffered damage as a result of member states' prior actions in breach of EC law. They may have paid levies which were wrongfully imposed (e.g., *Alfons Lütticke GmbH* v *Commission* (case 48/65)); or deprived of rights, for example under Directives, which they would have enjoyed had states fulfilled their Community obligations.

Thirdly, even where the Commission proceeds to action before the Court under Article 169 and obtains a judgment under Article 171 that the state has 'failed to fulfil its Community obligations' the Court has no power to impose sanctions to guarantee compliance. The state is simply required to 'take the necessary measures' to comply with the Court's judgment. If the State fails to take the necessary measures the Commission must resort to fresh Article 169 proceedings for the state's failure to comply with the Court's judgment under Article 171. The Maastricht treaty amended Article 171 to enable the Court to impose, at the request of the Commission, an 'appropriate' lump sum or penalty payment on member states in these (second) proceedings if, following a time limit for compliance set by the Commission, they fail to take action. However only a lump sum or penalty payment may be imposed; there is no provision, as in the competition provisions (e.g., Regulation 17/62, Article 16) for periodic payments, or for the enforcement of fines and penalties. The Court has no power to withhold payment of Community funds to member states. Moreover even a second declaration that a state has failed to fulfil its Community obligations will not remedy past failures or provide compensation for those who suffer damage as a result of such failures.

Proceedings under Article 170 by a member state against a member state correspond closely to those of Article 169 and are subject to the same weaknesses as regards enforcement. Few such actions have reached the final stage before the Court.

As well as a need for an effective system of enforcement of EC law against *member states*, it was necessary to ensure that *EC institutions*, in exercising their extensive powers, particularly in the enactment of legislation binding on states and individuals, acted within the law. These institutions are obliged under Article 4 EC to act within the limits of the powers conferred upon them by the Treaty.

Although the EC Treaty provides for direct action before the ECJ by member states, EC institutions and even individuals ('natural or legal persons') for judicial review of acts and omissions of the EC institutions (Articles 173, 175, 184), and for actions for damages in respect of damage resulting from unlawful Community acts (Article 215(2)), access to these remedies for individuals and the remedies themselves are limited (see Chapters 9 and 10).

Thus in the absence of an effective and comprehensive system of enforcement of Community law against member states or Community institutions it was left to the Court to supplement the provisions of the Treaty, by providing alternative routes whereby individuals' Community rights might be protected, and Community obligations challenged, in actions before their national courts. This was achieved by the introduction of a number of important principles of Community law, the principles of direct effects, indirect effects, and state liability in damages on the principles laid down in *Francovich* v *Italian State* (cases C 6 and 9/90). These principles will now be considered.

TWO

The means of enforcement

THE PRINCIPLE OF DIRECT EFFECTS

Directly effective Community law is Community law which may be invoked directly by individuals before their national courts. Where it is directly effective it can be invoked to challenge or avoid the application of domestic measures which are inconsistent with Community law. It is not a new principle in international law. Treaty provisions are not infrequently given direct effect where the Treaty has been incorporated into domestic law and the provision in question was clearly designed to protect individual rights. However, the principle is significant in EC law because of the extent to which it applies, both to treaty provisions and secondary legislation, and the fact that it is applied to provisions which might not have been expected by reason of their nature to be directly effective.

Treaty Articles

The principle was introduced by the Court in the context of Treaty Articles in *Van Gend en Loos* (case 26/62). Here an individual was held entitled to invoke Article 12 EEC, which requires member states to 'refrain from introducing between themselves any new customs duties on imports or exports or any charges having equivalent effect', in order to challenge a domestic levy imposed in breach of this provision. Despite the fact that the obligation was addressed to states, and, as Advocate-General Roemer suggested, was too complex for application by national courts, it was held directly effective. The Court's decision was clearly policy based, designed both to protect individuals' Community rights and to secure the enforcement of EC law against states which had failed to fulfil their Community obligations. As the Court said,

The vigilance of individuals interested in protecting their rights creates an effective control additional to that entrusted by Articles 169 and 170 [see Chapter 11] to the diligence of the Commission and the member states.

It may be noted that the obligation in Article 12 EEC, although addressed to member states, was construed in *Van Gend en Loos* as intended to confer rights on individuals.

EC Secondary Legislation

Since only Regulations are described in Article 189 as 'directly applicable', that is, not requiring implementation by member states but intended to be applied directly, it was thought that only Regulations could be directly effective. This has not proved to be the case. In a series of cases the Court has held that Directives, Decisions, and even provisions of international agreements entered into by the Community institutions are capable of direct effects. In *Van Duyn* v *Home Office* (case 41/74) the plaintiff, Ms Van Duyn, a Dutch national, was held entitled to invoke provisions of EC Directive 64/221 against the Home Office in order to challenge its refusal to allow her to work in the UK. In *Grad* v *Finanzamt Traunstein* (case 9/70) a Decision, addressed to the German government was held directly effective. In *Sevince* (case C 192/89) the plaintiff, a Turk working in the Netherlands, was held entitled to invoke Decisions made under an agreement between the EC and Turkey, in order to claim an extension to his residence permit in the Netherlands.

As in *Van Gend en Loos*, the Court's reasoning was based on the need to protect individuals' Community rights and to ensure the effectiveness ('*effet utile*') of Community law.

However, not all Community law is directly effective. In order to be directly effective it must first satisfy the criteria for direct effects. It must be unconditional and sufficiently precise; it must leave no discretion in implementation to member states or Community institutions. It must be 'legally perfect', capable of application by national courts. However, except in the case of international agreements, where the principles are construed more restrictively, in line with these agreements' more limited purposes (see, e.g., *Bulk Oil (Zug) AG* v *Sun International* (case 174/84)), the criteria for direct effects are not strictly applied. Many provisions which are far from clear and precise as to their scope of application have been held directly effective. In *Van Duyn* v *Home Office* (case 41/74), faced with a provision ('personal conduct') the scope of which was far from clear, the Court suggested that what was not clear to a national judge could be referred to the Court of Justice for interpretation under Article 177.

Secondly even if the criteria for direct effects are satisfied not all provisions of Community law can be invoked against *all* parties, that is against the state, or an 'emanation of the state', a 'public' body (known as 'vertical' effect) and against 'private' parties, individuals, whether natural or legal persons (known as 'horizontal' effect).

Where *Treaty articles* are concerned they may, if they satisfy the criteria for direct effects, be invoked vertically or horizontally, even though the obligation in question may be *expressly imposed on the state*. In *Defrenne* v *Sabena (No. 2)* (case 43/75) the Court held that Article 119, which provides that 'Each member state shall during the first stage ensure and subsequently maintain the application of the principle that men and women should receive equal pay for equal work' could be invoked against all employers:

> The prohibition on discrimination between men and women applies not only to the action of public authorities, but also extends to all agreements which are intended to regulate paid labour collectively, as well as to contracts between individuals.

Following *Defrenne* many other Treaty articles have been invoked against public and private parties (e.g., Article 6 EC (formerly Article 7 EEC), principle of non-discrimination on grounds of nationality, *Walrave and Koch* v *Association Union Cycliste Internationale* (case 36/74); Article 30, prohibition on measures having equivalent effect to quantitative restrictions, *Walter Rau* v *De Smedt* (case 261/81)).

Regulations, being 'of general application' and 'directly applicable' in all member states, were clearly intended to be directly effective. Therefore, provided they satisfy the criteria for direct effects they will be enforceable against all parties.

Directives are more problematic. Because the obligations in Directives are imposed on member states, requiring implementation by the state within a specific time limit, it was thought that they could not be directly effective. They were never intended to be invoked directly. Yet the Court has consistently maintained that once the time limit for their implementation has expired, they can be directly effective, provided they satisfy the criteria for direct effects (*Pubblico Ministero* v *Ratti* (case 148/78)). This principle has been held to apply even where the Directive has been implemented, on the grounds that the useful effect of Directives might be weakened if individuals were not able to invoke them before their national courts to ensure that national authorities have kept within the limits of their discretion (*Verbond van Nederlandse Ondernemingen* v *Inspecteur der Invoerrechten en Accijnzen* (case 51/76)).

Some national courts were unconvinced of the legitimacy of applying Directives directly. A few courts refused to do so (e.g., French Conseil d'Etat; see *Minister of the Interior* v *Cohn-Bendit* [1980] 1 CMLR 543). They pointed to Article 189, which seemed to suggest that only 'directly applicable' Regulations could be directly effective. Whilst it might be acceptable to allow a Directive to be invoked against a state, on which the obligation to implement the Directive had been imposed, it seemed unfair, in breach of the principle of legal certainty, to allow those obligations to be invoked horizontally, against 'private' parties, whose actions were unimpeachable under national law. Yet as long as states failed to implement Directives on time, or implemented them incorrectly, individuals were deprived of their Community rights; and Community law was unequally enforced. Thus there was a pressing need to secure the effective enforcement of Directives.

A compromise was reached in *Marshall* v *Southampton & South West Hampshire Area Health Authority (Teaching)* (case 152/84). Here, in a claim based on Directive 76/207 on the Equal Treatment of Men and Women in Employment, the Court held, following reasoning introduced in *Becker* v *Finanzamt Münster-Innenstadt* (case 8/81) that since the obligation contained in a Directive was addressed to the state, the state could not, in an action against it based on the Directive, plead its own wrong in failing to implement the Directive. The defendant hospital authority could be treated for these purposes as an agency or emanation of the state. Thus the Directive could be invoked against it, even though it was acting in its 'private' capacity, as an employer. Having chosen this line of reasoning the Court could not but conclude that the Directive could not be invoked directly against 'private' parties; it was not horizontally effective. If this distinction was arbitrary and unfair

such distinction may easily be avoided if the member state concerned has correctly implemented the Directive in national law.

Apart from the unfairness for individuals unable to invoke Directives against 'private' parties (e.g., employers), the 'public'/'private' distinction drawn in *Marshall* has also created problems of definition. What constitutes a 'public' body for the purposes of enforcement of Directives? Is it a question of status, function or control? Clearly this concept, and its interpretation, will vary from state to state and even from court to court, militating against the uniform application and enforcement of EC law. Perhaps in response to this problem, the Court has opted for a generous definition. In *Foster* v *British Gas plc* (case C 188/89) 'public' bodies were defined as

... organisations which (are) subject to the authority or control of the state or (have) special powers beyond those which result from the normal rules applicable to relations between individuals' (para. 18).

Ruling in the specific context of the claim against British Gas (which was at the relevant time a nationalised undertaking) the Court held that

A body, whatever its legal form, which has been made responsible, pursuant to a measure adopted by the state, for providing a public service under the control of the state and has for that purpose special powers beyond those which result from the normal rules applicable in relations between individuals is included in any event among the bodies against which the provisions of a Directive capable of having a direct effect may be relied upon (para. 20).

The application of *Foster* v *British Gas* is not without its problems. In *Doughty* v *Rolls Royce plc* [1992] 1 CMLR 1045, the Court of Appeal, purportedly applying *Foster*, found that Rolls Royce, which was at the relevant time a nationalised undertaking, was not a 'public' body. Applying the specific ruling of para. 20 it found that although Rolls Royce was responsible for providing a public service, the services which it provided, for example in the defence of the realm, were provided to the state and not to the public for the purposes of benefit to the state; nor did the company possess special powers of the type enjoyed by British Gas.

Such fine distinctions are not convincing. Clearly the Court of Appeal was not happy applying the Directive directly against a commercial undertaking which, even if it was arguably 'public' according to the broader definition of para. 18, and even within para. 20, of *Foster* clearly held no responsibility for the non-implementation of the Directive.

Despite the clear distinction drawn in *Marshall*, the question of whether Directives might be horizontally effective was raised once again, and referred to the ECJ, in 1993, in the case of *Faccini Dori* (case C 91/92), in a claim against a private undertaking allegedly acting in breach of EC Consumer Directive 85/577. Although the date for implementation had passed, the Directive had not been implemented by the Italian authorities at the relevant time. Advocate-General Lenz urged the court to reconsider its position in *Marshall* and extend the principle of direct effects of Directives to claims against all parties, in the interest of the correct and uniform application of Community law. This departure, he suggested, was justified in the light of the completion of the internal market and the entry into force of the TEU, in order to meet the legitimate demands of citizens of the Union seeking to rely on Community law.

The Court declined to follow his advice. In a judgment delivered in July 1994, reasserting the principles laid down in *Marshall* and the reasoning of *Becker*, it held that the Directive could not be invoked directly against private parties. In taking this difficult decision it was no doubt influenced by national courts' past reluctance, based on the wording of Article 189, to apply Directives directly, and their cautious acceptance, persuaded by the reasoning of *Becker*, of the principle of vertical effects. However, in deciding that Directives could not be applied horizontally, the Court noted the possibility of an alternative route for the plaintiff via the principle of indirect effects and state liability under *Francovich* (see further below).

Decisions, being 'binding upon those to whom they are addressed', will be directly effective against their addressees. Although it has not arisen before the Court, it would seem, following the Court's reasoning in *Marshall*, that a decision could not be invoked against third parties, not the addressees, although if it is addressed to a member state, it could perhaps be invoked against 'public' bodies.

Provisions of international treaties entered into by the EC, as binding obligations of Community law, can, where directly effective, in theory be invoked against any party, in line with provisions of the EC Treaty. However, in view of the more limited purposes of such agreements and the Court's more cautious approach in this area, it is more likely that such provisions will only be permitted to be invoked vertically; alternatively, where the effects fall horizontally, they may simply be denied direct effects (e.g., *Bulk Oil (Zug) AG v Sun International Ltd* (case 174/84)).

The application of the principle of direct effects has met little resistance in the Courts of member states in the case of Treaty Articles, Regulations and Decisions. As noted above the criteria for direct effects are not strictly applied.

As a result, and subject to the exceptions noted, direct effects have become the norm, rather than the exception. Clearly the Court has an interest in maximising the direct application of Community law. Buttressed by judicious use by national courts of the Article 177 procedure (see Chapter 4) its direct application facilitates the development of Community law and its integration into national legal systems. But in the case of Treaty Articles, which are by their nature expressed in broad general terms, the principle of direct effects can operate to the detriment of individuals, since the precise meaning and scope is often unclear (e.g., Article 119; see *Barber* v *Guardian Royal Exchange Assurance Group* (case C 262/88); see also Article 6 EC, formerly Article 7 EEC). This lack of stringency in the application of the criteria for direct effects provides further reason for protecting individuals' legitimate expectations that they are acting in accordance with the law and denying horizontal effects to Directives, especially when their meaning and scope are unclear.

Because of the arbitrary effect of a rule which allows Directives a vertical but not a horizontal effect, and the difficulty of drawing the line between public and private parties, the Court has attempted to provide alternative means of securing the effective application of Directives, notably via the principle of indirect effect and the principle of state liability in damages for breaches of Community law.

THE PRINCIPLE OF INDIRECT EFFECT

This principle was introduced in the cases of *Von Colson* v *Land Nordrhein-Westfalen* (case 14/83) and *Harz* v *Deutsche Tradax GmbH* (case 79/83). These cases, which came before the Court on the same day, highlighted the anomaly of the 'public'/'private' distinction in the context of Directives. Both plaintiffs sought to invoke Directive 76/207 (on the Equal Treatment of Men and Women in Employment) in almost identical circumstances of discrimination, Von Colson in an action against the German prison service, a 'public' body, Harz against a 'private' employer. The cases were decided in identical terms. Side-stepping the public/private distinction the Court held that Article 5 EC, which requires states to 'take all appropriate measures' to ensure the fulfilment of their community obligation, was binding on all the authorities of member states, including the courts. It thus fell to the courts of member states to *interpret* national law in such a way as to ensure that the objectives of the Directive were achieved. In this way EC law could be applied indirectly, by way of interpretation, even if it was not directly effective.

For some time it was unclear whether national courts were obliged to comply with this principle (the '*Von Colson* principle'), to interpret EC law to comply with an EC Directive when the domestic measure had been introduced *prior* to the Directive, perhaps without the Directive in mind at all. These questions were raised in *Marleasing SA* v *La Comercial Internacional de Alimentación SA* (case C 106/89). Here the Court held, in response to a direct question on this point, that national courts' obligation to interpret domestic law to comply with EC Directives applied whether the national provision in question were adopted before or after the Directive. This requirement 'precluded the interpretation of provisions of national law in a manner inconsistent with the Directive'. In fact at the time when the dispute in *Marleasing* arose no attempt had been made by the Spanish authorities to implement the Directive. Thus as far as the Court of Justice is concerned it appears that national courts' duty to interpret domestic law to comply with EC law does not depend on the intentions of national Parliaments.

However, even the Court of Justice has conceded that there may be limits to the principle of indirect effect. In *Von Colson* national courts' obligation to give indirect effect to Community Directives was expressed to exist 'insofar as they have a discretion to do so under national law'. In *Marleasing*, they were obliged 'as far as possible' to give effect to EC law. In *Officier van Justitie* v *Kolpinghuis Nijmegen* (case 80/86) the Court of Justice held that national courts' obligation to interpret domestic law to comply with EC law was 'limited by the general principles of law which form part of Community law, and particularly the principles of legal certainty and non-retroactivity'. So even under Community law it seems that national courts may refrain from 'interpreting' domestic law against its clear and intended meaning where to do so would breach the legitimate expectations of individuals.

THE PRINCIPLE OF STATE LIABILITY FOR BREACH OF COMMUNITY LAW

Although the state, or any 'public' body, might be liable to individuals for breach of directly effective Community law, and such liability might involve the award of damages (e.g., *Steinhauser* v *City of Biarritz* (case 197/84), *Bourgoin SA* v *Ministry of Agriculture, Fisheries & Food* [1985] 3 All ER 585, CA), there was, until *Francovich* v *Italian State* (cases C 6 and 9/90), no general principle of state liability in damages for breaches of Community law in the absence of direct or indirect effects. Many breaches of Community law by member states concerned the non- or inadequate implementation of Directives. Many of these Directives (e.g., employee, consumer protection) were designed to confer rights on individuals. As long as states failed to implement them, or to implement them correctly, or on time, individuals were deprived of their Community rights. States were increasingly failing to fulfil their EC obligations, particularly in respect of Directives, even following judgments against them under Article 169. In 1991 the Commission received more than 1,000 complaints from individuals claiming to have suffered as a result of infringements of EC law. The principle of direct effects was effective to provide a remedy in the individual case, where the individual was aware of his rights and willing to enforce them. But it was not available against 'private' bodies, nor could the principle of indirect effects be relied on. Neither principle remedied the primary problem, the non-implementation of the Directive by the state. To overcome these difficulties the Court, in *Francovich*, established a new principle that, under certain circumstances, a state may be 'liable to make good damage to individuals caused by a breach of Community law for which it is responsible'.

The breach in question was the non-implementation of a Directive (80/987) by the Italian state. The Directive, on the protection of employees in the event of their employers' insolvency, required states, inter alia, to set up a guarantee institution to ensure that employees' arrears of wages were paid in the event of their employers' insolvency. Despite the expiry of the time limit for implementation, and a judgment from the Court of Justice under Article 169 on the state's failure in this respect, at the time when the plaintiffs' claim arose the Directive had still not been implemented. The plaintiffs, who were owed arrears of wages, and whose employers were insolvent, sought compensation. Since their former employers were insolvent, they sued the state in the Italian courts. There were two heads of claim; one based on the direct effects of the provisions of the Directive (relating to arrears of pay) which were breached; the second for the state's breach of its primary obligation to implement the Directive. Questions as to the liability of the State under these claims were referred to the Court of Justice under Article 177 EC.

As regards the first claim, the Court found, contrary to the view of the Commission, that the provision was not directly effective. Applying the criteria for direct effects, the Court found that although the content of the right invoked (arrears of wages) and the beneficiaries of that right (employees) were sufficiently clear and precise for direct effects, the nature of the guarantee institution was not. Under the Directive it was not necessary that the state should be responsible for payment.

The state would however be liable under the second claim. The Court held that failure by a member state to take all necessary steps to achieve the results required by a Directive gives rise to a right to obtain damages based directly on Community law where three conditions are met:

(1)   the result required by the Directive includes the conferring of rights for the benefit of individuals;
(2)   the content of these rights may be determined by reference to the provisions of the Directive; and
(3)   there is a causal link between breach of the obligation of the state and the damage suffered by the person affected.

Thus in *Francovich* the Court laid down a new principle of state liability *wholly independent of the principle of direct and indirect effect*. It would not have been difficult to interpret the relevant provisions, as did the Commission, as directly effective. The Court clearly chose not to do so. It is likely that the Court denied them direct effects precisely because it wished to establish such a principle. Not only would it supplement, for individuals, the inadequacies of the principles of direct and indirect effect; it would also provide states with a powerful incentive to fulfil their obligations under Community law.

The Court's reasoning in *Francovich* was based largely on its case law in *Van Gend en Loos* (case 26/62), *Costa v ENEL* (case 6/64), *Simmenthal SpA* (case 106/77), and *Factortame (No. 2)* (case C 213/89) (see further below). Certain provisions of EC law give rise to rights for individuals; national courts are obliged to ensure the full effect of these provisions; their full effectiveness would be weakened and the rights they recognised undermined if individuals were not able to recover damages when their rights were infringed by a breach of Community law attributable to a member state. States were bound under Article 5 EEC to 'take all appropriate measures ... to ensure fulfilment of the obligations arising under Community law'. A principle of state liability for damage to individuals caused by a breach of Community law for which it is responsible was 'inherent in the scheme of the treaty'.

The reasoning is convincing. The decision in *Francovich* does however raise many problems. Does a principle of state liability only apply to cases such as *Francovich*, concerning the non-implementation of Directives, or can it apply, as Advocate-General Mischo and the terms of the judgment suggest, to any breach of EC law 'for which a member state is responsible'? Must the state's breach be established by the Court under Article 169 or Article 177 (see Chapters 4 and 11)? Must that breach of EC law be culpable? Given the imprecise nature of much EC law, at least until interpreted by the Court, a state's breach of EC law will sometimes be inadvertent. Is a principle of state liability restricted to actions for damages, or may other remedies be claimed? On what principles should damages be awarded? To what extent will *Francovich* supplement or supplant remedies based on direct or indirect effect? This will depend on future interpretations of *Francovich*. Clearly, if *Francovich* is to be uniformly applied in all member states, guidance on all these questions will be needed from the Court. Answers to some of these questions relating to fault, and damages, and liability for breaches of Treaty rules will be provided when the Court rules on questions referred by the English High Court (QBD) in *Factortame (No. 3)* (case C 48/93) and by the German Bundesgerichtshof in *Brasserie du Pêcheur SA* (case C 46/93), see further Chapter 5. But even after these rulings many uncertainties will remain. Therefore until the full implications of *Francovich* are revealed individuals seeking to enforce community rights will be advised, where appropriate, to claim on the basis of direct effects, for breach of substantive provisions of EC law or on the principle of indirect effects, as well as against the state under *Francovich*, for its primary failure to implement Community law. We shall return to these problems in later chapters of this book.

THE PRINCIPLE OF SUPREMACY OF EC LAW

The principles of direct and indirect effects and the principle of state liability under *Francovich* would be of no avail if they were not buttressed by a further principle, the principle of supremacy of EC law. This principle too is the creation of the Court, designed to ensure the effective and uniform application of Community law. In a series of cases, starting in 1964, the Court has held that in the case of conflict between Community law and national law, *prior or subsequent*, Community law must prevail (*Costa* v *ENEL* (case 6/64)). It must even prevail over provisions of a national Constitution (*Internationale Handelsgesellschaft mbH* (case 11/70)). In *Amministrazione delle Finanze dello Stato* v *Simmenthal SpA* (case 106/77) the Court held that directly applicable rules of Community law must be fully and uniformly applied in all the member states from the date of their entry into force in accordance with the principle of precedence of Community law ... A national court which is called upon ... to apply provisions of Community law is under a duty to give full effect to those provisions, if necessary refusing ... to apply any conflicting provision of national legislation, even if adopted subsequently, ... it is not necessary for the court to request or await the prior setting aside of such provision by legislative or other constitutional means.

These principles apply to all Community law, Treaty law, Regulations, Directives, Decisions and even provisions of international treaties entered into by the EC. In *Commission v Council (Re European Road Transport Agreement) (ERTA)* (case 22/70) the Court held that

Once the Community, in implementing a common policy, lays down common rules, member states no longer have the right, individually or collectively, to contract obligations towards non-member states affecting these common rules.

Although the principle of supremacy of EC law was expressed originally in terms of directly effective law, it is inherent in the principle of indirect effect and the principle of state liability under *Francovich*, both of which must be observed by national courts, that it can no longer be confined to such law.

Despite initial constitutional problems national courts have largely accepted the principle of the supremacy of *directly effective* Community law, no doubt convinced by the Court's reasoning of the necessity of doing so. Only by giving primacy to Community law can it be uniformly and effectively enforced. Without uniform enforcement 'solidarity' between member states would be lost. However, there has been greater reluctance to give indirect effect to Community law, and the principle of state liability under *Francovich* has yet to be put to the test in the English courts.This will occur following the Court of Justice's ruling in *Factortame (No. 3)* (case C 48/93).

APPLICATION OF COMMUNITY LAW IN THE UK

As a matter of English constitutional law international law does not become binding within the UK until incorporated by Act of Parliament. The European Communities Act 1972 was passed to this end. EC law takes effect within the UK solely by virtue of and according to the terms of this Act.

Section 2(1) provides for the reception of Community law.

All such rights, powers, liabilities, obligations and restrictions from time to time created or arising by or under the Treaties, and all such remedies and procedures from time to time provided for by or under the Treaties, as in accordance with the Treaties are without further enactment to be given legal effect or used in the United Kingdom shall be recognised and available in law, and be enforced, allowed and followed accordingly; and the expression 'enforceable Community right' and similar expressions shall be read as referring to one to which this subsection applies.

Section 2(2) provides blanket authority (subject to certain exceptions listed in Schedule 2; see Table 4 in the Appendix) for the issuing of domestic secondary legislation for the purpose of implementing 'any Community obligation' without recourse to Parliament.

Section 2(4) provides guidance as to the effect of Community law. It provides that any domestic measure, 'any enactment passed or to be passed, other than one contained in this part of this Act [i.e., provision relating to Community law], shall be construed and have effect subject to the foregoing provisions of this section'.

Finally, under s. 3(1)

For the purposes of all legal proceedings any question as to the meaning or effect of any of the Treaties, or as to the validity, meaning or effect of any Community instrument, shall be treated as a question of law (and, if not referred to the European Court, be for determination as such in accordance with the principles laid down by and any relevant decision of the European Court or any court attached thereto).

To what extent do these provisions enable our courts to apply Community law according to the principles established by the Court, the principles of direct and indirect effects, of state liability under *Francovich*, and the supremacy of EC law?

Section 2(1) provides for the incorporation of EC law within the UK legal system. EC law is directly effective in the UK by virtue of s. 2(1). Where EC law is directly effective our courts have been prepared to accord it supremacy over domestic law. They have done so in most cases by treating s. 2(4) as providing a rule of construction. But their approach to 'construction' is very different from the normal approach, even as applied to international law. Lord Diplock, in *Garland* v *British Rail Engineering Ltd* [1983] 2 AC 751, suggested (without committing himself), that in the context of directly effective law national courts must construe domestic law to conform with EC law, 'no matter how wide a departure from the prima facie meaning may be needed to achieve consistency'. The House of Lords in *Pickstone* v *Freemans plc* [1988] 2 All ER 803, was prepared to imply words into domestic legislation to achieve a result compatible with Article 119. In *Factortame* v *Secretary of State for Transport (No. 2)* [1991] 1 All ER 106, faced with a clear (alleged) conflict between certain provisions of the EC treaty and the Merchant Shipping Act 1988, Lord Bridge said that it was 'as if a section were incorporated into Part 11 (the impugned part) of the Merchant Shipping Act which in terms enacted that the provisions (in conflict with EC law) ... were to be without prejudice to the directly enforceable (i.e., applicable/effective) Community rights of nationals of any member state of the EEC'. It seems that only where no 'interpretation' of domestic law is possible will British courts apply EC law directly, in 'priority' over national law (e.g., *McKecknie* v *UBM Building Supplies (Southern) Ltd* [1991] ICR 710, EAT).

Our courts have, however, been less willing to give indirect effect to Community law. Some have suggested that s. 2(1) of the 1972 Act only applies to directly effective law. In *Duke* v *GEC Reliance Ltd* [1988] AC 618, the House of Lords refused to interpret the Sex Discrimination Act 1975 against the defendant employer, a 'private' undertaking, in order to comply with certain provisions of Equal Treatment Directive 76/207 (as interpreted by the Court of Justice in *Marshall* v *Southampton AHA* (case 152/84)) because it was convinced from the evidence that the Act was never intended to have the meaning contended for. Lord Templeman went further, and suggested that 'Section 2(4) European Communities Act (did) not .... enable or constrain a British court to distort the meaning of a British statute in order to enforce against an individual a Community Directive which has no direct effect between individuals'.

In *Finnegan* v *Clowney* [1990] 2 All ER 546, the House of Lords followed *Duke* v *Reliance*, in a case on very similar facts, except that the legislation in question, the Sex Discrimination (Northern Ireland) Order 1976, had been passed after Directive 76/207. Nevertheless the House refused to interpret the Order to comply with the Directive on the grounds that the relevant provisions of the Order, having been enacted in the same terms as the Sex Discrimination Act under discussion in *Duke* v *Reliance*, must have been intended to have the same effect.

However, in *Litster* v *Forth Dry Dock and Engineering Co Ltd* [1989] 1 All ER 1134, the House of Lords was prepared to 'interpret' the English Transfer of Undertakings Regulations generously, against the defendant employers, a 'private' body, to the extent of 'supplying the necessary words by implication', to meet the demands of Directive 77/187, because it was clear, from evidence supplied, inter alia from Hansard, that the Regulations were introduced *specifically in order to implement the Directive*.

Duke v *Reliance*, *Finnegan* v *Clowney* and *Litster* were all decided prior to the Court of Justice's decision in *Marleasing*. It remains to be seen whether our courts will only give indirect effect to Directives in cases such as *Litster*, where domestic law has been introduced specifically in order to implement a Directive, or whether they will follow *Marleasing* and interpret domestic law to give effect to Directives regardless of chronology or even statutory wording or intent. The latter is unlikely. If domestic law is clearly irreconcilable with the Directive they may legitimately refuse to 'interpret ' it to comply with the Directive on the principles expressed by the European Court in *Officier van Justitie* v *Kolpinghuis Nijmegen* (case 80/86), in order to respect the legitimate expectations of individuals. This would be preferable to following Lord Templeman's sweeping and dangerous dicta that s. 2(4) of the European Communities Act 1972 'applies, and only applies, to Community law which is directly applicable (i.e., effective)'. It is submitted that in an appropriate case (such as *Litster*, where it is clear that the national authorities intended fully to implement Community law) s. 2(1) and (4), together with s. 3(1) would provide an adequate base for the application of the *Von Colson* principle.

The application of *Francovich* (cases C 6 and 9/90) has yet to be tested in the British courts. It too could be justified under ss. 2(1) and (4) and 3(1) of the

1972 Act. Inasmuch as it could require the award of damages against the state
for acts or omissions of *Parliament* it will break new constitutional ground. The
House of Lords was willing in *Factortame (No. 2)* [1991] 1 All ER 70, following
a ruling from the ECJ and on the principles laid down in *Simmenthal SpA* (case
106/77) cited above, to grant an interim injunction against the Crown to
prevent the application of the Merchant Shipping Act 1988 in order to protect
the plaintiffs' (claimed) Community rights. In *EOC* v *Secretary of State for
Employment* [1994] 1 All ER 910, it granted a declaration that certain
provisions of the Employment Protection (Consolidation) Act 1978 were
incompatible with EC law. It may be argued that it is but a small step to
proceed from these cases to an award of damages. There might be serious
difficulties however, and not just in the UK, if liability were to be required to be
imposed in the absence of fault (see further Chapters 5 and 7).

Despite the UK courts' willingness to jettison entrenched constitutional
rules and espouse new modes of interpretation in order to give supremacy to
EC law which is directly effective, and even, as in *Litster*, to EC law which is not
directly effective but was intended to comply with Community law, the
principle of parliamentary sovereignty has not been wholly abandoned in the
context of the application of EC law. Both the Court of Appeal and the House
of Lords have held that

> If the time should come when our Parliament deliberately passes an Act with
> the intention of repudiating the Treaty or any provision in it – or intentionally
> of acting inconsistently with it – and says so in express terms, then ... it
> would be the duty of our courts to follow the statute of our Parliament' (per
> Lord Denning in *Macarthys* v *Smith* [1979] 3 All ER 32; see also Lord
> Diplock in *Garland* v *British Rail*)

Whilst it is unlikely that this will happen, traditionalists would argue that it
is important that it should remain a theoretical possibility.

PART TWO

Enforcing community rights before national courts

THREE
Introduction

Most EC law, whether Treaty law or secondary legislation, imposes obligations on member states. States are required to abolish, or refrain from introducing, measures which restrict the free movement of goods, persons, services and capital or impede free competition in the provision of goods and services in the single internal Community market. They are required to implement Directives to achieve the harmonisation of national standards: these include measures to eliminate barriers to trade, physical, technical and fiscal, within the single internal market; measures in the field of health and safety or to protect employees, shareholders, investors, consumers or the environment; to abolish discrimination on the grounds of sex; to ensure that substantial public procurement contracts for the supply of goods and services are open to competitive tender in all member states.

States are also required to comply with Community policies laid down by Regulation or Decision, for example in the sphere of agriculture and fisheries, or transport, or regulating the import and export of goods from and to countries outside the Community under the Common Customs Tariff or the Common Commercial policy .

Given the range and extent of states' obligations under Community law it was inevitable that they would on occasions be breached, whether deliberately, negligently or innocently. As was noted in Chapter 1, the procedures provided by the treaty under Articles 169 and 170 proved of limited effect in securing compliance, and the Court of Justice has turned to alternative means of enforcement, at the suit of individuals, before their national courts. In doing so the emphasis has shifted from the enforcement of obligations against member states to the *protection of individuals' Community rights*. These rights may be enforced against the state, against 'public' bodies representing the state, and even against 'private' bodies, according to, and subject to the limitations of, the principles of direct and indirect effects and state liability under *Francovich*.

Thus national courts have become the principal fora in which Community rights are enforced. Although a successful action does not remedy a state's breach, or result necessarily in the annulment or amendment of domestic measures which conflict with EC law, it does provide a remedy in the individual case: inconsistent national law is either 'interpreted' to comply with EC law or, following the principles laid down in *Simmenthal SpA* (case 106/77) (and see below, Chapter 5), simply not applied. Where national law is found to be clearly incompatible with Community law a state is obliged to amend its laws. It is not enough for a state to argue that the provision of EC law in question is directly effective or is in practice observed (*Commission* v *Greece: Commission* v *Spain* (cases 119, 120 and 159/89), [1991] ECR 691).

Where an individual seeks to enforce his Community rights he may invoke those rights, as a shield or a sword, in any proceedings in public or private law, in pursuit of any remedy, interim or final, available under national law. They have been invoked, for example, as a defence to a criminal (regulatory) charge (*Pubblico Ministero* v *Ratti* (case 148/78)); to challenge acts or omissions of the public authorities of the member states, including legislative acts (*Factortame* v *Secretary of State for Transport (No. 2)* [1991] 1 All ER 70; *EOC* v *Secretary of State for Employment* [1994] 1 All ER 910 (HL)); in claims for restitution (*Amministrazione delle Finanze dello Stato* v *SpA San Giorgio* (case 199/82) and actions involving breach of contract (*Walter Rau Lebensmittelwerke* v *De Smedt* (case 261/81)) and tort (*Bourgoin SA* v *Ministry of Agriculture, Fisheries and Food* [1985] 3 All ER 585 (QBD and CA)).

Although the Community has not provided for a system of harmonised remedies in respect of actions before national courts based on EC law, the Court has laid down a number of principles to be applied by national courts in the context of such actions, the most important being the 'effectiveness' principle; the remedies provided must be adequate to ensure the effective protection of individuals' Community rights and deter parties from breaching Community law. This has resulted in some modification of national law. These principles, and the resulting modifications, will be examined in Chapters 5–7. But first, since effective protection for individuals' rights depends on the correct interpretation and application of Community law, the role of Article 177 in assisting national courts in this task will be considered.

In addition to this formal procedure for access to the Court of Justice under Article 177 EC the Court has suggested that the Community institutions, particularly the Commission, whose task it is under Article 155 EC to see that 'the provisions of [the] Treaty and the measures taken by the [EC] institutions are applied', are under a duty to give 'active assistance' to national courts in their task of guaranteeing the application and effectiveness of Community law. This obligation is based on Article 5 EC, which imposes on member states and Community institutions 'mutual duties of sincere co-operation' (*Zwartveld* (case C 2/88 Imm) at para. 17). Such active assistance, in the form of documents and witnesses, was ordered by the Court to be supplied by the Commission in *Zwartveld*, following a request for judicial co-operation by a Groningen court investigating a case of alleged fraud in the management of the fish market, in breach of EC law. The Court of Justice suggested that a refusal to co-operate could only be justified to avoid interference in the functioning and independence of the Commission. It seems that the EC institutions' duty of confidentiality under Article 214 EC (and the Commission's under EC competition law (Regulation 17/62)) does not preclude such 'co-operation' with national authorities, provided that the use of the information provided (for example in an investigation into anti-competitive practices) is consistent with the purpose for which it was granted (*Dirección General de Defensa de la Competencia* v *Asociación Española de Banca Privada* (case C 67/91)).

FOUR

The role of Article 177 in the interpretation of EC law

In order to assist national courts in their task of interpretation and application of Community law the EC treaty provided, in Article 177, a procedure whereby a national judge, faced with a question of interpretation of EC law, can, and in some cases must, refer to the Court of Justice for a preliminary ruling on the interpretation of that law prior to himself applying the ruling in the case before him. The primary purpose of this procedure is to ensure the correct and uniform application of EC law in all member states. Designed originally to assist national courts in the application of 'directly applicable' Regulations, its role has been greatly increased with the extended application of the principles of direct and indirect effect, and now the principle of state liability under *Francovich*. These developments have in turn substantially enhanced the role of the Court of Justice in shaping and developing EC law. All the major principles of Community law have been established in Article 177 proceedings.

THE PROCEDURE

Article 177 provides

> The Court of Justice shall have jurisdiction to give preliminary rulings concerning:
> (a)   the interpretation of this Treaty;
> (b)   the validity and interpretation of acts of the institutions of the Community;
> (c)   the interpretation of the statutes of bodies established by an act of the Council, where those statutes so provide.
> Where such a question is raised before any court or tribunal of a member state, that court or tribunal may, if it considers that a decision on the question

is necessary to enable it to give judgment, request the Court of Justice to give a ruling thereon.

Where any such question is raised in a case pending before a court or tribunal of a member state against whose decisions there is no judicial remedy under national law, that court or tribunal shall bring the matter before the Court of Justice.

Thus the jurisdiction of the Court of Justice is two-fold, embracing questions of interpretation and validity of Community law. Its role in determining the validity of Community law will be considered later, in the context of challenging Community obligations and actions for damages against the Community (see Chapter 8). The present chapter is concerned only with the role of Article 177 in the *interpretation* of Community law.

Article 177 is an example of shared jurisdiction, based on a clear division of function and requiring close co-operation between national courts and the Court of Justice. As Advocate-General Lagrange commented in *De Geus en Uitdenbogerd* v *R Bosch GmbH* (case 13/61), the first case to reach the court on an application under Article 177

Applied judiciously – one is tempted to say loyally – the provisions of Article 177 must lead to a fruitful collaboration between the municipal courts and the Court of Justice of the Communities with mutual regard for their respective jurisdiction.

Thus the attitudes of both national courts and the Court of Justice to Article 177 are vital to its success.

JURISDICTION OF NATIONAL COURTS

Jurisdiction to refer under Article 177 is conferred on 'any court or tribunal of a member state'. This has been interpreted widely, to include 'any court acting in the general context of a duty to act, independently and in accordance with the law, upon cases in which the law has conferred jurisdiction upon it' (*Pretore di Salo* v *Persons Unknown* (case 14/86)). It is not necessary that the body be acting in a judicial capacity. In *Pretore di Salo*, the Italian Pretore, whose functions combine those of public prosecutor and examining magistrate, and whose decision not to prosecute had been challenged, was held entitled to refer to the Court under Article 177 'even though certain functions of that court or tribunal in the proceedings which (gave) rise to the reference for a preliminary ruling (were) not strictly of a judicial nature. . .'. In *Broekmeulen* (case 246/80) the appeal committee of the Dutch professional medical body was held entitled to refer:

... In the practical absence of an effective means of redress before the ordinary courts, in a matter concerning the application of Community law, the appeal committee, which performs its duties with the approval of public authorities and operates with their assistance, and whose decisions are accepted following contentious proceedings and are in fact recognised as final, must be deemed a court of a member state for the purposes of Article 177.

By contrast in *Nordsee Deutsche Hochseefischerei GmbH* (case 102/81) the Court found that an independent arbitrator, appointed by the parties to a joint shipbuilding contract involving the pooling of European aid, was not a court or tribunal for the purposes of Article 177 since 'the public authorities of member states were not involved in the decision to opt for arbitration, nor were they called upon to intervene automatically before the arbitrator'. If questions of Community law were raised before such a body, the Court suggested, the 'ordinary courts' might be called upon to give them assistance, or review their decision; it would be for them to refer to the European Court under Article 177.

These decisions suggest that in order for a body to constitute a court or tribunal for the purposes of Article 177 it must be subject to some element of *public* authority or control. This view, if unmodified, must be questioned. The Court's decision in *Nordsee* has been criticised. It proceeded on the assumption that the parties concerned had recourse to the ordinary courts, which they did not. As a result the arbitrator was required to interpret a difficult point of EC law, of central importance to the proceedings, unaided. Many similar privately constituted tribunals, for example the Jockey Club in the UK, are empowered to make decisions affecting individuals' Community rights. These decisions may not be subject to review. Since, as the Court pointed out in *Nordsee*, 'Community law must be observed in its entirety throughout the territory of all the member states', and 'parties to a contract are not free to create exceptions to it', it may be argued that where privately constituted bodies take decisions affecting individuals' Community rights access to the Court for interpretation concerning these rights must be not be denied. Either national law must guarantee review of their decisions by the ordinary courts (see further Chapter 6) or these bodies, whether they be publicly or privately constituted, should themselves be entitled to refer to the Court under Article 177.

A Decision on the Question must be Necessary

The jurisdiction of national courts and tribunals to refer to the Court of Justice under Article 177 arises where the court considers 'that a decision on the question (of EC law) is necessary to enable it to give judgment'. Although on a literal reading of Article 177 it would appear that this question was only relevant to courts with a discretionary jurisdiction under Article 177(2), the Court has held that 'it followed from the relationship between Article 177(2) and 177(3) that the courts or tribunals referred to under Article 177(3) have the same discretion as any other national court to ascertain whether a decision on a question of Community law is necessary to enable it to give judgment' (*CILFIT Srl* v *Ministro della Sanità* (case 283/81)). Thus national courts may not invoke Article 177 in order to embark on 'fishing expeditions', nor may they refer general or hypothetical questions; the ruling sought must relate to a genuine issue between the parties (*Foglia* v *Novello (Nos 1 and 2)* (cases 104/79 and 244/80); *Weinand Meilicke* v *ADV/ORGA F.A. Meyer AG* (case C 83/91)). On the same principle national courts may not refer to the Court when national proceedings have been terminated (*Pardini* (case 338/85)). These limitations apart, the Court of Justice has in the past given national courts the strongest encouragement to refer. In *Pretore di Salo* v *Persons Unknown* (case 14/86) the Court accepted a referral from the Italian pretore even though the proceedings in which the reference was made were against persons unknown, and a decision from the pretore might never be required in the case. The Court did however adopt a more restrictive approach and refuse its jurisdiction in a recent request for a ruling on the *validity* of a Community measure (TWD *Textilwerke Deggendorf GmbH* v *Bundesrepublik Deutschland* (case C 188/92), see further Chapters 8 and 9).

When will a decision on a question of Community law be necessary to enable a national court to give judgment?

Guidelines laid down on this matter by national courts must be treated with caution. Although the decision as to whether or not to refer rests with the national judge the question of whether it is necessary to refer is a matter of Community law, requiring a uniform approach by national courts, following principles established by the Court of Justice. These principles were provided in *CILFIT* (case 283/81). Here the Court of Justice suggested that it would not be necessary to refer if

(a)   the question of EC law is irrelevant, or
(b)   the provision has already been interpreted by the Court of Justice, even though the question at issue is not strictly identical, or
(c)   the correct application is so obvious as to leave no scope for reasonable doubt. This matter must be assessed in the light of the specific characteristics of Community law, the peculiar difficulties to which its interpretation gives rise, and the risk of divergence in judicial interpretation within the Community.

Because of the fundamental importance of Article 177 to the uniform application of EC law, as well as for the protection of individuals' Community rights, these criteria must be rigorously applied.

Question irrelevant   Clearly if the question is irrelevant a ruling as to its interpretation will not be 'necessary'. However this matter cannot be lightly decided. Whether or not it is relevant requires an inquiry into the facts and issues of national law, as well as an understanding of the principles of interpretation relevant to EC law.

Question already interpreted by the Court of Justice   This principle was established by the Court in the case of *Da Costa en Schaake* (cases 28–30/62), in which the issues involved and the EC provision to be interpreted (Article 12 EEC) were materially identical to those already decided by the Court in *Van Gend en Loos* (case 26/62). In such circumstances the Court held it was not necessary to refer. However, where a previous interpretation has been given in a different factual context it may well be necessary to refer. In *R v Secretary of State for the Home Department (ex parte Sandhu) The Times* 10 May 1985, the House of Lords refused to refer a question concerning the rights of residence in the UK of Mr Sandhu, on the grounds that the matter had already been decided by the Court of Justice in the case of *Diatta v Land Berlin* (case 267/83). Whilst both cases concerned the rights of residence of a separated spouse who was not an EC national their facts were materially different, and the 'ruling' followed in *Sandhu* was delivered obiter. In *Diatta* the issue was decided in the spouse's favour; Mr Sandhu on the other hand was held to have forfeited his right of residence. Surely a decision of such consequence to Mr Sandhu, based on EC law, should not have been made without reference to the Court of Justice.

Even where the issues appear materially identical a court is not precluded from referring. Although the Court of Justice will normally follow its prior judgments it is not bound, as is an English court, by precedent. As it pointed out in *Da Costa en Schaake*, it retains a legal right to depart from its previous judgments. It may recognise its errors in the light of new facts. It has on occasions changed its mind (see *Marshall v Southampton AHA* (case 152/84); and compare that case with *Burton v British Railways Board* (case 19/81)).

Provision so obvious as to leave no scope for reasonable doubt   This is a version of the French doctrine of *acte clair*. Unlike that doctrine's application in French administrative law, in the context of EC law it must be applied restrictively, in the light of the purposes of Article 177. It is not enough that a provision be 'reasonably clear and free from doubt', as Lord Denning suggested in *Bulmer v Bollinger* [1974] 2 All ER 1226. A lax, subjective approach based on a test of reasonableness would militate against referral. It could be used to avoid referral (see, e.g., *Minister of the Interior v Cohn-Bendit* (Conseil d'Etat) [1980] 1 CMLR 543). Above all this principle must be applied in the light of its rider, taking into account the 'special nature' and 'particular difficulties' of EC law. These are its lack of precision and uncertainty of scope, providing a wide berth for interpretation. If national judges from twelve (and, from 1 January 1995, fifteen) member states, with their different legal concepts and traditions of interpretation, applying different language versions of EC law, were to take it upon themselves to interpret EC law without guidance from the Court, there would be a real risk of divergence in judicial interpretation, unless the provision in question was unequivocally clear. (For an exemplary approach to *acte clair* by the British courts see Bingham J in *Customs & Excise Commissioners v Samex ApS* [1983] 3 CMLR 194 (commercial court); Kerr LJ in *R v Pharmaceutical Society of Great Britain* [1987] 3 CMLR 951).

Permissive and Mandatory Jurisdiction

Even where, applying the *CILFIT* criteria, a decision from the Court of Justice on a question of EC law is 'necessary', not all national courts are bound to refer. Under Article 177(3) only courts and tribunals 'against whose decision there is no judicial remedy under national law' *must* bring the matter before the Court of Justice ('mandatory' jurisdiction). All other courts have a discretion to do so ('permissive' jurisdiction).

Mandatory jurisdiction; which courts 'shall' refer?   The purpose of the mandatory jurisdiction under Article 177(3) is to ensure that where a decision on a question of EC law is necessary to enable the national court to give judgment, a referral will eventually be made. There are conflicting views as to which courts are those against whose decision there is no judicial remedy under national law. One theory, the 'abstract' theory, holds that only those courts which are supreme within the national legal system fall within this category. In *Bulmer* v *Bollinger* Lord Denning suggested that in the UK 'only the House of Lords is bound to refer'. This view has not won widespread acceptance, as being too restrictive and contrary to the purpose of Article 177(3). The better view, the 'concrete' theory, is that it refers to all courts from which there is no appeal in the case in question, regardless of their position in the judicial hierarchy. The Court of Justice appeared to endorse this view in *Costa* v *ENEL* (case 6/64) when it held, in the context of a reference from the Italian pretore (magistrates' court), from which the plaintiff had no right of appeal, the sum of money involved being so small, that 'by the terms of this article (177(3)), national courts against whose decisions, as in the present case, there is no judicial remedy, must refer to the Court of Justice'.

Difficulties arise when the right to appeal depends on the granting of leave by a higher court, subsequent to judgment, for example by the House of Lords, following a refusal of leave by the Court of Appeal. Even applying the 'concrete' theory the Court of Appeal is not a 'court against whose decisions no judicial remedy exists' at the time when the decision is made. It becomes so only when leave to appeal is refused. By this time it is too late to refer. In such situations, if access to the Court of Justice is not to be denied, a lower court must be persuaded either to grant leave to appeal or itself to refer to the Court of Justice. Alternatively the higher court must grant leave to appeal.

Permissive jurisdiction: which courts 'may' refer?   Courts falling within the permissive jurisdiction of Article 177(2) have a discretion as to whether or not to refer. On what principles should they exercise their discretion? Lord Denning in *Bulmer* v *Bollinger* suggested that national courts should take into account factors such as time and cost, the difficulty and importance of the point, the wishes of the parties and the workload of the Court of Justice. Such guidelines may be persuasive, but they should not be treated as rules of law. A ruling from the Court of Justice will take time, involving on average at least eighteen months' delay; clearly it will add to costs. But, as Bingham J pointed out in *Commissioners of Customs & Excise* v *Samex ApS*, where a decision on the point of EC law is necessary, an early referral to the Court of Justice, particularly where the point is difficult and important, may save time and money. The wishes of the parties must be considered, since they must finance the ruling; but it is not necessary, indeed not likely, that both parties will have an equal interest in referring. The workload of the Court should never deter a national court from referring where it needs assistance on the interpretation of Community law. Thus where there appears to be a genuine claim based on EC law, and the point of law is difficult and novel, and an interpretation would prove conclusive, a fortiori when other similar cases are pending (see e.g., *Polydor Ltd v Harlequin Record Shops Ltd* [1980] 2 CMLR 413 (CA), there is little to be gained by delay.

Not unnaturally superior courts have on occasions warned inferior courts against early referral. In *R v Henn* [1980] 2 All ER 166 (HL), Lord Diplock suggested that in a criminal trial on indictment it might be better for the question to be decided by the national court and reviewed if necessary through the hierarchy of the national courts. Clearly if lower courts are unsure as to the genuineness of the claim under EC law (and it has not infrequently been invoked as a 'last ditch' defence in criminal or injunctive proceedings, see *Quietlynn v Southend BC* (case C 23/89)), or its application to the case in hand, it may be wise to leave the decision to a higher court. But rarely if ever will it be desirable to pursue a claim through the judicial hierarchy when it is clear that a reference to the Court of Justice must in the end be made. As the body of EC case law develops and national courts at all levels acquire greater confidence and expertise in applying EC law, so there will be less need for national courts to refer. The crucial question will always be whether a decision is 'necessary' to enable a national court to give judgment.

The effect of national precedent   One factor which should never operate to prevent a national court from seeking a ruling under Article 177 is the existence of national precedent. A previous ruling from a superior national court on a question of EC law is never binding; it cannot take away the power of a lower domestic court to refer to the supreme authority on matters of Community law, i.e., the Court of Justice. This issue arose in *Rheinmühlen-Düsseldorf* (case 166/73). Here the German federal tax court (*Bundesfinanzhof*), hearing a case on appeal from the Hessian tax court, referred certain questions to the Court of Justice and, as a result of that ruling quashed the Hessian court's decision and referred the case back to that court for a final decision. The Hessian court, dissatisfied with the *Bundesfinanzhof*'s decision on the matter of EC law, sought a further ruling from the Court of Justice. Both German courts referred certain questions to that Court concerning the Hessian court's right, in these circumstances, to refer. The Court held that, since the object of the Article 177 procedure was to ensure that the law was the same in all member states, a lower court must be free to make a reference to the Court of Justice if it considers that a superior court's ruling could lead it to give judgment contrary to Community law. It would only be otherwise if the decision put by the lower court were substantially the same.

Scope of discretion in matters concerning referral   Just as the decision whether or not to refer rests solely with the national judge, so does the timing and form of referral. As the Court said in *Simmenthal v Italian Finance Administration* (case 70/77) 'every court or tribunal of a member state is entitled to request a preliminary ruling under Article 177, regardless of the stage reached in the proceedings pending before it and regardless of the nature of the decision which it is called upon to give'. It may even make a second reference in the same case if it considers that a further ruling is necessary. This may be justified 'when the national court encounters difficulty in understanding or applying the judgment, or when it refers a fresh question of law to the Court, or when it submits new considerations which might lead the Court to give a different answer to the question submitted earlier' (*Pretore di Salo* (case 14/86)). Nor are there any special requirements as to the form of the ruling. Where the questions referred are inappropriate the Court will reformulate them, often extensively (see e.g., *Adoui and Cornuaille* v *Belgian States* (case 115 and 116/81)), in such a way as will best assist the national judge to decide the case before him. To ascertain this matter the Court has suggested to national courts that the facts of the case should be established and questions of purely national law be settled at the time the reference is made (*Irish Creamery Milk Suppliers Association* v *Ireland* (cases 36 and 71/80)). In this way the Court can 'take cognisance of all the features of fact and law which may be relevant to the interpretation of Community law which it is called upon to give'. In *Telemarsicabruzzo SpA* (cases C 320, 321 and 322/90) the Court rejected an application for a ruling from an Italian magistrates' court on the grounds that the reference had provided no background factual information and only fragmentary observations on the case. However, the Court has stressed its desire 'not in any way (to) restrict the discretion of the national court, which alone has a direct knowledge of the facts of the case and of the arguments of the parties, which will have to take responsibility for giving judgment in the case and which is ... in the best position to appreciate at what stage it requires a preliminary ruling from the Court of Justice' (*Irish Creamery Milk Suppliers*). As a result of the Court of Justice's ability to reformulate questions in the light of the relevant issues of fact and national law, the referring judge may receive guidance which is sufficiently specific as to leave him little choice in the application of Community law. This undoubtedly promotes the uniform application of Community law .

JURISDICTION OF THE COURT OF JUSTICE

The Article 177 procedure rests on a strict separation of powers. The Court of Justice has no power to compel national courts to refer and no control over the application of its rulings. Its jurisdiction depends 'solely on the existence of a request from the national court' (*De Geus en Uitdenbogerd* v *Bosch* (case 13/61)). Under Article 177 it may give preliminary rulings on questions of interpretation and validity of EC law. Its interpretative role is very wide. It may rule on the interpretation of the EC treaties, of acts of the institutions, and of statutes of bodies established by an act of the Council, where those statutes so provide. Its interpretative jurisdiction thus extends over the whole field of EC law. It is not necessary that the EC law be directly effective (*Mazzalai* (case 111/75)) or even that the measure in question be legally binding. An interpretation on any provision of EC law, even a recommendation or opinion, may be relevant to the interpretation of domestic implementing measures (see *Grimaldi* v *Fonds des Maladies Professionnelles* (case C 322/88)).

The Court is confined however to the interpretation of *Community* law. It has no jurisdiction to interpret domestic law or pass judgment on the compatibility of domestic law with EC law, although it is often asked to do so (*Van Gend en Loos* (case 26/62)). Nevertheless its rulings on questions of EC law, delivered in the context of the relevant facts and issues of national law, usually leave the matter in little doubt, and a national judge often has little discretion in the application of the ruling if he is to comply with his duty to give priority to EC law.

THE EFFECT OF A RULING

A ruling from the Court of Justice under Article 177 is clearly binding on the referring court. As a representative of the state the judge requesting the ruling has a duty under Article 5 EC to apply it in deciding the case before him. In addition, a ruling will normally be binding generally and retrospective in its effect. As the Court held in *Ariete SpA* (case 811/79), an interpretation under Article 177 of a rule of Community law 'clarifies and defines where necessary the meaning and scope of that rule as it must or ought to be understood from the time of its coming into force'. Thus, subject to national limitation rules (which must now be applied in the light of the Court's ruling in *Emmott* v *Minister for Social Welfare* (case C 208/90), see Chapter 5, it can form the basis for a claim in respect of situations occurring prior to judgment. However in certain cases, in the interests of legal certainty, and taking into account the serious effects which its judgments might have as regards the past on legal relationships established in good faith, it may limit the effects of its judgment to future claims, or claims already lodged at the time of judgment. It did so in *Defrenne* v *Sabena (No. 2)* (case 43/75), in *Blaizot* (case 24/86) and *Barber* v *Guardian Royal Exchange Assurance Group* (case C 262/88). These were exceptional cases, examples of highly 'creative' interpretations by the Court. To apply them retrospectively would undoubtedly have breached the legitimate expectations of the parties on whom the obligations under the rulings had been imposed. But the court has been sparing in allowing such exceptions, even when its rulings have changed, with significant effect, what appeared to be the law (e.g, *Marshall* v *Southampton AHA (Nos. 1 and 2)* (cases 152/84 and 271/91)). Despite the urgings of Advocate-General Mischo it did not limit the effect of its ruling in *Francovich* (cases 6 and 9/90). Moreover only the Court itself has the power to limit its rulings, and it may only do so in the case in which the ruling is given (*Ariete SpA*), unless some new issue of EC law is raised (e.g., *Blaizot*). Thus if a party, for example an employer, or a member state wishes to limit the effect of a ruling he must persuade the Court to do so *in the case in which the ruling is given*. All member states are notified of references to the Court and member states and persons who can establish an interest in the case are entitled to intervene in Article 177 proceedings, although submissions are limited to supporting the submissions of one of the parties (Articles 20 and 37 Protocol on the Statute of the Court of Justice 1988). In *Defrenne, Blaizot* and *Barber* strong arguments were adduced by some member states as to the disruptive and unforeseen effects of the ruling were it to apply retrospectively.

In the absence of special pleading the Court is unlikely to limit the effects of a ruling on interpretation. To do so freely would be to undermine respect for the law, to encourage the belief that the Court is making, not simply declaring, EC law.

Although a ruling under Article 177 is not directed at a member state (unless the state is a party to the domestic proceedings) where it reveals a breach by a state of its Community obligations, that state, by reason of its duty under Article 5 EC to 'take all appropriate measures' to fulfil its Community obligations, should rectify national law to bring it into line with that ruling. If it fails to do so it may now be liable in damages under *Francovich* v *Italian State* (cases C 6 and 9/90) (see Chapters 2, 5 and 7).

FIVE

Remedies: relevant principles and rules of Community law

BASIC PRINCIPLES

If the Court of Justice has provided the means of enforcement of Community rights before national courts via the principles of direct and indirect effects and state liability in damages, the question arises what remedies and procedures are appropriate for the enforcement of these rights? Do national rules apply, or are there special, Community rules? As has been seen in Chapters 1–4, the application of Community law requires national judges to adopt new modes of interpretation, to adapt to new procedures. Does it also require the provision of new remedies?

The answer to these questions has been provided almost entirely by the Court through its rulings on the interpretation of Community law in Article 177 proceedings. There are three basic principles in this area:

(a) the principle of national treatment or equivalence;
(b) the principle of non-discrimination, which embraces, as elsewhere in EC law, both direct and indirect discrimination, and
(c) the principle of effectiveness.

The classic formula, containing all three principles, was introduced in *Rewe-Zentralfinanz* v *Landwirtschaftskammer Saarland* ((case 33/76); see also *Comet BV* v *Produktschap voor Siergevassen* (case 45/76)), in the following terms

In the absence of Community rules, it is for the domestic system of each member state to designate the courts having jurisdiction and the procedural conditions governing actions at law intended to ensure the protection of the rights which subjects derive from the direct effects of Community law, it being understood that such conditions cannot be less favourable than those relating to similar actions of a domestic nature . . .

. . . The position would be different only if these rules made it impossible in practice to exercise rights which the national courts have a duty to protect

Similarly in *Rewe* v *Hauptzollampt Kiel* (case 158/80)

Although the Treaty has made it possible . . . for private persons to bring a direct action (before domestic courts based on EC law), it was not intended to create new remedies in the national courts to ensure the observance of Community law . . . On the other hand . . . it must be possible for every type of action provided for by national law to be available for the purpose of ensuring observance of Community provisions having direct effect, on the same conditions as would apply were it a question of observing national law.

Thus the 'normal' rules applicable to claims before national courts based on EC law are the relevant national rules governing the equivalent claim under domestic law: it is only where national rules are ineffective, making it 'impossible in practice' to protect individuals' Community rights that it will be necessary for national courts to provide new rules.

Although originally expressed in terms of the protection of directly effective Community rights, the Court in *Francovich* (cases 6 and 9/90) extended these principles to apply to 'all rights which persons enjoy under Community law'. This was clearly necessary to ensure the effective application by national courts of the principles of indirect effects and state liability under *Francovich*.

THE EFFECTIVENESS PRINCIPLE

Whilst the first two principles of national treatment and non-discrimination are relatively clear (although, as will be seen below, the former particularly is not without its problems), and have been consistently applied, the principle of effectiveness has developed over the years. As introduced in *Rewe* and *Comet* (cases 33 and 45/76) an effective remedy was one which did not make it 'impossible in practice' for an individual to exercise his Community rights. It has since been extended to exclude the application of national rules which make it 'virtually impossible' or 'excessively difficult' (*Express Dairy Foods* (case 130/79)) to do so. In *Von Colson* v *Land Nordrhein-Westfalen* (case 14/83), the Court, in interpreting Article 6 of Equal Treatment Directive 76/207, which requires states to

introduce into their national legal systems such measures as are necessary to enable all persons who consider themselves wronged by failure to apply the principle of equal treatment to pursue their claims by judicial process . . .

held that this obligation required all member states

to adopt measures which are *sufficiently* effective to achieve the objective of the Directive. Although the Directive does not require any specific form of sanction for unlawful discrimination it does entail that that sanction be such as to guarantee real and effective judicial protection. It must also have a real deterrent effect on the employer (para 23).

Thus the concept of effectiveness has a two-fold application. It must be effective both to protect individuals' Community rights and to deter parties from breaching Community law. Whilst the former function is alluded to more consistently by the Court, the latter must not be forgotten. It is especially important in certain fields, such as public procurement and environmental protection, where prevention may be more effective than cure.

Although the *Von Colson* judgment concerned the interpretation of a specific Article contained in a Directive, it is generally agreed that it represents a particular application of the wider Community principle of effective judicial protection based on Article 5 of the EC Treaty.

In *Amministrazione delle Finanze dello Stato* v *Simmenthal SpA* (case 106/77) the ECJ, arguing from member states' obligation under Article 5 EC to protect the rights which persons derive from direct effective provisions of EC law, held that

Any provisions of a national legal system and any legal, administrative or judicial practice which might impair the effectiveness of Community law by withholding from the national court having jurisdiction to apply such law the power to do everything necessary, at the moment of its application, to set aside provisions which might prevent, even temporarily, Community rules having their full force and effect, are incompatible with these requirements, which are the very essence of Community law.

This potent principle was applied in *Factortame* v *Secretary of State for Transport (No. 2)* [1991] 1 All ER 70 to enable the applicants to claim and obtain from the House of Lords an interim injunction against the Crown, to prevent the application of a British statute, a remedy regarded by that House at the time to be unobtainable as a matter of English law.

Finally in *Marshall* v *Southampton AHA (No. 2)* (case C 271/91), in a challenge based, as in *Von Colson*, on Article 6 of Directive 76/207, to the effectiveness of the remedy in damages provided under the Sex Discrimination Act 1975, which were subject at the time to fixed statutory limits, the Court ruled that the remedies required to be provided under Article 6 must be 'sufficiently effective to achieve the objectives of the Directive'. Despite, indeed citing, its statement in *Von Colson* that Article 6 was not sufficiently clear and precise to provide a specific sanction against discrimination, the Court went on to decide that in order to comply with the principle of non-discrimination and its obligations under Article 6 of Directive 76/207 the state must provide full compensation for those damaged as a result of its breach.

Thus the principle of effectiveness has broadened since its introduction in *Rewe-Zentralfinanz* v *Landwirtschaftskammer Saarland* (case 33/76) resulting in some uncertainty. Whilst it may not be hard to establish that a rule of national law, whether of substance or procedure, makes it 'impossible in practice' or even 'excessively difficult' to protect an individual's Community rights, the question of whether it is 'effective' or 'sufficiently effective' to achieve that end, and, if not, what remedy will be so regarded, is far from clear. A test of 'effectiveness' or 'sufficient effectiveness' does not lend itself to objective assessment. Moreover some limitations and exclusions which may undermine the full effectiveness of national remedies may be justified; a factor which has served to restrict the protection of individuals in claims against the Community (see Chapters 9 and 10) but which has rarely been considered by the Court when assessing the effectiveness of national remedies for breaches of EC law.

As well as providing a basis for the award by national courts of full compensation for individuals suffering loss as a result of infringements of their Community rights, the effectiveness principle has also been invoked in the context of the imposition of penalties. In *Commission* v *Greek Republic* (case 68/88) the Commission instituted Article 169 proceedings against Greece for failing to take action against a fraud, perpetrated against the Community, designed to avoid the imposition of agricultural levies on the import of maize from Yugoslavia. The consignments in question had been officially declared by the Greek authorities to originate in Greece. The Court held that

> By failing to institute criminal or disciplinary proceedings against the persons who took part in the perpetration and concealment of the transactions which made it possible to evade the above-mentioned agricultural duties the Hellenic Republic had failed to fulfil its obligations under Article 5 of the EEC Treaty.

Thus where Community rules do not provide for sanctions for infringements of its rules Member States are obliged under Article 5 EC to take all necessary steps to ensure the effectiveness of Community law. Whilst states are free to choose the penalties, they must ensure that infringements of EC law are subject to sanctions which are, in substance and procedure, analogous to those applicable to infringements of national law of a similar nature and importance, and which are 'effective, proportionate and dissuasive' in character.

Thus, despite the Court's purported adherence to the principles of national procedural and remedial autonomy in matters concerning the enforcement of EC law, the effectiveness principle has on occasions required the modification of national law, even the provision of new remedies and sanctions. National laws are not always effective, or sufficiently effective, to protect individuals' Community rights, or to deter breaches of Community law. As will be seen in the following chapters, access to the courts may be limited, as may access to remedies; procedural rules relating for example to standing, or time limitation, or evidence, or the giving of reasons, may stand in the way of effective enforcement. The remedies provided by way of damages may not be adequate to compensate for the loss of Community rights, or to prevent their breach. Such lacunae may result from statutory limitations, as in *Marshall*, or from established privileges and immunities. Whilst some may be justified for sound policy reasons, many will not. Furthermore, even if national remedies are deemed effective to protect individuals' Community rights, and their application results in equal protection for individuals as regards matters of domestic and matters of Community law *within* member states, the wide variation in rules from state to state (Hartley has noted (1980) 5 EL Rev 366) that limitation periods in respect of the same claim can range from two months to ten years) gives rise to unequal protection for individuals *across* the Community.

The Court has long been aware of this problem. In *Rewe-Zentralfinanz* v *Landwirtschaftskammer Saarland* (case 33/76) and *Comet* (45/76) it averted to the distortions in trade and competition which might result from the application of diverse national rules. It suggested that steps should be taken by the EC institutions to 'eliminate the differences between the provisions laid down in such matters by law, regulatory and administrative action in member states if those differences are found to be such as to cause distortion or to affect the functioning of the common market'. In *Express Dairy Foods* (case 130/79) it 'regretted' the absence of Community provision harmonising procedures and time limits, noting that their absence resulted in 'differences of treatment on a Community scale'. But it was 'not for the Court to issue general rules of substance and procedure, these being provisions which only the competent institutions can adopt' (para. 12).

Despite the Court's urgings, and those of many commentators, attempts by the Commission to introduce measures to harmonise national rules in this area have so far met with little success. Thus it has been left to the Court to decide, on a case-by-case basis, on reference from national courts under Article 177, whether particular national rules, in particular contexts, provide effective protection for individuals' Community rights. In ruling on questions of interpretation of EC law in the context of such referrals, the ECJ, contrary to its original position in *Express Dairy Foods* (case 130/79) that it was 'not for the Court' to do so, has laid down, in increasingly specific terms, pursuant to the effectiveness principle, a number of 'general rules of substance and procedure' to be applied by national courts in the context of enforcement of EC law. These will now be considered

SPECIFIC PRINCIPLES AND RULES OF COMMUNITY LAW

Restitution

There have been many claims before national courts for the return of money paid in breach of Community law. The EC Treaty prohibits the imposition of customs duties, or charges of equivalent effect, on imports and exports from member states. Discriminatory taxation, whether directly or indirectly imposed, is forbidden. These provisions, which are directly effective, are not infrequently breached. Similarly, in implementing the Community's Common Customs tariff or Common Commercial Policy, levies may be imposed by national authorities in breach of EC Regulations, or pursuant to EC Regulations alleged, or found (in previous Article 173 or Article 177 proceedings, see

Chapters 8 and 9) to be invalid. As early as 1960 the Court held, in a claim for the repayment of taxes levied in breach of the ECSC treaty (*Humblet* v *Etat Belge* (case 6/60) (1960) Receuil 1131), that once a state has been found to have breached Community law it must take the necessary measures to make good the unlawful effects of the breach (*'réparer les effets illicites'*), making restitution for sums wrongfully levied as a result of that breach (*'faire restituer au requérant les sommes éventuellement perçus à tort'*). *Rewe-Zentralfinanz* v *Landwirtschaftskammer Saarland, Comet* and *Express Dairy Foods* all concerned claims for restitution of sums levied in breach of EC law in which their right to restitution was presumed.

Questions have arisen whether restitution can be denied where the cost has been passed on to third parties. In *Denkavit* ((case 61/79) [1980] ECR 1205, see also *Hans Just* v *Minister for Fiscal Affairs* (case 68/79) [1980] ECR 501) the Court ruled, in Article 177 proceedings, that the principle of effective judicial protection did not require the recovery of sums paid to national authorities in breach of EC law where this would involve an unjustified enrichment of the party concerned. This prompted some states to introduce legislation precluding recovery in these circumstances and imposing onerous requirements of proof that the cost incurred by the party seeking restitution had not been passed on. The legality of such measures was challenged before the Court in *Amministrazione delle Finanze dello Stato* v *SpA San Giorgio* (case 199/82). The Court, ruling under Article 177, found that rules such as those introduced by the Italian government, which imposed on those seeking restitution a negative burden of proof and demanded the production of documentary evidence that the sums wrongfully levied had been passed on, thereby rendering the recovery of such sums 'virtually impossible' or 'excessively difficult', would be incompatible with EC law. Although expressed in terms of a claim for restitution, this ruling, as an application of the effectiveness principle, could be invoked in other contexts to challenge similarly restrictive presumptions or rules of evidence prescribed under national law, a fortiori when they are introduced by the state deliberately, as appeared to be the case with the Italian legislation challenged in *San Giorgio*, in order to avoid financial liability for actions taken in breach of EC law.

Interim Relief

The principle of national treatment has also been found inadequate in the UK in relation to interim relief. Whilst there should be little difficulty in principle in obtaining interim relief in private law actions, the position was unclear in respect of actions against public authorities, and it was generally (but see Wade (1992) NLJ 1275) thought that in English law an interim injunction was not available against the Crown. This question arose in *Factortame* v *Secretary of State for Transport* [1990] 2 AC 85. Here the applicants, a group of Spanish fishermen, were seeking an interim injunction to prevent the application of a statute, the Merchant Shipping Act 1988, which they claimed was in breach of Community law. At this stage the Community 'rights' claimed under Articles 7 and 52 EEC were putative, since it had not been proved that the statute was in fact in breach of Community law. This question had been referred to the Court of Justice by the English Divisional Court, but had not yet been decided: hence the request for interim relief. When the matter came before the House of Lords, the House found that it had no jurisdiction under English law to grant interim relief against the Crown. However, recognising that it was obliged, under the European Communities Act 1972, to protect individuals' directly effective Community rights, it referred to the Court of Justice to ascertain whether it was obliged to provide the relief requested to protect the applicants' putative rights as a matter of Community law. The Court's ruling was unequivocal. Citing *Simmenthal SpA* (case 106/77) that a national court must do 'everything necessary ... to set aside provisions (of national law) which might prevent, even temporarily, Community rules from having their full force and effect', it concluded (at para. 21) that

> the full effectiveness of Community law would be just as much impaired if a rule of national law could prevent a court seized of a dispute governed by Community law from granting interim relief in order to ensure the full effectiveness of the judgment to be given on the existence of the rights claimed under Community law. It follows that a court, which in those circumstances would grant interim relief if it were not for a rule of national law, is obliged to set aside that rule.

Therefore (at para. 23)

> Community law must be interpreted as meaning that a national court which, in a case before it concerning Community law, considers that the sole obstacle which precludes it from granting interim relief is a rule of national law, must set aside that rule.

The Court went further in *Zuckerfabrik Süderdithmarschen AG* v *Hauptzollamt Itzehoe* (cases C 143/88 and C 92/89). The applicants here were attempting to resist a demand from their national authorities, based on an EC Regulation, for the payment of an 'elimination levy', on the grounds that the EC Regulation was invalid. They applied to their national court for an interim injunction to prevent the application of the Regulation against them, pending a ruling from the ECJ, under Article 177, on its validity. The national court sought a ruling from the ECJ on this point, and on the question of whether national courts were obliged under Community law to grant interim relief when the invalidity of the impugned Regulation had not yet been established. Citing *Factortame*, the Court confirmed that they were so obliged:

> In cases where national authorities are responsible for the administrative implementation of Community Regulations the legal protection guaranteed by EEC law includes the right of individuals to challenge, as a preliminary issue, the legality of such Regulations before national courts ... and to induce these courts to refer questions to the ECJ for a preliminary ruling. That right would be compromised if, pending delivery of a judgment by the

Court, which alone has jurisdiction to declare EEC Regulations invalid, individuals were not in a position to obtain a decision granting suspension of enforcement which would make it possible for the effects of the disputed Regulation to be rendered for the time being inoperative against them' (paras. 16, 17).

In the context of actions for annulment Article 185 EEC enables an applicant to request suspension of the enforcement of the contested act and empowers the Court of Justice to order such suspension. The coherence of the system of interim protection requires that national courts should also be able to order the suspension of enforcement of national administrative measures based on an EEC Regulation, the legality of which is contested (para. 18) . . .

The interim legal protection which Community law ensures for individuals before national courts must remain the same, irrespective of whether they contest the compatibility of national legal provisions with Community law or the validity of secondary Community law, in view of the fact that the dispute in both cases is based on Community law itself (para. 20).

Having established a general obligation to grant interim relief, and pointing out that the application of different rules of procedure according to the different rules of member states 'may jeopardise the uniform application of Community law', the Court proceeded to lay down specific conditions to be observed by national courts in the granting of such relief. Borrowing from its own jurisdiction under Article 185 EC it suggested that interim measures should be granted by national courts only

(a) if the facts and legal circumstances are such as to persuade the court that *serious doubts exist* as to the validity of the Community measure on which the contested administrative measure is based. In seeking a ruling on the validity of the measure in question the national court must set out the reasons for which it believes that the provision is invalid;
(b) in cases of *urgency* (i.e., if it is necessary to adopt them); and
(c) *to avoid serious and irreparable damage* to the party seeking them.

Furthermore, the damage must be likely to materialise before the ECJ's ruling on the validity of the Community act. Purely financial damage will not be regarded as irreparable. In deciding whether to grant interim relief the national court must also take into account the interests of the Community. Regulations should not be set aside without appropriate guarantees. If suspension of enforcement is liable to involve a financial risk to the Community the national court must be in a position to provide adequate guarantees such as the deposit of money or other security (para. 32).

Although *Zuckerfabrik* concerned the granting of interim relief pending a ruling on the validity of Community law paragraph 20 of the Court's judgment suggests that the conditions laid down in *Zuckerfabrik* will also apply in cases such as *Factortame*, where the individual is seeking an injunction to prevent the application of national law pending a ruling on interpretation designed to assess the compatibility of national law with Community law.

But *Zuckerfabrik* has a wider significance in that it represents the first attempt on the part of the Court to lay down specific *Community* rules for the application of *particular* remedies in the context of actions before national courts based on EC law. The careful reasoning, founded on the need for coherence and uniformity, will no doubt provide the basis for the development of further Community rules.

Damages

Since, in actions based on individuals' Community rights, national courts are obliged to apply the principle of national treatment, it is clear that individuals should be entitled, at least under the conditions appropriate to similar or equivalent claims under national law, to damages. This has long been accepted in the context of claims based on directly effective Community law. There are two situations in which damages may be claimed

(a)   on the basis of direct or indirect effects, for breach of substantive provisions of Community law; and

(b)   on the principles laid down in *Francovich*.

Damages based on direct and indirect effects   As noted above, in *Humblet* (case 6/60) in 1960, the Court suggested, in a claim based on inter alia Article 43 of the ECSC treaty, that the defendant state was obliged to '*réparer les effets illicites*' of its actions in breach of the Treaty. In *Russo* v *AIMA* ((case 60/75) [1976] ECR 45), in a claim by an Italian cereal producer against the Italian Intervention Agency for losses suffered as a result of the Agency's having sold cereals, imported from third countries, at prices below Community intervention prices, in breach of EC law, the Court held

If damage has been caused through an infringement of EC law the state is liable to the injured party for the consequences, in the context of provisions of national law on the liability of the state.

In fact a number of successful claims for damages have been brought before national courts based on directly effective EC law (e.g., *Roussel*, Hague District Court, 1984; *Steinhauser* v *City of Biarritz*, Tribunal Adminstratif de Pau, 1985 (case 197/84); *Bourgoin* v *Minister of Agriculture Fisheries and Food*, English Court of Appeal, defendants potentially liable under the tort of misfeasance in public office [1985] 3 All ER 585). But it was not until *Von Colson and Kamann* and *Harz* v *Deutsche Tradax* that the Court of Justice had an opportunity to rule more specifically on the question of damages.

The claims in *Von Colson and Kamann* (case 14/83) and *Harz* v *Deutsche Tradax* (case 79/83) were for damages, in respect of sexual discrimination, contrary to EC Directive 76/207. Both plaintiffs claimed that the damages available under German law, which were limited to expenses, were in breach of Article 6 of the Directive. However in Harz's case the Directive under which she claimed was not directly effective, since the defendant was not a 'public' body. It is here, no doubt to overcome the problem of enforcing Directives against 'private' bodies, that the Court introduced the principle of indirect effect. This required national courts, as agencies of the State, to 'interpret' domestic law in such a way as to give effect to the Directive (see Chapter 2). On the question of damages, although it found that Article 6 of the Directive was not sufficiently clear and precise to give rise to a specific Community sanction, and a member state was 'free to choose between different solutions for achieving its objective', it suggested that in accordance with their obligation to provide 'real and effective' remedies, states must provide compensation which is more than nominal; it must be 'adequate in relation to the damage sustained'.

A more significant step was taken in *Marshall* v *Southampton AHA (No. 2)* (case C 271/91). Having established a claim to damages under Directive 76/207 against the health authority on the principle of direct effects, Ms Marshall questioned the adequacy of the damages awarded under the Sex Discrimination Act 1975. The ceiling of £6,250, to which the award was subject at the relevant time, was not, she suggested, adequate to protect her Community rights. The House of Lords asked the ECJ inter alia whether the statutory figure was adequate to protect her rights under the Directive or whether Article 6 of the Directive obliged member states to provide for the award of full compensation. It also asked whether she was entitled to interest on the award running from the date of discrimination to the date when compensation was paid.

The Court reiterated its view in *Von Colson* that Article 6 did not prescribe a specific remedy for breach of Community sex discrimination rules, but went on to hold that although states were free under Article 6 to choose between different solutions, the Article implied that the solutions chosen must be suitable for achieving the objectives of the Directive. Since the objective of the Directive was to achieve real equality of opportunity, where financial compensation was the measure adopted to achieve this objective, it had to enable the loss actually sustained to be made good in full, in accordance with the applicable rules of national law. It followed that the compensation provided under national law could not be limited a priori in amount. Following the same principle the award of interest 'in accordance with the applicable national rules' was an 'essential component of compensation'.

The application of this ruling left little discretion to the industrial tribunal deciding Marshall's case. The concept of full compensation, the basic principle underlying tort compensation, is fully developed in English law. Ms Marshall would be entitled to be put into the position she would have been in had the discrimination not occurred, and she had worked, as she wished to do, until the age of 65, with interest as from the date of discrimination, when her dismissal occurred. But the wider implications of the case remain unclear. Was the Court simply responding, as it appeared to be, to questions referred concerning the applicability and adequacy of *particular* rules of English law? Or was it attempting to establish a new Community rule governing the award of damages? Does the principle of full compensation only apply, as seems unlikely, to claims based on sex discrimination, or does it apply to all claims for compensation for damage resulting from infringements of individuals' Community rights, including claims based on *Francovich*?

If it is desirable, for the reasons suggested by the Court in *Zuckerfabrik*, that the rules for the protection of individuals' Community rights be uniform throughout the Community, the principle of full compensation should apply, *under the same conditions*, in all member states. Anything less would 'cause distortion and affect the functioning of the common market' (see *Express Dairy Foods*, case 130/79)). It would result in unequal treatment for persons suffering the same loss. But even if the principle of full compensation is held to apply in all member states, as long as it is applied 'in accordance with the applicable rules of national law' there will be no uniformity.

Whatever the answer to the questions raised by *Marshall (No. 2)*, which in the absence of legislation will have to be decided by the ECJ, it is clear from the cases considered above that individuals may claim damages for infringements of their Community rights under the principles of direct and indirect effects, although their chances of success will be more limited under the latter for the reason outlined in Chapter 2. In the interest of legal certainty, national courts may be reluctant to award, by means of 'interpretation', against a 'private' body, a remedy different from that which is available in respect of a comparable claim under national law in order to ensure that the remedy provided is 'sufficiently effective'.

Damages under Francovich　A claim for damages against the state, based on *Francovich*, is different in kind from one based on direct or indirect effects. *Francovich* introduced a new Community principle of state liability. Although the Court suggested that it should be applied by national courts 'within the context of national law on liability' (para. 42), therefore subject to the principle of national treatment, it is clear that in most, if not all, member states, national law will not be effective (in any sense of the word) to protect individuals' rights under *Francovich*. Whilst all member states provide (albeit to different degrees and subject to different conditions) for the liability of public authorities for damage resulting from invalid or ultra vires acts (or failure to act), in the majority of cases damages are available only in respect of administrative or executive acts. Largely for reasons relating to the sovereignty of Parliament, they are not available against *legislative* acts, even if they can be found to be 'wrongful'. Yet liability under *Francovich*, even if confined to the non-implementation of Directives, as seems unlikely, will more often than not arise from legislative acts or omissions. If national courts are effectively to protect individuals' rights under *Francovich*, damages must be paid in respect of such acts. It is even possible, following *Marshall (No. 2)* that the compensation provided will have to be 'full'.

Moreover, although the principle of state liability was laid down in specific terms in *Francovich*, expressed as arising where a state has failed to implement a Directive, it was also expressed in broader terms, that 'a state is liable to make good damage to individuals caused by a breach of Community law for which it is responsible'. It has yet to be decided whether states can be liable under *Francovich* for 'every failure to observe Community law . . . whether that failure is in breach of the Treaty, Regulations or Directives, whether they have direct effect or not', as suggested by Advocate-General Mischo, and if so, whether such failures must be culpable in order to attract liability. A principle of strict liability would render member states highly vulnerable in view of the imprecise nature of much EC law.

Answers to some of these questions will be provided when the Court of Justice rules on the questions referred in *Brasserie du Pêcheur SA* (case C 46/93, 1993 OJC 92/4) and *Factortame (No. 3)* (case C 48/93, 1993 OJC 94/13). In *Brasserie du Pêcheur* the German *Bundesgerichtshof* asked whether liability under *Francovich* might be engaged in the case of breach of (EC) Treaty rules; whether fault in the form of intention or negligence could be imposed as a condition of liability; whether a state could be liable for losses suffered prior to a formal finding of failure by the Court. Both *Brasserie du Pêcheur* and *Factortame (No 3)* raised questions relating to damages; whether compensation entitled claimants to all financial losses, including lost profits (*Brasserie du Pêcheur*); whether compensation was available for purely economic loss; whether exemplary damages should be available (*Factortame (No. 3)*. Answers to these questions will create a degree of certainty, but they will not solve all the problems. The questions submitted reflect, and will be applied within the context of, particular rules of national law. These rules differ from state to state, as do other relevant rules relating, for example, to causation and remoteness of damage, which were not referred for consideration by the Court. If claims under *Francovich* continue to be decided 'within the context of national law on liability' albeit subject to rulings on interpretation from the Court, there will still be no uniformity. For reasons to be explored below, it is not desirable that these matters, of profound importance to member states and to Community solidarity, should be resolved ad hoc under the Article 177 procedure.

Limitation Periods

A number of cases considered above (*Rewe-Zentralfinanz* v *Landwirtschaftskam-mer Saarland* (case 33/76); *Comet* (case 45/76); *Express Dairy Foods* (case 130/79)) have raised questions concerning the applicability of national limitation rules to claims based on EC law. Clearly the rules vary greatly, depending on the nature of the action, both within a state and from state to state. Apart from the anomaly this creates, and the lack of equality in the protection of individuals' Community rights, limitation rules have operated in the Community context to undermine the effective protection of these rights. Uncertainty as to the nature and effect of Community law and the scope of the principles of direct and indirect effects has resulted in individuals failing to act in time to enforce their rights.

Initially, and cautiously, in *Rewe-Zentralfinanz* v *Landwirtschaftskammer Saarland* and *Comet* (cases 33 and 45/76) in ruling on the question of the applicability of national limitation rules as well as on the matter of restitution, the Court was content to assert the principle of national treatment, simply suggesting that a 'reasonable period of limitation' would not make it 'imposs-ible in practice' for national courts to protect individuals' Community rights.

The fixing of time limits, the Court said, was an 'application of the fundamental principle of legal certainty', which protects both the authority concerned and the party from whom payment is claimed. In *Express Dairy Foods* it 'regretted' the absence of Community provisions harmonising time limits, but refrained from attempting itself to lay down general rules.

It changed its mind in *Emmott v Minister for Social Welfare* (case C 208/90). This case concerned a challenge to the Irish authorities' refusal of disability benefit which the applicant, Mrs Emmott, claimed was discriminatory, in breach of EC Directive 79/7 on the Equal Treatment of Men and Women in matters of Social Security. At the time when her cause of action arose Mrs Emmott was unaware that the Directive was directly effective. When she became aware that it was, following a ruling from the ECJ in *McDermott v Minister for Social Welfare* (case 286/85), she applied to the Minister for her case to be reviewed. Her application was deferred pending a ruling from the ECJ in *Cotter and McDermott* (case 377/89). Following that ruling, when the Irish High Court finally granted leave to institute proceedings for judicial review, the Minister argued that she was out of time. The Irish Judge referred to the ECJ the question of whether it was contrary to Community law for the relevant authorities of a member state to rely on national procedural rules, in particular rules relating to time limits, in defending claims based on Community Directives.

The Court of Justice, citing *Rewe-Zentralfinanz v Landwirtschaftskammer Saarland's* classic three principles and the compatibility with these principles of 'reasonable' limitation rules, went on to establish a new rule of Community law, based on the 'particular nature of Directives'. It reasoned as follows: states are obliged under Article 189(3) to adopt all the measures necessary to ensure the full application of Directives. The principle of direct effects provides only a minimum guarantee for individuals' Community rights under Directives: it cannot justify a member state absolving itself from taking, in good time, implementing measures appropriate to the purpose of the Directive. As long as the state has failed fully to implement the Directive, the individual is in a state of uncertainty; he is unable to ascertain the full extent of his rights. Therefore the competent authorities of a member state cannot rely, in an action against them based on the Directive, on national procedural rules relating to time limits for bringing proceedings as long as that member state has not properly transposed that Directive into domestic law.

Thus, although national limitation rules continue to apply (provided they are 'reasonable'), time will not begin to run in an action against a (public) party acting in breach of the Directive until the Directive has been fully and correctly implemented. Whilst the reasoning of *Emmott* is consistent with the principle invoked in *Becker* (case 8/81) to justify the vertical effect of Directives (that a state cannot plead its own wrong in failing to implement a Directive in an action against it based on the Directive), the implications of the decision are profound. Although expressed in terms of the inability of the 'competent authorities' to rely in these circumstances on national limitation rules, it is likely to be invoked against other 'public' bodies against which Directives can be invoked, such as British Gas or the Health Authority in *Marshall*, which have no control over, and bear no responsibility for, the non-implementation of the Directive. This fact has not in the past prevented a Directive from being enforced against such bodies. If 'public' bodies, as broadly defined in *Foster* v *British Gas* ((case C 188/89) see Chapter 1) are to be subject to the rules laid down in *Emmott*, arguably they should be entitled to seek indemnity from the state under *Francovich*. It could also be argued that *Emmott* might be invoked to postpone the running of time in a case based on *Francovich*.

Another question arising from *Emmott* is at what stage will a member state be deemed to have 'properly transposed' a Directive into domestic law? A state may have implemented the Directive in good faith, on time and, in its view, correctly. It may have done nothing, genuinely and reasonably believing that domestic law was consistent with the Directive. An unexpected interpretation from the Court of Justice under Article 177 may prove otherwise. The state may then change its law to comply with that ruling. Unless the ECJ has expressly (and exceptionally) limited the effect of its ruling (see Chapter 4), claims in respect of prior, hitherto unrecognised breaches may at that stage be made. Will *Emmott* allow time to begin to run in respect of all these claims? Following the amendment of the Sex Discrimination Act 1975 by the Sex Discrimination and Equal Pay (Remedies) Regulations 1993 (SI 1993/2798), bringing the Act into line with the law as declared in *Marshall (No 2)*, many claims for full compensation have been lodged in respect of acts of discrimination dating from 9 August 1978, the date on which the Equal Treatment Directive (76/207) became directly effective. If *Emmott* is to apply without modification there is no reason why these claims should not succeed.

Perhaps having become aware of the problems raised by *Emmott*, the ECJ was more cautious in *Steenhorst-Neerings* (case C 338/91). This case concerned a claim based on EC Equal Treatment (Social Security) Directive 79/7 in respect of past discrimination (between 1984 and 1988, remedied in 1988) in the granting of invalidity benefit under Dutch law. The claim was barred under Dutch law, which imposed a statutory limit of one year on the retrospective payment of invalidity benefit. The applicant, invoking *Emmott*, argued that this was inconsistent with EC law. The Court, in a ruling on interpretation under Article 177, distinguished *Emmott*. *Emmott*, it argued, concerned national rules fixing *time limits for bringing an action*, which prevented individuals from asserting their rights under the Directive. The rule challenged in *Steenhorst-Neerings* on the other hand did not affect the individual's right to rely on Directive 79/7; it merely *limited the retroactive effects of claims* made for the purpose of obtaining the relevant benefits. Whilst the former limitation was designed to ensure that the legality of administrative decisions cannot be challenged indefinitely, the latter served a different purpose, namely to establish the degree of the applicant's incapacity, which might vary over time, and to preserve the financial equilibrium in a scheme in which claims submitted in one year must be covered by the contributions collected during that same year. As such it was justified and was not contrary to EC law.

Such fine distinctions are not convincing. Whilst it is true that the two limitation rules served different purposes, surely their *effect* in both cases was to prevent the applicant from relying on the Directive. *Steenhorst-Neerings* suggests that the Court may be prepared to impose some limits on the application of *Emmott* where a genuine justification for a restriction on recovery can be proved. *Steenhorst-Neerings* was approved and followed in a claim involving similar facts, also based on Directive 79/7, in *Johnson* v *Chief Adjudication Officer* (case C 410/92 judgment of 6 December 1994, unreported).

LEGISLATIVE PROVISION

As well as the three basic principles of Community law, and the specific rules developed by the Court pursuant to the principle of effectiveness, there are a number of areas in which, in addition to laying down substantive rules, EC legislation (usually in the form of Directives) makes some provision in respect of remedies. Such provision ranges from the most general, such as the requirement in Directive 76/207 for member states to introduce 'such measures as are necessary ... for persons wronged to pursue their claim by judicial process', to the particular, as in Directive 64/221 (OJ Sp Ed 1964 No. 850/64 p117), which lays down certain procedural safeguards (e.g., a right to reasons for decisions (Article 6), to due process (Article 9)) for EC workers and their families whom member states seek to deprive of their rights of free movement within the Community on the grounds of public policy, public security and public health. Although, in implementing EC Directives, states have a discretion as to the 'form and method' of implementation, the measures adopted, as the Court pointed out in *Marshall (No. 2)* (case C 271/91), must be 'sufficiently effective to achieve the objectives of the Directive'. Thus a minimal implementation, even if within the strict letter of the Directive, may not suffice. The measures adopted must comply with the effectiveness principle. Subject to this important qualification Community legislation plays a useful role in fostering legal certainty and uniformity by providing for the creation of specific rights, in particular situations, which may not be available under national law.

Since it is clearly impossible in a book of this nature comprehensively to examine Community legislative provision touching on the question of remedies, two areas have been selected, both as examples of a trend towards more specific Community provision in the field of remedies and in order to demonstrate the approach to implementation and interpretation required of these provisions and their relationship with the more general principles and rules of Community law. Where a remedy is sought in an area governed by Community law, the relevant EC legislation should always be consulted, as it should on matters of substance; but it, and the measures adopted to implement the legislation, must be interpreted and applied in the light of the principles of Community law, particularly the effectiveness principle.

Public Procurement

Community legislation in the field of public procurement comprises the Works, Supply and Services Directives (Directive 71/305 (1971) OJ L 185/5, as amended, Directive 77/62 (1977) OJ L 13/1, as amended, and Directive 92/50 (1992) OJ L 209/1 respectively). These Directives lay down the procedures to be followed by public bodies in the awarding of major public contracts, with a view to ensuring an opportunity for contractors in all member states to compete for the contracts on an equal basis. Provision for the enforcement of the Directives was made under separate 'Compliance' Directives, Compliance Directive 89/665 ((1989) OJ L 395/33) and Utilities Compliance Directive 92/13 (OJ L 76/14) as amended by Directive 93/38 (adopted 14 June 1993). The Directives lay down rules on remedies in the public and utilities sectors respectively. They are significant in that they embody, for the first time, separate, complementary legislation designed to secure compliance by those charged with obligations under the Directives with substantive Community rules.

Compliance Directive 89/65 begins by asserting the general principles of non-discrimination and effectiveness, the latter reinforced by the requirement that decisions taken by contracting authorities be reviewed 'as rapidly as possible' (Article 1). Whilst it does not define effectiveness, or lay down specific time limits within which decisions must be made, it is submitted that the principle of effectiveness should be applied in its two-fold sense, as laid down in *Von Colson* (case 14/83). The remedies provided must be effective both to protect individuals' Community rights and to provide a real deterrent against breach of Community public procurement rules. Clearly one of the primary purposes of the Compliance Directives is to secure compliance by public authorities with their obligations under the Works and Supply Directives.

The Directive also sets out specific forms of relief which must be made available. All states are required to make provision for the power (to be exercised by a responsible body) to award interim measures, to set aside unlawful decisions, and to award damages (Article 2). In addition the Directive provides for safeguards where a review body is not judicial in character (Article 2(8)) and it provides that decisions are to be capable of being effectively enforced (Article 2(7)). It also requires that review procedures are to be available, in effect, to interested contractors (Article 1(3)).

It could be argued that these provisions are simply concrete examples of the general principles already established in Community law. Nevertheless they provide a degree of certainty and uniformity at least as to the minimum required of national authorities in this field. However, whilst the Directive provides for specific forms of relief, and specific procedural safeguards, the detailed application of these remedies, and some discretion, is left to member states. The provision of interim relief, set aside and damages, the enforcement and review procedures will be governed by national law. It is open to doubt whether the English Regulations implementing these provisions (SI 1991/2679, 1991/2680, 1992/3297), which fail to provide for the setting aside of *concluded* contracts, although in conformity with the strict words of the Directive, will satisfy the effectiveness principle. A remedy in damages, although available for persons such as contractors precluded from tendering as a result of breach of the rules, may not be effective to protect their rights. Moreover, although courts have the power to grant injunctions or set aside 'decisions' or 'actions' relating to the award of contracts, this power will not be effective either to protect individuals' rights or deter breaches of public procurement rules unless these powers are *exercised* with these objectives in mind. These matters will be considered further in Chapters 6 and 7.

Consumer Protection

Directive 84/450 on Misleading Advertising (1984 OJ L 250/17) and Directive 93/13 on Unfair Terms in Consumer Contracts (1993 OJ L 95/29) both make some specific provision in respect of remedies. Both contain the standard requirement that member states must ensure that 'adequate and effective' means exist for the enforcement of their substantive provisions. More specifically, Directive 86/450 requires states

(a)   to provide means whereby 'persons and organisations regarded under national law as having a legitimate interest' may

(i)   take legal action against such advertising (Article 4(1)(a)) or
(ii)   bring such advertising before an administrative authority competent either to decide on complaints or to initiate appropriate legal proceedings (Article 4(1)(b)), and

(b)   to empower national courts to order the cessation of ... misleading advertising or to order or to institute the appropriate legal proceedings for the prohibition of such publication 'even without proof of actual loss or damage or of intention or negligence on the part of the advertiser (Article 4(2)), such authority being empowered to take measures under an accelerated procedure with (according to choice) interim or definitive effect (Article 4(2)).

Directive 93/13 provides that 'adequate and effective' means of enforcement

shall include provisions whereby persons or organisations having a legitimate interest under national law in protecting consumers, may take action according to the national law concerned before the courts or before competent administrative bodies for a decision as to whether contractual terms drawn up for general use are unfair, so that they can apply appropriate and effective means to prevent the continued use of these terms (Art 7(2)).

Also

with due regard for national laws, the legal remedies referred to in [Article 7(2)] may be directed separately or jointly against a number of sellers or suppliers from the same economic sector or their associations which use or recommend the use of the same general contractual terms or similar terms' (Article 7(3)).

Thus as well as providing for specific remedies against specific defendants the Directives provide for enforcement by persons and organisations regarded as having a 'legitimate interest' in protecting consumers. Although these requirements are expressed to be 'according' or 'with due regard' to national law, the discretion of member states is limited by the need to ensure that national law is sufficiently effective to achieve the objectives of the Directives. Where member states interpret or implement these provisions in an unnecessarily restrictive manner they risk breaching EC law. Unless the courts can bridge the gap by 'interpreting' the domestic provision in such a way as to ensure an effective remedy, which they may not feel able to do in a 'horizontal' claim, the only possible remedy for individuals whose rights had not been effectively protected would be against the state, under *Francovich*, a point made by the Court in *Faccini Dori* (case C 91/92), noted Chapter 2), itself a consumer claim.

CONCLUSIONS

As will be seen in the next two chapters, the application of the principles and rules of Community law as outlined above creates problems for national courts.

First there is the problem of classification. If national courts are to enforce EC law according to the principle of national treatment, the first question to arise is the question of equivalence. What is a 'similar action of a domestic nature'? EC law is sui generis. It extends over an ever increasing range of human activity, conferring rights and imposing obligations in private and public law. It cuts across traditional legal boundaries. In some areas, for example in UK competition law, the enforcement of private rights has developed ad hoc, not always coherently. A plaintiff's interests may be protected by the rules of equity, for example in an action for breach of confidence (e.g., *Seager* v *Copydex* [1967] 2 All ER 415), by specific economic torts, such as passing off (e.g., *Cadbury Schweppes* v *Pub Squash* [1981] 1 All ER 213), or through the doctrine of restraint of trade (e.g., *Esso* v *Harpers Garage* [1968] AC 269). Only if a claim can be fitted within existing categories of tort, or the laws relating to restitution, can full damages be obtained. This raises a question as to which action is appropriate, in the EC context, to provide compensation? These are matters of national law, to be discussed in Chapters 6 and 7. But it is important to note that from the point of view of Community law it is of little relevance which remedy in which area of law is deemed to be equivalent, as long as it is applied without discrimination and is effective, both to protect individuals' Community rights and to secure compliance, by public and private parties, with EC law.

Secondly there is the problem raised by the principle of effectiveness. The main problem is its uncertainty. Whilst it may not be difficult to establish that a particular rule of national law, whether of substance or procedure, makes 'it impossible in practice' for an individual to exercise his Community rights, the question of whether it is 'effective' or 'sufficiently effective', or 'adequate', will often be unclear. Where it is it invites litigation. In the absence of Community rules, legislative or judicial, the matter can only be decided by the European Court. Whilst it is theoretically possible for the matter to be raised by the Commission under Article 169 EC, being politically sensitive this is highly unlikely in practice. It will normally be raised in Article 177 proceedings.

This is not satisfactory. The very nature of the Article 177 procedure, which is based on a strict separation of powers between national and Community courts, means that the ECJ's jurisdiction is limited to particular questions referred in a particular factual context. Although the Court is ingenious in rephrasing the questions referred, and member states and Community institutions and even individuals who can establish 'an interest in the case' (Article 37, Protocol on the Statute of the Court) are permitted to intervene, thereby widening the enquiry, questions are decided in relative isolation. Submissions made in an application to intervene are limited to supporting the submissions of one of the parties (Article 37, Protocol). Thus the wider implications of a ruling are often not explored. As soon as one question is resolved, for example the issue of principle of state liability in *Francovich*, or of time limitation in *Emmott*, further questions arise as to their scope, again requiring resolution by the European Court. If they are not referred to the Court, and are decided 'according to the applicable national rules', the application of important principles of Community law, with serious consequences for states and for public and even private bodies, will not be uniform. Despite the Court's continuing adherence to the principle of national treatment the list of exceptions to that principle is growing and will continue to grow. The development of a coherent and uniform system of protection for individuals' Community rights would be more effectively achieved by legislation than through incremental development by the Court of Justice, subject to the hazards of litigation.

SIX

Impact on judicial review

It is clear from an examination of the scope and objectives of EC law as outlined in Chapter 1 that much, indeed the majority, of EC law, imposes obligations in public law on the authorities of the member states. In carrying out their duties they are obliged to act in accordance with EC law. They are required to implement Community policies laid down in EC Regulations, Directives and Decisions. In fulfilling their duties of implementation, whether by legislative or administrative action, they must respect the rules and principles, written and unwritten, of Community law. Any act or failure to act in breach of these rules will be subject to challenge for illegality.

Whilst the rules and procedures governing actions before domestic courts for judicial review of acts or omissions of public authorities based on EC law are, following the principle of national treatment, the same as those governing similar actions based on domestic law, two factors operate in the Community context to modify these rules. First, the remedies available under national systems must be *effective* to protect individuals' Community rights and deter national authorities from breaching EC law; secondly the grounds for review may need to take into account general principles of law declared by the Court of Justice to be part of Community law.

The purpose of this chapter, and Chapter 7, is not to attempt to define or precisely to draw the line between matters of public and matters of private law, but to focus on the remedies available under both, and the ways in which both may need to be modified to meet the demands of Community law. Clearly public bodies may be liable in the UK under public or private law, depending on the nature of their acts and the context in which they operate. However, whilst acts which belong in the purely 'private' sphere will not be subject to judicial review, the concept of what may be regarded as 'public' may, pursuant to the effectiveness principle, be required to be generously construed for the purpose of the protection of rights derived from Community law.

JUDICIAL REVIEW IN THE UK: ITS EFFECTIVENESS

Judicial review has been described as the 'process by which the High Court exercises its supervisory jurisdiction over the proceedings and decisions of inferior courts, tribunals or other bodies or persons who carry out quasi-judicial functions, or who are charged with the performance of public acts or duties' (Supperstone & Goudie 1992). It is concerned, not with the decision itself, or with the merits of the decision, but with the decision-making process. The duty of the court is confined to testing the legality of action of public bodies performing public acts or duties. It is intended to protect the individual against the abuse of power. Derived from the common law it is now regulated by statute (Supreme Court Act 1981) and Rules of Court (Rules of the Supreme Court (RSC Order 53)). Under these rules the applicant can seek the old prerogative remedies of certiorari, mandamus or prohibition or, following amendments introduced in 1977, injunctions or declarations (RSC Order 53 r. 1 (2)) and, where appropriate, damages (Order 53 r. 7). The remedies are discretionary. In order to obtain access to judicial review the applicant must show a 'sufficient interest' (Order 53 r. 7) and must obtain the leave of the court to proceed. His action is subject to a three-month time limit, running from the date when the decision was made, unless 'good reason' can be shown for the delay (Order 53 r. 4). These limitations are seen as a necessary filter both to protect the administration and to exclude vexatious or frivolous claims. The discretionary nature of the remedies enables the court to take into account the interests of third parties and the wider public interest.

However the High Court is not the only forum, nor Order 53 the only procedure, whereby public action may be challenged in the UK. The legality of public acts or omissions may be challenged indirectly, as an ancillary matter, in any court or tribunal, in an action based on private law, for example to support a claim for damages in tort (e.g., *Bourgoin* v *Ministry of Agriculture, Fisheries and Food* [1985] 3 All ER 585 (CA)), or restitution, or to defend an action in civil or criminal proceedings (e.g., *Wandsworth BC* v *Winder* [1985] AC 461; *Stoke-on-Trent City Council* v *B&Q plc* [1991] 4 All ER 221 (Ch D); *Portsmouth City Council* v *Quietlynne* [1989] 1 CMLR 673), subject to the rules and procedures appropriate to the principal action. Public action may also be challenged under statutory procedures (e.g., *Foster* v *Chief Adjudication Officer* [1993] 1 All ER 705 (HL)). However, whilst an injunction or a declaration may be obtained in these proceedings, the prerogative orders are not obtainable. There may also be statutory limits on remedies. Thus any assessment of the effectiveness of the domestic system of judicial review must take into account the advantages and limitations of all these avenues of review.

A number of factors operate to undermine the effectiveness of the British system of judicial review. Access may be denied on the basis that the decision challenged is not a public law matter, or on technical procedural grounds, that the applicant's action is inappropriate to judicial review. Action may be barred or impeded by statutory or prerogative immunities. There may be limits on the remedies available. Procedural hurdles governing standing or leave, or time limitation, or evidence, may stand in the way of otherwise viable claims. These will now be considered.

Decision not Amenable to Judicial Review

Whether a decision is challenged in an action begun by writ, indirectly, or under Order 53, there is considerable uncertainty over the scope of judicial review; that is the question of which matters emanating from which bodies are sufficiently 'public' to be susceptible to judicial review. The line between public and private acts and between public and private bodies is far from clear. This uncertainty has increased with the growing range and diversity of public involvement in private activities and the vesting of private bodies with public powers. Traditional tests, based on the source of power, whether derived from statute or prerogative, have proved inadequate as a means of assessing whether a decision taken by a particular body involves an element of public law. Many of the acts of public bodies pertain to the private sphere. Conversely, many bodies, such as the City Panel on Takeovers and Mergers have no statutory or prerogative powers, yet they clearly exercise public regulatory functions. For this reason the House of Lords suggested in *R v Panel for Takeovers and Mergers ex parte Datafin plc* [1986] AC 484, that although in some circumstances the source of power may be decisive of the question whether an exercise of that power is a matter of public or private law, in many cases it will be necessary to look at the nature of the power.

If the body in question is exercising public law functions, or if the exercise of its functions have public law consequences, then that may be sufficient to bring the body within the reach of judicial review.

However, whilst the 'function' test has gained widespread acceptance, and is undoubtedly more effective than one based simply on the source of power, the question of what will constitute a 'public law function' or have 'public law consequences' may be unclear. Nor has the 'source' test been abandoned. Where a body's powers are derived from contract, actions taken under these powers will not be subject to judicial review. Although some decisions of domestic tribunals such as trade unions and universities may be deemed to involve matters of a 'public' nature, such as to warrant judicial review, decisions of such bodies concerning 'internal' matters are normally regarded as matters of private law. Thus only those with contractual rights, such as students or trade union members, are able to assert them, and only in pursuit of private law remedies. Although members of clubs or incorporated associations have a contractual relationship, they often have few contractual rights against their decision-making bodies, notwithstanding those bodies' extensive, sometimes monopolistic powers. Where individuals have no contractual rights, and seek to challenge the 'private' decisions of domestic bodies such as the Jockey Club or the Football Association, they may have no effective remedy, even when those decisions profoundly affect their lives.

The UK courts have recognised this problem and regretted the lacuna. In *R v Jockey Club ex parte RAM Racecourses* [1990] COD 346, Simon Brown J, whilst not dissenting from the Divisional Court's decision refusing judicial review of a decision of the Jockey Club on the grounds of its essentially private nature, wondered whether the court's jurisdiction might not be extended to certain functions of what might normally be regarded as non-governmental institutions when those functions could be seen as having an essentially public character. It is clear that had it not been for authority the court would have found the decisions of the Jockey Club in issue in the case to be capable of review. In *R* v *Disciplinary Committee of the Jockey Club ex parte Aga Khan* [1993] 2 All ER 853, the Court of Appeal felt similarly constrained by precedent. Whilst acknowledging that the Jockey Club regulated a significant national activity, exercising powers affecting the public, and that those who wanted to take part in racing had no choice but to agree to be bound by its rules, the Court of Appeal felt bound by authority to conclude that decisions such as those in issue in the case made under powers derived from contract were not subject to judicial review. Similarly in *Page* v *Hull University Visitor* [1993] 1 All ER 97, the House of Lords, expressing regret at the anomalous position of University visitors, whose actions within and without their jurisdiction may not be challenged even for error of law, was not prepared to 'sweep away the law which has for so long regulated the conduct of charitable organisations'. Whilst decisions of universities not subject to visitorial powers may be challenged in some situations (e.g., *R* v *Manchester University, ex parte Nolan*, noted NLJ 27 May 1994), the position is unpredictable; thus access to judicial review even in these cases cannot be guaranteed.

These rules cannot be allowed to prevail in the context of a claim based on EC law. Since tribunals of a private nature may take decisions in breach of individuals' Community rights, for example the right of migrant EC nationals to equal access to employment, whether as employees or self-employed, the right of their families to equality of treatment in the host state, it is essential that decisions emanating from such bodies affecting these rights should be capable of judicial review. It would only be otherwise if the applicant possessed an adequate and effective alternative private law remedy. Whilst in the context of employment many Community rights constitute private rights, best protected by action based on private law, decisions by regulatory bodies concerning admission to professions or institutions, or conditions of work within those professions, will undoubtedly operate in the public sphere, and must be capable of being reviewed for their compatibility with EC law.

Despite the more extreme precedent-bound view taken in the *Jockey Club* cases and *Page* (see also *R* v *Football Association ex parte Football League* [1992] COD 32), there is ample authority in British law that the decisions of private bodies can be subject to review when they are exercising public powers (see e.g., *Nagle* v *Fielden* (1966) 2 QB 633; *Eastham* v *Newcastle United Football Club* [1964] Ch 413). In Scotland, the USA and New Zealand the law has taken this view. Thus it is but a small (but essential) step for English courts to extend access to judicial review to enable individuals to challenge decisions of a 'public' nature, albeit made by a private body, under powers derived from contract, for breaches of Community law.

Jurisdictional Hurdles

The lack of a clear distinction between matters of public and private law has led to further difficulties of a procedural nature. Prior to 1982 the public/private dichotomy was less marked than it is today. The terms 'public' and 'private' were 'convenient expressions for descriptive purposes, embracing miscellaneous cases where special considerations arise relating not only to public authorities, but also to public interest issues relating to non-governmental bodies' (Alder (1993) JSPTL 88). Public decisions were open to challenge via the full range of judicial procedures. It was not until *O'Reilly* v *Mackman* [1983] 2 AC 237, that the decision became significant. In that case the House of Lords refused to admit an action for a declaration that a decision of the Board of Visitors of Hull prison was null and void, for breach of the rules of natural justice, on the grounds that the action, which was commenced by writ, should have been brought under Order 53. Lord Diplock, who delivered the principal judgment, pointed out that the Order 53 procedure had been amended in 1977, and given statutory confirmation in the Supreme Court Act 1981, in order to eliminate the procedural disadvantages of the old Order 53 procedure, by extending the range of remedies available and providing more flexible rules for discovery and cross-examination. Whilst the courts had been prepared prior to these changes to entertain actions involving public law issues commenced by writ or originating summons to overcome inequities resulting from the limitations of Order 53, this was no longer necessary. The Order 53 procedure was specifically designed to promote good administration and protect public authorities. Procedures needed to be speedy in the interest of legal certainty, to ensure that authorities and third parties should not be kept in suspense as to the legal validity of a decision for longer than was necessary. The requirement of a prior application for leave, supported by full and candid affidavits, was necessary to provide a safeguard against groundless and unmeritorious claims. Since the new Order 53 had removed all the disadvantages, from the procedural point of view, of the old system of judicial review it would be

> contrary to public policy and as such an abuse of the process of the court to permit a person seeking to establish that a decision of a public authority infringed rights to which he was entitled to protection under public law to proceed by way of an ordinary action and by this means evade the provisions of Order 53 for the protection of such authorities.

Lord Diplock's reasoning is convincing. But whilst it is unobjectionable when applied to cases involving exclusively public law issues (as was the case in *O'Reilly* v *Mackman*), the decision raises serious problems for those with 'mixed' claims, particularly when both private and public claims arise from the same facts, or where the private right depends on a prior finding of invalidity. Following *O'Reilly* v *Mackman* a number of seemingly genuine claims instituted by writ, but raising, either independently or as a necessary precondition of the private rights claimed, issues of public law, were rejected on the grounds that the applicant should have proceeded by way of judicial review (e.g., *Cocks* v *Thanet District Council* [1983] 2 AC 286; *Davy* v *Spelthorne BC* [1984] AC 282). Whilst the decisions were no doubt correct on a strict and logical application of *O'Reilly* v *Mackman* it is doubtful that they achieved a just result. The assessment as to which is the appropriate procedure in such cases is a fine one, depending on the relative weight of the private and public law claims and the relationship between them. Moreover, whilst under Order 53 r. 9 the court may direct that an action begun by judicial review may continue as if begun by writ, the reverse is not possible. A court has no power to treat an action begun by writ or originating summons as if it had been commenced by an application for judicial review. Thus an applicant who mistakenly and bona fide proceeds by writ in a matter found to involve what is essentially a question of public law must make a fresh application for judicial review. Since the application is likely to be made more than three months after the impugned decision was made it will be out of time, unless 'good reason' can be shown. Choosing the wrong procedure, even in a mixed claim, may not be regarded as sufficient reason. In such circumstances the applicant will be denied relief regardless of the merits of his claim.

No doubt because of this, the rule of *O'Reilly* v *Mackman* has been criticised (see Justice/All Souls Report 1988) and often distinguished. As Alder has pointed out 'the ten year history of the *O'Reilly* rule has seen a steady retreat from the principles laid down by Lord Diplock and a weakening of the Order 53 jurisdiction'. Lord Diplock himself suggested in *O'Reilly* v *Mackman* that these principles would only provide a 'general rule'; that neither Order 53 nor s. 31, Supreme Court Act 1981

expressly provided that the procedure by application for judicial review shall be the exclusive procedure by which the remedy of a declaration or injunction may be obtained for infringement of rights that are entitled to protection under public law: there may be exceptions, particularly where the invalidity of the decision arises as a collateral issue in a claim for infringement of a right of the plaintiff arising under private law, or where none of the parties objects to the adoption of the procedure by writ or originating summons.

The exception appears to be moving, if not consistently, towards the rule. There have been a number of cases in which the applicant's private and public rights have been found 'inextricably linked' or in which his public law rights have been viewed as collateral to his private law rights where the applicant has been allowed to proceed by writ (e.g., *An Bord Bainne* v *Milk Marketing Board* [1984] 2 CMLR 584). Furthermore the concept of a private right was extended in *Roy* v *Kensington and Chelsea and Westminster Family Practitioner Committee* [1992] 1 All ER 705 (HL), in a mixed claim admitted in proceeding begun by writ to include a bundle of rights of a quasi-contractual nature. This has led to the suggestion that *Roy* has made the *O'Reilly* v *Mackman* rule virtually meaningless, and that Order 53 is exclusive only where no private rights are involved at all (Alder (1993)). Further support for a 'flexible' approach to *O'Reilly* v *Mackman* was provided by the House of Lords in *EOC* v *Secretary of State for Employment* [1994] 1 All ER 910.

Nevertheless inconsistent caselaw and a lack of precision as to what may constitute a 'private' or 'public' law right, and what matters may be deemed to be 'inextricably linked' with, or collateral to, public law rights, renders outcomes uncertain. Applicants may still find themselves trapped in the wrong procedure. This is not satisfactory A system of effective protection for individuals' Community rights requires that genuine, non-abusive challenges to public acts or omissions should not fall prey to procedural technicalities.

What guidelines can be offered as to the appropriate procedure for claims involving challenges to public acts or omissions allegedly in breach of Community law?

EC law imposes obligations on bodies, whatever their nature, which perform public functions, in both private and public law. As a general rule, measures of a regulatory nature, such as Articles 12 and 30 (prohibition on member states imposing customs duties or quantitative restrictions, or equivalent measures, on imports and exports between member states), and Directive 64/221 (member states' permitted justification from free movement of persons provisions), take effect in public law. Measures imposing obligations on the state as employer or entrepreneur, such as Article 119 (equal pay for equal work for men and women) or Articles 85 and 86 (competition provisions) fall within the private sphere. Some EC obligations, such as Article 6 EC (principle of non-discrimination on grounds of nationality, formerly Article 7 EEC) may impose obligations in public or private law, depending on the context in which they occur. Even when EC obligations clearly fall in the public sphere, they may, and often will, if breached, give rise to rights in private law, for example to restitution or damages. Therefore it is not possible or desirable to categorise issues involving particular EC rights as amenable to review under Order 53 or in ordinary civil proceedings.

Where the matter is clearly and only a public law matter, a fortiori where the applicant seeks one of the prerogative remedies, he should proceed under Order 53. Where the claim is mixed, but the private claim is contingent on a prior finding that domestic law is invalid, or inapplicable, being incompatible with EC law the Order 53 procedure might again seem more appropriate, since the court is able under this procedure to award the full range of remedies. The policy reasons for deciding matters of public law under Order 53 advanced by Lord Diplock in *O'Reilly* v *Mackman* continue to hold good; in matters of public law it is necessary to provide safeguards against abuse, to protect the interests of good administration against groundless claims. On the other hand where there is little doubt as to the existence of a private Community right, simply requiring a finding that a public act is incompatible with EC law, and therefore 'inapplicable' (see *Simmenthal SpA* (case 106/77) Chapter 2) in order that that right may be enjoyed, ordinary proceedings should suffice. But there should be no rigid rule. In the absence of evidence of abuse a claimant with a seemingly meritorious claim based on EC law who chooses to proceed by writ should not be turned away. The best solution might be, as Alder suggests, that the Order 53 procedure and its safeguards be extended, not circumvented, to matters involving public law wherever they are raised. Alternatively, courts in civil or criminal proceedings might be given the power to refer questions of public law to the High Court to determine as though they had been raised under Order 53 (see Emery (1992) CLJ 342), This would guarantee the necessary expertise and uniformity in the adjudication of matters of public law, particularly important where the claim is based on EC law.

Decision Immune from Judicial Review

Even where a decision clearly belongs in the public law sphere there are circumstances in which decisions made under public powers are immune from judicial review. Some prerogative powers may be deemed non-justiciable. Statute may provide that a particular decision is 'final' or 'will not be subject to question in any court of law'. To what extent are these rules contrary to EC law?

Judicial review of prerogative powers was traditionally limited. The courts could enquire into the existence and extent of such powers but could not review the manner in which they were exercised. In *Council of Civil Service Unions* v *Minister for the Civil Service* [1985] AC 374 (the *CCSU* case), these limitations were swept away. The House of Lords held that the only limitation on the courts' power of review of prerogative acts was the justiciability of the issue. Only where the issues were inherently unsuitable for judicial resolution would review not be available. In that case the minister's decision not to consult the Civil Service Trade Union when deciding to change members' conditions of service, removing their right to join a trade union, was held to be, in principle, reviewable, although on the facts immunity was justified by the need to safeguard national security. Following that case there would appear to be few prerogative powers which would as a matter of principle be wholly immune from judicial review.

Many prerogative powers have now been held reviewable (e.g., Home Secretary's residual powers over matters of immigration). In some cases, where they have been so found they have been put on a statutory footing (e.g., Criminal Injuries Compensation Scheme, Criminal Justice Act 1988, recently threatened but reprieved). A few powers continue to be non-justiciable. Lord Roskill suggested in the *CCSU* case that powers in relation to the making of treaties, the defence of the realm, the prerogative of mercy, the grant of honours, the dissolution of Parliament and the appointment of ministers would not be amenable to judicial review. It has been suggested that even these immunities may be open to question, and that in some circumstances, on some grounds, and with limitations as to the remedies available, decisions in these areas might be open to review (see Lewis C 1992). It can be argued that few prerogative powers should per se be unreviewable.

With regard to statutory exclusions and limitations, our courts have long interpreted these restrictively. Even though a decision may be declared to be 'final' or 'not to be questioned in any court of law' they will grant certiorari to quash ultra vires acts. But statutory provisions, where unequivocal, cannot be ignored. Moreover, although a certificate, declared by statute to be 'conclusive evidence' of a particular matter, cannot itself wholly preclude judicial review, applications for such review are doomed to failure if evidence cannot be adduced that the certificate was unlawful.

Thus although the ambit of prerogative and statutory immunities has been limited by the courts these immunities may still stand in the way of an individual seeking to assert his Community rights.

The Court of Justice had an opportunity to rule in a case involving such an immunity in *Johnston* v *Royal Ulster Constabulary* (case 222/84). This case, considered in Chapters 1 and 5, involved a claim of sex discrimination based on EC Equal Treatment Directive 76/207. The applicant claimed that the RUC, in refusing to renew her contract of full-time employment on the grounds of her sex, was acting, without justification, in breach of EC law. Directive 76/207, Article 2, provides specific grounds for derogation from the non-discrimination principle in respect of 'activities for which the sex of the worker constitutes a determining factor', and for 'provisions 'concerning the protection of women as regards pregnancy and maternity'. The Secretary of State for Northern Ireland had certified that the act of refusal of employment of Mrs Johnston was for the purposes of safeguarding national security and public order. Under Article 53(2), Northern Ireland (Sex Discrimination) Order 1976 a certificate from the Secretary of State that an act was done for that purpose was 'conclusive evidence' that it was so done. On a reference from the Irish Industrial Tribunal to the ECJ, raising a number of questions concerning the legality of the RUC's action under EC law, that court held (although it was not directly asked this question) that Article 53(2), requiring the Secretary of State's certificate to be treated as 'conclusive evidence' that the conditions for derogation had been fulfilled, was 'contrary to the principle of effective judicial control laid down in the Directive'. Although the decision was based on Article 6 of the Directive, the Court held that Article 6 reflected

a general principle of law which underlines the constitutions of member states. That principle is also laid down in Articles 6 and 13 of the European Convention of Human Rights and Fundamental Freedoms ... It is for member states to ensure effective judicial control as regards compliance with the applicable provisions of Community law and of national legislation intended to give effect to the rights which the Directive provides.

It is submitted that this ruling does not apply simply to certificates concerning 'conclusive evidence', as in *Johnston*. The principle of effective judicial control, derived from Articles 6 and 13 of the European Convention of Human Rights and adopted as a general principle of Community law (see Chapter 1) can be invoked in any situation in which prerogative or statutory immunities operate to undermine the effective judicial protection of individuals' Community rights.

This does not mean however that restrictions on access to judicial review can never be justified. Although this point has rarely been considered by the ECJ it is submitted that there will be occasions when access to, and conditions governing, judicial review may be limited without infringing EC law. EC rights, which include the right to effective remedies, are not absolute. Even the most basic Community rights such as the right to freedom of movement for goods and persons are subject to derogation in order to safeguard fundamental national requirements of public policy and public security (see Articles 36, 48(3), 56). But EC law does not permit blanket immunities. It requires that any derogation from a fundamental Community right be 'objectively justified'. In every case, both the grounds for derogation and its proportionality must be proved. The principle of proportionality requires that the measure adopted or immunity claimed must be both appropriate and necessary to achieve its stated (and legitimate) purpose. This approach was adopted by the House of Lords in the *CCSU* case. After examining the case for immunity the Court concluded that it was in fact justified.

Limitations on Remedies

In asserting his right to challenge public acts or omissions for breaches of Community law, the individual should in principle have access to all the public law remedies available under English law, namely certiorari, mandamus, prohibition, injunction and declaration, where they are necessary to protect his community rights or to deter a public authority from breaching Community law. He will not be entitled to damages for infringement of his Community rights as a matter of *public* law. To what extent will the remedies currently provided under public law be available and/or necessary for the protection of these rights? Here it may be helpful to separate claims against public bodies based on the principle of direct and indirect effects from claims against the state based on *Francovich*.

Claims against public bodies: prerogative orders, declarations, injunctions Since the prerogative orders of certiorari, mandamus and prohibition can only be obtained in an action under Order 53 RSC, it is essential that this procedure be available where it is needed in a genuine public law claim based on EC law, regardless of the nature of the body against which it is invoked and the source of its power.

Prerogative orders are now available in principle against all bodies exercising public law functions, including government ministers acting or failing to act pursuant to statutory powers and duties, regardless of the capacity in which they are acting, although not all remedies will be available against all claims. Provided that an effective remedy exists it is not necessary that all remedies be available in claims based on EC law. As was suggested regarding access to judicial review, some limitations and even total immunity may be 'objectively justified' in the individual case.

Until the UK's entry into the EC a prerogative remedy could only be sought in respect of unlawful administrative or executive acts or omissions. Under the principle of parliamentary sovereignty a challenge to the legality of a *legislative* act (or omission), and a remedy based on that challenge, was unthinkable. The principle of the supremacy of EC law over all domestic law, including statute law, together with national courts' obligation to provide effective protection for individuals' community rights, both established by the Court of Justice and binding on the UK courts by virtue of Article 5 EC and the European Communities Act 1972, have changed that position (see Chapter 2). Where a British statute is inconsistent with Community law, and cannot be interpreted to comply with that law, it is, according to the Court of Justice in *Simmenthal SpA* (case 106/77) automatically 'inapplicable'. Although British courts have not been prepared to declare a statute 'unlawful' for breach of EC law, they have been willing to 'disapply' it and even, as in *Factortame* v *Secretary of State for Transport (No. 2)* [1991] 1 All ER 70 to grant an injunction to restrain its application. Does it follow that they will also be obliged to grant prerogative remedies?

In *EOC* v *Secretary of State for Employment* (1994), in an action by the Equal Opportunities Commission seeking a declaration that provisions of the Employment Protection (Consolidation) Act 1978 were contrary to EC law and a declaration and mandamus against the Secretary of State in respect of his failure to amend the Act, the High Court (QBD) and a majority of the Court of Appeal (Dillon LJ dissenting) held that it would be 'wrong and unconstitutional for the courts to make the latter orders in an attempt to enforce obligations which if they existed did so only in international law' (per Kennedy LJ [1993] 1 All ER 1022 at p. 1043 (CA)). On appeal to the House of Lords [1994] 1 All ER 910) the House did not address the question of mandamus. However Lord Keith, speaking for the House, which was unanimous on this issue, held on the question of the court's jurisdiction to grant a declaration that there was no need to declare that the United Kingdom or the Secretary of State were *in breach* of their obligations under Community law. A declaration that the relevant provisions of the 1978 Act were *incompatible* with EC law would suffice for the purposes sought by the EOC and was capable of being granted consistently with the precedent afforded by *Factortame*. This would not involve any attempt by the EOC to enforce the international obligations of the Treaty (at p. 920). A declaration was granted accordingly.

This judgment suggests, it is submitted correctly, that our courts will not be prepared to grant prerogative orders in actions based on statutory infringements of EC law, but also that *it will not be necessary to do so*. A declaration that particular provisions of a statute are incompatible with EC law and/or an injunction preventing their application will be sufficient to guarantee effective protection for individuals' Community rights. These remedies are available under Order 53 procedures and in private law actions. Lords Jauncey, Lowry and Browne Wilkinson suggested that the court had jurisdiction to grant a declaration in Order 53 proceedings even though it could not in the circumstances of the case make a prerogative order. They were not 'entirely happy' with the procedural restrictions for which *O'Reilly* v *Mackman* was an authority (at p. 925).

Following the House of Lords' decision in *Factortame* there is no doubt that injunctive relief, including interim relief, is available against the Crown, even to prevent the application of statutory provisions, as a matter of Community law, where it is necessary to protect individuals' Community rights. The House of Lords has now decided, following extensive argument concerning the history of injunctive relief in civil and criminal proceedings in England and Wales, that, contrary to its original view in *Factortame*, interim injunctions, including interlocutory injunctions (as well as proceedings for contempt of court) were available against ministers of the Crown, regardless of the capacity in which they were acting, as a matter of English law (*M* v *Home Office* [1993] 3 All ER 537). As Lord Donaldson MR remarked in the Court of Appeal ([1992] 4 All

ER at p. 141a), it would be 'anomalous and wrong in principle' if the powers
of the court were limited in matters of domestic law when these limitations had
been removed by European Community law if the dispute concerns rights
under that law.

Nevertheless there may be difficulty in obtaining interim relief. It is a
discretionary remedy. Whether the courts apply national criteria or (as they
should) the Community criteria prescribed by the Court of Justice in
Zuckerfabrik Süderdithmarschen (cases C 143/88 and C 92/89), see Chapter 5),
in the absence of a strong prima facie case national courts may be reluctant to
grant such relief against a public body seeking to enforce the law, particularly
when the application is based on uncertain provisions of EC law. The courts
are understandably wary of abusive claims, of 'virtual paralysis of the law
enforcement system' (see *Portsmouth City Council* v *Quietlynne* [1989] 1 CMLR
673; *R* v *Secretary of State for National Heritage ex parte Continental Television BV*
[1993] 2 CMLR 333 (QBD)). Damages at trial may be considered to offer
sufficient protection for individuals' rights. Yet a breach of EC law may not give
rise to a private right to damages. Even where actionable damage occurs, for
example in relation to public procurement, it may be hard to prove, or quantify.
In areas such as public procurement or environmental law, interim relief may
be the only effective means whereby interests, individual or public, may be
protected or public bodies deterred from breaching Community law. As
Schiemann J pointed out in *R* v *Secretary of State for Environment ex parte Rose
Theatre Trust Co.*, *Independent*, 4 July 1989, in an action by the Secretary of State
to discharge an interim injunction which had been granted ex parte to prevent
further development of the Rose Theatre site, the grant of an injunction in final
proceedings may be rendered 'nugatory' in the absence of interim relief.
Regrettably these considerations did not prevent him from discharging the
injunction on the grounds of the applicants' lack of standing. These factors
should be weighed when interim relief is sought in the context of a genuine,
albeit uncertain, claim based on EC law.

Interim declarations are not available under Order 53, and there may be
statutory bars to interim relief. Although access to an injunction may now
provide an effective alternative remedy, statutory limitations must not be
allowed to prevent the granting of a declaration where this is the only effective
way to protect an individual's Community rights. *Factortame* could be invoked
to support this view. (See also Woolf, Sir H., 'Judicial Review; a possible
programme for Reform', 221 at p. 225.)

Claims against public bodies: damages   Although the courts now have power,
under s. 31(7), Supreme Court Act 1981 and Order 53 r. 7(1), to award
damages, this provision does not create a new substantive right to damages. It
simply enables damages to be awarded in 'mixed' proceedings brought under
Order 53 where the plaintiff is entitled to damages in private law. Interest may
also be awarded on damages and debts under s. 35A, Supreme Court Act 1981.

In *R* v *Secretary of State for Transport ex parte Sheriff & Sons Ltd (No. 2)* (see
[1989] PL 197) the Court of Appeal held that since payment of a statutory
grant does not represent a 'debt' or 'damages', interest on such payments

would not be available under Order 53. This position will have to be revised in the light of EC law and the decision of the Court of Justice in *Marshall* v *Southampton AHA (No. 2)* ((case C 271/91) discussed in Chapter 5).

Damages for breach of private law right should be distinguished from damages resulting from a cross-undertaking demanded as a condition for the granting (or refusal) of interim relief. There has been some debate as to whether the latter can be demanded of public authorities when they are seeking an interlocutory injunction in order to enforce the law. In *Hoffman La Roche & Co Ltd* v *Secretary of State for Trade and Industry* [1975] AC 295, the House of Lords suggested that whilst in principle an undertaking in damages could be required of the Crown to protect its own private (i.e., proprietary or contractual) rights, and the courts had a discretion to impose such a requirement in all cases, no such undertaking should be required when it was acting in the public interest to enforce the law. This limitation appeared to be presumed by Schiemann J in *R* v *Secretary of State for the Environment ex parte Rose Theatre Trust Co., Independent*, 4 July 1989, and was described by Hoffmann J in *Director General of Fair Trading* v *Tobyward Ltd* [1989] 2 All ER 266 (with reservations as to its merits) as 'well established' as regards the Crown. With regard to public authorities the matter was less clear. Whilst they could be required to give cross-undertakings in a relator action, regardless of the capacity in which they were acting, it was uncertain whether they could be so obliged when acting in their own capacity to enforce the law. In *Kirklees Borough Council* v *Wickes Building Supplies Ltd* [1991] 4 All ER 240, in the context of an action to enforce the Sunday trading laws which the defendants claimed were in breach of Article 30 EC, the Court of Appeal held that local authorities could and should be required to give a cross-undertaking where this was necessary to guarantee effective protection for the defendants' (alleged) Community rights. The House of Lords [1992] 3 All ER 717) disagreed. It saw no material distinction between this case, involving a local authority, and the position of the Crown in *Hoffman La Roche*. Both were fulfilling functions of law enforcement; therefore neither should be required to give a cross-undertaking in damages.

There is little doubt that the House of Lords was influenced in *Kirklees* by the (tenuous) merits of the defendants' claim and the remoteness of their chance of success. A ruling from the ECJ in two similar cases (*Conforama, Marchandise* (cases C 312 and C 332/89)) pointed strongly in the local authority's favour. Their lordships also pointed out that should the defendants' claim be vindicated at trial they might make good their loss by suing the state in a claim based on *Francovich*.

Whilst the courts' concern to protect public bodies against exploitative claims based on alleged Community rights is understandable, from the standpoint of individuals with a legitimate claim under EC law the decision in *Kirklees* is not satisfactory. If a public body, whether Minister of the Crown or public authority, seeks and obtains an interim injunction to enforce national law, and that law is subsequently found to be in breach of Community law, the individual seeking to rely on his Community rights will have no effective remedy in respect of damage suffered prior to the final decision *unless he can establish a breach of a private right sounding in damages.* It was this argument which swayed the Court of Appeal in *Kirklees*. Similarly, if an individual seeks an interim injunction to prevent the application against him of national law and is refused (and, as Schiemann J noted in the *Rose Theatre* case, in the absence of a cross-undertaking the court will be 'extremely slow' to grant interim relief), even if he succeeds at trial, losses suffered prior to the trial may go uncompensated. As will be seen in Chapter 7, infringements of EC law by public authorities will not necessarily give rise to a private right to damages. The extent to which, and the basis on which, states may be liable under *Francovich* remains unclear. In order to have 'sufficient interest' to request an injunction under Order 53 it is not necessary to establish a private right to damages. If that interest does not receive interim protection, and damage is suffered as a result of what proves at trial to be unlawful action on the part of public authorities, the applicant should at least be compensated for the interim damage suffered. Such gaps in respect of damages under Order 53 have not gone unnoticed. Both Lord Woolf and the Justice/All Souls Committee suggested that a court should be able under Order 53 to grant compensation where other remedies will not 'secure substantial justice in the case'. Since individuals are entitled to assert their EC rights even when they carry no private law right to damages, by resisting an application for (or demanding) an interim injunction, they should be entitled to a cross-undertaking in damages for losses suffered as a result of that relief being granted (or refused) if their claim under EC law is vindicated at trial. To obtain such compensation it should not be necessary to prove a private law right to damages. Since, as the House of Lords conceded in *Hoffmann La Roche* and *Kirklees*, English courts have a discretion to require a cross-undertaking of both the Crown and public authorities, even in law enforcement cases, that discretion should be exercised, in appropriate cases involving Community law, in the individual claimant's favour. It may further be argued that where an individual applicant succeeds in obtaining interim relief, thereby 'paralysing' the law enforcement process, he too should be required to provide some guarantee or security to compensate for damage to the public interest, as was suggested in *Zuckerfabrik Süderdithmarschen* (cases C 143/88 and C 92/89, see Chapters 5 and 9) to compensate for financial risks to the Community. Although difficult to quantify, it would not be impossible. Such mutual provision for liquidated damages would provide fair and effective protection for individuals with a genuine claim whilst protecting the public interest, not least by deterring abusive claims based on Community law.

Claims based on Francovich   A claim for damages against the state based on *Francovich* is a claim in private law, akin to a tort. The basis of the claim is a right granted to certain groups of individuals, for example employees, subject to the satisfaction of certain criteria, by EC law. But the claim depends on a breach by the state of its obligation to act to safeguard that right, resulting in damage to the plaintiff. Thus liability depends on a finding that a particular act or omission on the part of the state is in breach of EC law. The scope of the tort and the nature of the breach required to give rise to liability, whether it applies only to central authorities, to obligations arising from Treaty provisions,

Regulations and Decisions as well as Directives, is not yet clear (see Chapters 2, 5 and 7). But even were it to be interpreted narrowly, to apply only in cases like *Francovich*, involving a clear failure by the state to implement a Directive (which is unlikely), liability will still be contingent on a finding of a breach of Community law on the part of the state. Such breaches will often comprise legislative failures. The question arises whether it is necessary to obtain a declaration of such a failure in order to claim damages under *Francovich*. As has been noted above, the impugning of acts of Parliament raises delicate constitutional problems for the British courts.

However, it may be argued that in order to succeed in a claim for damages under *Francovich* it is not necessary to obtain a formal declaration that domestic legislation is in breach of Community law. It simply requires a finding that national law is incompatible with EC law. This approach was taken by the House of Lords in *EOC v Secretary of State for Employment* [1994] 1 All ER 910, in the context of an action for a declaration that certain provisions of the Employment Protection (Consolidation) Act 1978 were in breach of EC law. As the Court of Justice held in *Simmenthal SpA* (case 106/77), in the event of a conflict between Community law and domestic law, whatever its nature, the national judge must simply apply Community law, if necessary ignoring conflicting provisions of national law. It is not necessary to request or await the prior setting aside of the offending national law. Applying this ruling by analogy to a claim for damages based on *Francovich*, provided that the requisite inconsistency between national law and EC law is established, along with the plaintiff's rights, the court may simply award the remedy. It will then be left to Parliament to take the necessary action to remedy the inconsistency. Although it cannot be required by a British court to repeal or amend or introduce legislation, the prospect of further liability in damages will no doubt provide a powerful incentive to do so Thus it is submitted that, depending on its interpretation, the application of *Francovich* need pose no greater constitutional problems than have already been faced by the British courts in coming to terms with the principle of supremacy of EC law.

Procedural Hurdles

Where action is brought under Order 53, a number of procedural hurdles need to be surmounted. The action is subject to special rules, tailored to the particular requirements of public law, designed to achieve a balance between the interests of the public in good administration and legal certainty and the interests of the individual citizen. The rules governing leave to apply for judicial review, and standing, and time limits protect the former. The rules concerning cross-examination and discovery, which were originally restrictive, were amended in 1977 to assist the latter. The fact that the remedies are discretionary enables the court to take into account their effect on the public interest and third parties.

None of these rules per se stands in the way of the effective protection of individuals' Community rights. It may be noted that the rules governing judicial review of Community law under Articles 173, 175 and 184 (see

Chapter 9), as interpreted by the European Court, impose more severe restrictions on standing and time, for similar reasons. Thus the need to apply for judicial review and for a sufficient interest (s. 31(3), Supreme Court Act 1981, Order 53 r. 7)), the three-month time limit, with the possibility of extension for 'good reason', and the element of discretion in the granting of remedies could all be regarded as appropriate and necessary to an action involving issues of public law. Similarly the power of the court to order discovery and cross-examination under Order 53 r. 8 is sufficiently wide to ensure that in the absence of some overriding justification they are available when they are needed.

However, to the extent that these rules are imprecise and provide wide scope for discretion on the part of the court, their application may result in a lack of effective protection for individuals' Community rights.

Leave to apply: standing   In order to apply for judicial review the applicant must first seek the leave of the court to proceed (Order 53 r. 1). This process was described in a Public Law Project in 1993 (*'Judicial Review in Perspective; The Future of Judicial Review'*) as 'something of a lottery'. Although the purpose of the leave requirement is to ensure that the applicant's claim is not frivolous or vexatious, that the applicant appears to have standing and a prima facie case, the precise criteria applied by the court in deciding whether or not to grant leave are unclear. The project found that although the decisions of individual judges were consistent, there was a wide and unpredictable variation in the granting of leave by different judges. It appeared that attitudinal factors played an important part in their decision, and the leave filter was being used for reasons of 'administrative efficiency', in order to reduce caseloads. Many applications were dealt with without an oral hearing: 15% of the sample had been rejected on paper alone. Whilst the effectiveness principle might not require that applicants receive an oral hearing, the lack of 'transparency', of clear and objectively verifiable criteria and the absence of reasons for decisions, could be subject to challenge under Community law. The Public Law Project's suggestion that judges should complete a questionnaire explaining their reasons, and that leave should be granted if judges refused to explain their reasons, or if their reasons were inadequate, would go some way to meet the demands of EC law.

The granting of leave is only the preliminary, albeit crucial step, in the application for judicial review The court must then decide if the applicant has standing, defined as a 'sufficient interest in the matter to which the application relates' (Order 53 r. 7). The leading case on this issue is *R v IRC ex parte National Federation of Self-Employed and Small Businesses* [1982] AC 617. In considering whether the applicant has a sufficient interest it is

necessary to consider the powers and duties in law of those against whom relief is asked, the position of the applicant in relation to those powers and duties, and to the breach said to have been committed' (per Lord Wilberforce at p. 630) . . .

It is a mixed question of fact and law; a question of fact and degree and the relationship between the applicant and the matter to which the application relates, having regard to all the circumstances of the case' (per Lord Roskill at p. 659).

Although it is not necessary for the applicant to prove that the action challenged affects him personally, or even as a member of a restricted class, or that he has a direct legal or financial interest in the matter, clearly a close relationship and a strong social or financial interest will greatly strengthen his claim.

However, these issues are not examined in isolation. Decisions as to whether an applicant has standing are also influenced by the merits of his case. Where the applicant's case appears to be strong, or raises serious questions of public interest, the court may be prepared to take a generous view (e.g., *Gillick* v *West Norfolk and Wisbech Area Health Authority* [1986] AC 112 (HL)). In *R* v *HM Treasury ex parte Smedley* [1985] 1 All ER 589, the Court of Appeal allowed a taxpayer to challenge a Treasury decision to approve a supplementary budget for the European Community, a matter in which he had an interest no greater than any other taxpayer. On the other hand, where the applicant's case is weak, a fortiori when he is seeking to challenge a discretionary act on *Wednesbury* principles, a more direct and personal interest will be required.

Where an individual is seeking to challenge a domestic measure for breach of a Community right intended for his benefit this right should prove 'a sufficient interest' for the purpose of locus standi. Even where the rights claimed are inchoate, or unclear, it would not be desirable, except in a clearly opportunistic case, to deny the applicant standing.

The problems however are less likely to arise with individual claims based on EC law than with group, or representative claims. Here it may be helpful to distinguish along the lines suggested by the EC Commission in its Green Paper on *Access to Justice* in the settlement of consumer disputes (COM (93) 576 Final) between representative claims, in which action is brought by a representative body on behalf of the public or a section of the public in order to protect a *collective* interest, and a joined cases facility, which allows for the collective exercise of *individual* rights. The Commission also identified a third 'hybrid' category, the 'joint representation action', which would allow for a cluster of individual suits to be co-ordinated and conducted by a representative body with power of attorney to act on the claimants' behalf in a single case. Although the categories are not exclusive to claims in public or private law, the most important from the point of view of the enforcement of public law rights is the first category, the representative action. The second and third categories will be considered more appropriately in Chapter 7 on the impact of EC law on actions based on private law.

Although English law does permit representative actions it cannot be said that the rules governing action by interested groups are sufficiently certain or comprehensive to ensure the effective enforcement of Community law in all situations. Where a particular claim, brought by an individual, is deemed to concern the public interest, the Attorney-General may intervene by way of a relator action and pursue the claim on the public's behalf. But the

Attorney-General is a representative of government and the decision whether or not to intervene lies within his discretion. Thus intervention cannot be guaranteed, even where it may be justified. Where the Attorney-General refuses to act or has not been asked to intervene the courts have allowed representative bodies 'having sufficient interest in the matter to which the application relates' to bring a claim. But their approach to the question of 'sufficient interest' has not been consistent. The criteria by which they operate are not clear. As with the question of individual standing, the decision on locus standi often appears to depend on the merits of the claim. (It may be noted that in the context of a claim based on EC law the merits of the case may not be immediately clear, especially to a judge conditioned by English methods of interpretation.)

Where a particular body is charged by statute to protect a particular interest, or the interest of a particular group, it will normally have 'sufficient interest' to bring proceedings with a view to protecting that interest. Thus the Equal Opportunities Commission has been permitted to bring proceedings in a number of cases (e.g., *EOC* v *Birmingham City Council* [1989] AC 1155 (HL); *R* v *Secretary of State for Social Security ex parte EOC* [1992] 3 All ER 577)). In *EOC* v *Secretary of State for Employment* [1994] 1 All ER 910, despite a difference of view in the High Court and the Court of Appeal, the standing of the EOC to challenge an exclusion from protection for part-time workers under the Employment (Consolidation) Act 1978 was confirmed by the House of Lords (Lord Jauncey dissenting). However, Lord Keith made it clear that 'the determination of this issue rested essentially on a consideration of the statutory duties and public law role of the EOC'. It is to be hoped that the courts, in deciding questions of standing of statutory bodies, will not adopt too restrictive an interpretation of their statutory powers and duties, particularly in the context of a claim based on EC law.

The courts have on occasions also allowed interest or pressure groups which are not statutory bodies to bring proceedings (e.g., *Covent Garden Community Association Ltd* v *GLC* [1981] JPL 183; *R* v *Secretary of State for Social Services ex parte Child Poverty Action Group* [1989] 1 All ER 1047; *R* v *Hammersmith and Fulham London Borough Council ex parte People before Profit* (1982) 80 LGR 322). More recently the Friends of the Earth were allowed to challenge the UK Water Supply (Water Quality) Regulations for breach of EC Drinking Water Directive 80/778 (*R* v *Secretary of State for the Environment ex parte Friends of the Earth and Lees, The Times*, 4 April 1994). But the courts' approach has not been consistent. In *R* v *Secretary of State for the Environment ex parte Rose Theatre Trust* [1990] 1 All ER 754, Schiemann J held that a trust comprising a number of eminent archaeologists, set up to preserve the remains of the ancient Rose Theatre, did not have sufficient standing to challenge the Secretary of State's decision not to list the remains under the schedule of monuments, thereby preserving them against future development. A company incorporated as a 'vehicle of campaign', he suggested, could enjoy no greater standing than its members could have enjoyed before incorporation. No 'agglomeration of individuals' could have standing which an individual lacked.

In reaching this decision on standing Schiemann J was clearly influenced by the merits of the case. Following an extensive survey of the substance of the claim he concluded that the applicants had no case; the Minister was clearly acting within the scope of his discretion. 'I cannot find' he said 'that the Minister has acted unlawfully'.

In the circumstances of the case it is regrettable that Schiemann J found it necessary to express himself so widely on the question of standing. This case should not be allowed to encourage a restrictive attitude towards the question of standing of non-statutory bodies, a fortiori in the context of claims based on EC law. In the absence of a statutory body charged with protecting a particular interest on behalf of the public, any recognised and respected pressure group with a genuine claim should be given standing to act to prevent a breach of Community law or to obtain a declaration that a particular national law or practice is contrary to EC law. Such groups, as well as having an interest, have considerable expertise in the matter which they seek to protect. In areas such as environmental protection, where private rights may be lacking, representative action may be the only effective way in which public interests may be protected and parties, public and private, deterred from breaching Community law. Even where individuals' private rights have been infringed, each individual's damage may be too small to justify the cost of litigation. Such considerations will also influence decisions concerning the granting of legal aid. As Kennedy LJ pointed out in *EOC* v *Secretary of State for Employment* [1993] 1 All ER 1022 case in the Court of Appeal, it is easier and more cost-effective for representative bodies to obtain a declaratory judgment than to support individual litigants in private law actions. Such a ruling would not be 'an empty exercise of the court's discretion', since an authoritative ruling from a competent court could form the basis for a claim in private law. Whilst the courts are understandably reluctant to open their doors to all and sundry pressure groups seeking to use the law for particular political ends, it may be argued that the need for leave to apply for judicial review, the severe limitations on challenge to discretionary acts, and the discretionary nature of the remedies are sufficient in themselves to provide a safeguard against abuse. Where the applicant body is clearly (and not necessarily officially) recognised as representative of a particular interest and appears to have a genuine claim based on EC law, it should be granted standing. This view was taken by Otton J, enabling the Greenpeace organisation to bring an action in respect of the activities of British Nuclear Fuel plc (BNFL) in *R* v *Pollution Inspectorate ex parte Greenpeace (No. 2)* [1994] 4 All ER 329, QBD.

Time limits Where the action, although involving issues of public law, is begun by writ and is based on private law, it will be subject to the time limits appropriate to the principal action. Where the action is under Order 53 application for leave must be made

promptly and in any event within three months from the date when grounds for application first arose unless the court considers there is good reason for extending the period within which the application shall be made' (Order 53 r. 4(1)).

Under s. 31(6), Supreme Court Act 1981, the High Court, where it considers that there has been undue delay in making the application for judicial review, may refuse to grant leave to apply. It may refuse any relief sought if it considers that the granting of the relief would be likely to cause substantial hardship to, or substantially prejudice, the rights of any person or would be detrimental to good administration.

Thus the limits are short, in the interests of legal certainty, but provide considerable scope for extension where this is justified, taking into account the interests of the public and third parties. It may be noted that actions under Article 173 for the annulment of Community law are subject to a two-month time limit, and may not be extended, although EC legislation may be challenged outside that time under Article 177 or Article 215(2) (see Chapters 8 and 10).

Despite the three-month limit (and the court may refuse leave even within that limit if it considers that there has been undue delay, see *Re Friends of the Earth* [1988] JPL 93) there is ample scope for the court's discretion if it finds 'good reason' for the delay. Thus, provided this requirement is interpreted broadly, an applicant seeking judicial review on the basis of EC law, even outside the three-month period, should not be readily turned away. In *R v Minister of Agriculture, Fisheries and Food ex parte Bostock* [1991] 1 CMLR 681 (CA), Purchas LJ granted the applicant leave to apply for judicial review even though he was 'wildly out of time'. His claim, which was lodged in 1990, was based on alleged infringements of EC law by the Ministry between 1984 and 1986, which deprived him of a share of his milk quota when he retired as a tenant farmer in 1986. Until 1989 and the Court of Justice's judgment in *Wachauf* (case 5/88 (see further below)) both the applicant and the minister were under a misapprehension as to the applicant's rights. Purchas LJ found that there was 'good reason' for the delay. It would 'ill lie in the mouth of the respondent' to rely on Rule 4(1) under such circumstances. *Bostock* (although it failed on its merits in its claim under EC law (case C 2/92, *The Times*, 11 May 1994)) would provide an admirable model for a claim based on EC law.

However, since *Emmott v Minister of Social Welfare*, and subject to its uncertainties (see Chapter 5), there may be no need to invoke 'good reason' to extend the limitation period, at least in the context of a claim based on an EC Directive, since time will not begin to run until the Directive has been fully implemented. Although the decision was based on the 'particular nature' of Directives, which require implementation by member states in order to take effect (the concept of direct effects providing only a minimum guarantee), its reasoning, based on the individual's state of uncertainty 'as to the full extent of his rights', could arguably be applied in other circumstances, such as *Bostock*, where states (may) have failed to comply with their EC obligations and the individual's rights are unclear.

Cross-examination and discovery   Although cross-examination and discovery of documents are not available as of right in judicial review proceedings, following the 1977 reforms both may now be granted under Order 53 r. 8. These rules, which reflect the special nature of judicial review, are designed to ensure speedy decision-making in the interests of good administration. Judicial review is not an appeal from a decision, but a review of the manner in which the decision was made. Therefore normally findings of fact are not disputed in such proceedings; the court is concerned with the legal consequences of the facts as found. If cross-examination on affidavits were routinely allowed the court would be drawn into a consideration of the merits of the case. Similarly too liberal an approach to discovery would tempt applicants to call it in aid of a simple 'fishing expedition or to supplement a challenge based on *Wednesbury* principles in the hope of finding some unsuspected defect in the reasoning' (Supperstone & Goudie at p. 369). However, where they are genuinely necessary to the applicant's case they can be made available. As Lord Diplock suggested in *O'Reilly* v *Mackman* [1983] 2 AC 237, both cross-examination and discovery should be available 'whenever and to the extent that the justice of the case requires'. Lord Donaldson's dicta in *R* v *Lancs CC ex parte Huddleston* [1986] 2 All ER 941, that judicial review is a process 'which falls to be conducted with all the cards face upwards on the table, and the vast majority of cards will start in the authority's hands' needs to be borne in mind. Certain questions of EC law, particularly concerning the circumstances in which member states are permitted to derogate from fundamental Community rules, inevitably raise factual issues. The question of objective justification requires proof that a particular measure is necessary to meet a genuine need. As Forbes J commented in *R* v *Minister of Agriculture, Fisheries and Food ex parte Bell Lines* [1984] 2 CMLR 502 (QBD), in an action challenging UK Regulations providing for authorised places of entry for milk products for breach of Article 30 EC, which required an enquiry into whether the rules in question were 'justified' under Article 36 EC, 'the court is drawn ineluctably into the business of fact finding'. He concluded 'I do not believe that persons with rights arising from (Community law) should be deprived of any means of enforcing them'. Similarly in other areas of EC law involving, for example, the free movement of persons, the enquiry whether measures taken by national authorities are appropriate and necessary, that is proportionate, to achieve a particular policy objective involves facts which must be proved. Where disclosure is necessary to enable an applicant to prove his case it should be ordered.

Discovery may be denied on the grounds of public interest immunity. As noted above, whilst EC law does not preclude such a claim, it would not be likely to endorse public interest immunity in respect of a class of documents, as was permitted in *Halford* v *Sharples* [1992] 3 All ER 624 (CA), Gibson LJ dissenting. On the other hand immunity might be permissible on the grounds of the *contents* of a document, provided that the necessity for the immunity, *in the particular circumstances of the case*, could be proved. This view was taken by the House of Lords in *R* v *Chief Constable of West Midlands Police ex parte Wiley*, *The Times*, 15 July 1994, when it refused to grant class immunity to documents originating in an investigation into complaints against the Police under the police complaints procedure.

The discretionary nature of public law remedies   Although the Court of Justice has not ruled on this point it is submitted that the obligation on national courts to provide effective remedies for the protection of individuals' Community rights does not require that these remedies be available as of right. The principles of legal certainty, which embrace the concept of vested rights and legitimate expectations, and which may weigh in the exercise of the court's discretion to protect third parties, are also respected as general principles of Community law. However, general principles of law also require that the reasons for refusing a particular remedy should be made explicit, in order that they may be examined for their objectivity, and open to challenge. In deciding whether or not to grant the relief requested the availability of an effective alternative remedy should also be considered.

THE REVIEW PROCESS: THE RELEVANCE OF GENERAL PRINCIPLES OF LAW

In the context of the enforcement of Community rights, the purpose of judicial review, whether conducted under Order 53 or as a collateral issue in ordinary proceedings, is to ensure that acts or omissions of national authorities falling within the public sphere are subject to challenge for breach of EC law. Where the act is successfully challenged, even if it is not set aside, it will be 'automatically inapplicable' (*Simmenthal SpA* (case 106/77)). Where a national authority is found to have failed to act, contrary to the requirements of Community law, it may be required to take action. In certain circumstances it may be liable in damages under *Francovich* v *Italian State* (case C 9/90). As has been noted above, in the case of challenge to legislative acts and omissions there may be limits to the remedies available.

Any national measure, executive, administrative or legislative, can be challenged for breach of any binding Community obligation contained in the EC Treaty, Regulations, Directives or Decisions, provided that the provision allegedly infringed is sufficiently clear and precise to constitute a defined Community obligation. Although Directives (normally) and some provisions of Regulations and Decisions require implementation by national authorities in order to take effect within national legal systems, and member states may have some discretion in implementation, national implementing authorities must ensure that the objectives of the legislation, particular and general, are achieved in full (see e.g., *Commission* v *UK* (case C 337/89) [1992] 1 ECR 6103), and that they do not exceed the limits of their discretion. To ascertain whether states have fulfilled their obligations in these respects it is necessary to examine the relevant Community legislation in its entirety, and to interpret its specific provisions in the light of its overall objectives, including the general objectives expressed in the preamble, in the manner of the Court of Justice. Even where states appear to have a margin of discretion in the implementation of specific provisions they may be required to provide some minimum guarantee that the objectives of the legislation are achieved (see e.g., *Francovich* (cases C 6 and 9/90), states to guarantee minimum three months' arrears of wages; *Marshall* v *Southampton AHA (No. 2)* (case C 271/91), damages for sex discrimination, in order to be effective, must be full). To establish the question of compatibility as between national and Community law, which will depend on the meaning and effect of the Community measure, it may be necessary to refer to the Court of Justice for a ruling on *interpretation* under Article 177 (see Chapter 4).

National measures, including legislative measures, may also be challenged on the grounds that they are based on an EC provision which is itself invalid. This matter may be established in the case in question by a ruling from the Court of Justice under Article 177 on the *validity* of the Community measure, or from a prior ruling under Article 177 or Article 173 (see Chapters 8 and 9), or under a prior action for damages against the Community under Article 215(2) (see Chapter 10).

As well as being open to challenge for breach of the EC Treaty, or secondary legislation, or as proceeding from an invalid Community act, national implementing acts or omissions may be challenged for breach of general principles of law. As noted in Chapter 1 these principles, although not expressed in the EC treaty, were invoked by the Court of Justice in the context of judicial review of Community law under Article 173, in order to ensure that Community law should not infringe general principles laid down in national constitutions or international treaties for the protection of human rights on which member states had collaborated or of which they were signatories. In deciding which general principles should be adopted as part of Community law the Court has drawn inspiration from 'constitutional traditions common to the member states' (*Nold KG* v *Commission* (case 4/73)). Since fundamental rights are expressed in different ways, and guaranteed in different degrees in different member states, the Court has sought to extract from these diverse provisions a number of underlying principles common to all member states to uphold as part of Community law. The main source of general principles has been the European Convention for the Protection of Human Rights and Fundamental Freedoms 1953, to which all member states have agreed.

The principles so far established in Community law are the principles of equality (e.g., *Royal Scholten-Honig* v *Intervention Board for Agricultural Produce* (cases 103 and 145/77)), legal certainty (*Defrenne* v *Sabena* *(No. 2)* (case 43/75)), which embraces the principles of non-retroactivity (*Officier van Justitie* v *Kolpinghuis Nijmegen* (case 80/86)) and legitimate expectations (*Töpfer* v *Commission* (case 112/77)), proportionality (*Internationale Handelsgesellschaft* (case 11/70)), the right to protection for private property (*Hauer* v *Rheinland Pfalz* (case 44/79)), the principle of unjust enrichment (*Amministrazione delle Finanze dello Stato* v *SpA San Giorgio* (case 199/82)) and procedural guarantees in the form of a right to be heard (*Hoffman-La Roche* v *Commission* (case 85/76)), a right to be given reasons for decisions (*UNECTEF* v *Heylens* (case 222/86)), a right of individuals to pursue their claim by judicial process ('due process'; *Johnston* v *RUC* (case 222/84)), a right to protection against self-incrimination in criminal proceedings (*Orkem* (case 374/87)) or (quaere) civil proceedings of a penal nature (*Funke* v *France* (case SA 256A) [1993] 1 CMLR 897 (ECHR)), and a limited right to privilege against disclosure (*A M & S Europe Ltd* v *Commission* (case 155/79)). The list cannot be regarded as closed.

Some of these general principles are expressed in specific terms in the EC Treaty, for example Article 40(3) which excludes 'any discrimination between producers and consumers within the Community' in the organisation of the common agricultural market, and Article 119, which provides for equal pay for equal work for men and women, or in EC secondary legislation such as Article 6 of Directive 76/207 on Equal Treatment for Men and Women, which requires member states to introduce measures to ensure that persons who consider themselves wronged by a breach of the equal treatment principle to 'pursue their claim by judicial process'. Others have been incorporated into treaty provisions or secondary legislation by judicial interpretation; for example exceptions to the provisions concerning the principles of free movement of goods and persons in Articles 36 and 48(2), which must be 'justified' on particular grounds, have been interpreted as incorporating the principle of proportionality. Derogations will be permitted as long as they do not exceed what is appropriate and necessary to achieve their particular (legitimate) ends. The former particular examples have been described by the Court as specific enunciations of the wider general principles which form the fundamental principles of Community law (*Klensch* (cases 201 and 202/85)).

Like all fundamental or constitutional rights, general principles of law do not constitute absolute rights. In the Community context

Restrictions may be imposed on the exercise of those rights as long as they correspond to objectives of general interests pursued by the Community and do not constitute, with regard to the aim pursued, a disproportionate and intolerable interference, impairing the very substance of those rights. (*Hubert Wachauf* v *Bundesampt Ehrnahrung unt Forstwirtschaft* (case 5/88).)

Thus, as with human rights protected under the European Convention of Human Rights, derogation is permitted as long as it is objectively justified. Since the question of justification involves a balancing of competing interests, and fundamental rights such as equality and legal certainty can themselves be competing, their precise scope of application is often unclear.

National authorities' obligation to comply with general principles of law as a matter of *Community* law arose initially from specific provisions of the EC treaty (e.g., Article 40(3), principle of equality of treatment between producers (*Klensch* (cases 201 and 202/85)), or from the Court's interpretation of Treaty provisions (e.g., Article 48, derogation from right to freedom of movement of persons subject to the principle of proportionality, *Criminal proceedings against Watson and Belmann* (case 118/75)), or from secondary legislation (Article 6, EC Directive 76/207, right to effective judicial control, *Johnston* v *RUC* (case 222/84)). In *Wachauf* the Court appeared to go further. Here, the applicant, a tenant dairy farmer, was seeking to challenge both the Community system of regulation of dairy production by the imposition of levies (to discourage over-production) and the award of levy-free 'reference quantities' to producers calculated by reference to production in a particular year, and the measures introduced by the German authorities to implement that system. Wachauf and others were seeking compensation for discontinuing production on the expiry of their lease and losing the benefit of 'reference quantities' earned during their tenancy. Under the relevant Community Regulations the lessor was entitled to take over the tenant's 'reference quantity' on the expiry of the lease. The tenant was entitled to compensation for discontinuing production, but only if he obtained the lessor's written consent. In the applicants' case the lessor had refused his consent. The applicants claimed that the Community system, and the measures introduced by the German authorities, were invalid, in breach of both Article 40(3) EC, which requires equal treatment for producers, and the general principles of equality and the right to protection of private property. In a reference for interpretation under Article 177 the ECJ found that the tenant had no right to compensation under the relevant Community Regulations. These simply gave member states a power to provide for compensation which the German authorities had failed to exercise. The Court suggested that the system introduced by the Germans, which 'deprived the tenant of the fruits of his labour', without compensation, and allowed the lessor to receive the benefit of the outgoing tenant's reference quantities, even where he had never engaged in milk production, was 'unacceptable' and 'incompatible with the fundamental requirements of Community law. These requirements, binding on Community authorities, were

> also binding on member states. When states implement community rules they must as far as possible apply those rules in accordance with these requirements . . .

Since Community law did not preclude national authorities from providing for compensation for tenants in these circumstances the implication of the ruling, although this was not expressed, was that the German authorities were obliged by general principles of Community law to respect the tenants' fundamental rights and guarantee compensation for loss of the applicants' property rights.

However, *Wachauf* must now be read in the light of the Court's rulings in *ERT* v *DEP* (case C 260/89) and R v *Minister of Agriculture, Fisheries and Food ex parte Bostock* (case C 2/92). In *ERT* v *DEP*, in a claim involving a challenge to ERT's monopoly in television broadcasting in Greece, granted by Greek law, based on breaches of the EC Treaty and the principle of freedom of expression laid down in Article 10 ECHR, the Court held that it had 'no power to examine the compatibility with the Convention on Human Rights of national rules *which do not fall within the scope of Community law* (emphasis added)'. This dictum was invoked in R v *Minister of Agriculture, Fisheries and Food ex parte Bostock* (case C 2/92). The claim here, involving facts very similar to *Wachauf*, was brought by another tenant dairy farmer seeking compensation for loss of the benefit of reference quantities transferred to his lessor on the expiry of his lease. The claim was brought, and allowed to proceed, 'wildly out of time', following, and encouraged by, the Court's judgment in *Wachauf*. When the applicant surrendered his tenancy in 1985 he had no right to compensation under British law. The law was amended in 1986 by the Agriculture Act (s. 13, Sch. 1) to provide for the award of compensation, but it did not apply retrospectively. The applicant sought to challenge the pre-existing law, which was applied to his case, invoking *Wachauf*, and alleging breach of general principles of law, namely the right to property and the principles of non-discrimination and unjust enrichment. In a reference under Article 177 from the Queen's Bench Division, the Court of Justice found that the right to property safeguarded under the Community legal order

> did not include the right to dispose, for profit, of an advantage, such as the reference quantities allocated in the context of the common organisation of the market, which did not derive from the assets or occupational activity of the person concerned.

Likewise, the Community principle of equality, invoked by the applicant to claim compensation under the same conditions as those claiming under the Agriculture Act 1986

> could not bring about retroactive modification of the relations to the parties to a lease to the detriment of a lessor by imposing on him an obligation to compensate the outgoing lessee, whether under national provisions which the member state in question might be required to adopt, or by means of direct effect.

On the question of unjust enrichment the Court simply concluded that the 'legal relations between lessees and lessors, particularly on the expiry of a lease, were, as Community law now stood, still governed by the law of the member state in question'.

This decision, arguably in breach of the applicant's legitimate expectations after *Wachauf*, did not deny that general principles of law can be binding on national authorities when implementing Community law. The Court simply found that the impugned acts were outside the scope of Community law. This case may serve as a warning to individuals seeking to challenge national authorities' acts (or omissions) in implementing Community law that, at the present stage of the Community's development too much should not be expected of general principles of law. Where national authorities are acting within a sphere of discretion permitted under Community law, their acts can only be challenged for breach of general principles of law where they are required to respect those principles as a matter of *national* law.

Nevertheless, in the context of challenge to acts or omissions of public authorities implementing Community law and falling 'within the scope' of Community law, general principles of law remain a valuable weapon in the armoury of judicial review, particularly in the UK. Although the UK has acceded to the European Convention of Human Rights, the Convention has not been incorporated into British law. Thus its provisions are not directly effective in the UK. Whilst they may, indeed must, be invoked as an aid to interpretation of domestic law, this can only occur where that law is ambiguous, and capable of being interpreted consistently with provisions of the Convention, without any undue straining of the words of the domestic enactment (see e.g., *Brind* v *Secretary of State for Home Department* [1991] 1 All ER 720 (HL)). Similarly, although most, if not all, of the general principles of law recognised under Community law may be found to exist in our common law, they are not established or applied systematically as principles of judicial review in the UK. In the context of a claim based on rights and obligations derived from Community law they may now under certain circumstances be applied.

Application of General Principles in the UK

Although some general principles of law, such as the duty to give reasons and the principle of legitimate expectations may be invoked in the context of judicial review in the UK, and others, such as the principle of proportionality, may inform the courts' approach to the question of *Wednesbury* unreasonableness, these principles are not routinely applied as a matter of English law. To what extent, and in what circumstances, may they now be invoked to challenge the acts or omissions of national authorities for breach of Community law, as falling 'within the scope' of Community law?

The case law of the ECJ is not well developed in this area, and consists largely of ad hoc decisions, delivered in Article 177 proceedings, concerning the application of particular general principles in specific and very different factual circumstances. It is submitted that a distinction may be drawn between general principles concerned with procedural rights and 'substantive' rights such as the principles of equality and legal certainty. The obligation of national courts to ensure effective judicial protection for individuals' Community rights, based on Article 5 EC (see Chapter 5) requires that fundamental rights of a procedural nature, such as the right to be heard, the right to reasons and the right to due process, *must* be observed whenever individuals seek to assert their Community rights. Although exceptions may be permitted, as was acknowledged in *Johnston* v *RUC* (case 222/84), they will be strictly controlled. In every case both the grounds for derogation, and its necessity, must be proved.

It was suggested by Sir Louis Blom-Cooper QC in *R* v *Lambeth LBC ex parte Walters, The Times,* 6 October) that a similar approach was applied to the duty to give reasons under English law

It is hard to envisage any situation, except possibly where the giving of reasons would reveal some aspect of national security, or unintentionally disclose confidential information or invade privacy, where an individual should not know the reasons for the decision which has been made. In many cases exceptions from the duty to give reasons might be regarded as justifying more limited forms of reasons, rather than an absence of reasons.

Despite Sir Louis Blom-Cooper's optimistic words, and the 'perceptible trend towards an insistence on greater openness in the making of decisions', approved by Lord Mustill in *R* v *Secretary of State for the Home Department ex parte Doody* [1993] 2 All ER 92, as Lord Bridge pointed out in *Lloyd* v *MacMahon* [1987] 1 All ER 1118, 'the so-called rules of natural justice are not engraved in tablets of stone' (at p. 1161)), English law does not yet recognise a *general* duty to give reasons, any more than it provides a *general* right to be heard or a *general* right to due process. To the extent that it does not, and fails to provide objective justification for this omission, it risks breaching EC law. Other rights of a procedural nature, such as the right against self incrimination, which, following the ECHR's decision in *Funke* v *France* should extend to civil proceedings of a penal nature, and the right to confidentiality, should also be observed by national authorities when seeking to enforce Community law, subject to exceptions which may be objectively justified.

By contrast with procedural rights, the scope for challenge to domestic implementing measures on the grounds of breach of the broader 'substantive' general principles of law such as equality, or legal certainty, or the protection of private property, or unjust enrichment, appears to be limited. Where these principles are expressed in specific terms in the EC Treaty or secondary legislation, or have been applied by the Court in interpreting Treaty provisions or secondary legislation, particularly, as the Court suggested in *ERT* v *DEP* (case C 260/89, at para. 43), when states are seeking to justify derogations from Community rules, they may be invoked to challenge national measures as falling 'within the scope' of Community law. Outside these areas, when invoked as free-standing rights, to challenge acts lying within the sphere of member states' discretion, *Bostock* indicates that their application is a matter for member states, to be determined according to the equivalent principles of *national* law, albeit interpreted as far as possible in a manner consistent with the general principles of Community law.

The principle of proportionality merits special consideration. In the context of a challenge to domestic law it has been invoked principally in the interpretation of the EC Treaty and secondary legislation, to control member states' derogations from basic principles of Community law, for example in the field of the free movement of goods and persons and sex discrimination. Exceptions to these principles are permitted under Community law provided that they can be proved to be 'necessary' or 'justified' on particular legitimate grounds. This may be expressed in the Treaty, for example Article 36, which provides for exemption from the prohibition on quantitative restrictions on the free movement of goods of Article 30 on specific exhaustive grounds; Articles 48(2) and 55, which allow for derogation from the principle of free movement of persons on grounds of public policy, public security and public health; or in secondary legislation, as in Article 2 of Directive 76/207, which allows for (strictly limited) exceptions to the prohibition on direct sex discrimination; or in rulings of the Court (e.g., *Cassis de Dijon* (case 120/78), the 'rule of reason' exception to Article 30); *Bilka-Kaufhaus* (case 170/84), principle of 'objective justification' for indirect sex discrimination). In deciding whether member states' derogations are 'necessary' or 'justified' the Court of Justice applies the proportionality principle. Derogations must be proportionate to the ends pursued, that is, they must be no more than is appropriate and necessary to achieve their intended (and legitimate) ends. Designed to control the exercise by public authorities of discretionary powers, particularly when derogating from fundamental rights, the principle is, as Lord Ackner commented in *Brind* v *Secretary of State for Home Department* [1991] 1 All ER 720, 'a different and severer test' than the *Wednesbury* test of reasonableness.

British courts have had some difficulty in applying the proportionality principle. Despite Lord Diplock's suggestion in the *CCSU* case [1985] AC 374, as to the 'possible adoption in the future of the principle of proportionality, which is recognised in the administrative law of several of our fellow members of the European Economic Community', the House of Lords refused to apply it in *Brind*. This case involved a challenge to Directives issued by the Home Secretary prohibiting the broadcasting of direct statements by representatives of proscribed organisations in Northern Ireland. Although the claim involved no issues of EC law the applicants, citing Lord Diplock's dicta in *CCSU*, sought to invoke the right to freedom of expression and the principle of proportionality from the European Convention of Human Rights. The court held that since the Convention had not been incorporated into domestic law it would be a 'judicial usurpation of the legislative function' to apply its provisions directly. As Lord Ackner pointed out, in applying the proportionality principle 'an enquiry into the merits of a decision cannot be avoided'. Thus the case was 'not one in which the first step might be taken'. Their Lordships were clearly wary of being drawn into a review of the merits of a decision, of 'substituting (their) own judgment of what was needed to achieve a particular objective for the judgment of the Secretary of State upon whom the duty had been laid by Parliament' (per Lord Roskill at p. 725).

In *Brind* the challenge was to an administrative act. The courts' difficulties increase when the challenge is to an Act of Parliament, which it may be when that challenge is based on a breach of Community law. In *Stoke-on-Trent City Council* v *B & Q* [1991] 4 All ER 221 (Ch D)) Hoffman J was required to examine provisions of the Shops Act 1950 limiting Sunday trading, alleged by B & Q, in defending an action by the Council for an injunction to prevent them from trading on Sunday, to be contrary to Article 30 EC, in the light of the principle of proportionality. Since the rules were 'indistinctly applicable', that is applicable equally to both domestically produced and imported goods they fell to be judged according to the *Cassis de Dijon* test: i.e., they would be permissible if proved to be necessary to satisfy mandatory requirements relating, in this case, to characteristics of 'national or regional socio-economic policy'. As Hoffman J, speaking of the impugned provisions of the Shops Act, pointed out

this is a case of a sovereign legislature acting to further what the European Court has held to be legitimate objectives. It is subject only to a requirement that the measure should not be disproportionate to the importance of its objectives. The question is one on which strong and differing views may be held . . . It is not my function to carry out the balancing exercise or to form my own view on whether the legislative objective could be achieved by other means . . . The function of the court is to review the acts of the legislature but not to substitute its own policy or values.

Questions of proportionality were

essentially legislative questions involving a balance of interests and the judiciary cannot do more than decide whether the view of the legislature is one which could reasonably be held.

Despite these strong words, applying the test, as he felt bound by EC law to do, he concluded that the rules in question were not disproportionate.

Hoffman J's reaction to the principle of proportionality in *Stoke-on-Trent* v *B & Q* was on the facts understandable. The alleged incompatibility of the impugned provisions of the Shops Act with Article 30 EC was far from clear. B & Q's defence, if logical, was exploitative, designed to maintain a lucrative Sunday trading advantage. But Hoffman J's approach was clearly at odds with the European view. The principle of proportionality does not require national courts to substitute their own policy views for those of national administrative or legislative bodies; it is designed simply to limit their discretion when they are acting, albeit within a permitted sphere of derogation, contrary to the fundamental rules of Community law. In weighing, as is required by the proportionality principle, the damage caused by the alleged infringement of Community law by the Shops Act against the justification for limiting Sunday trading, there can be little doubt that the rule was proportionate.

The principle of proportionality was applied successfully by the English High Court in *R* v *Minister of Agriculture, Fisheries and Food ex parte Bell Lines* [1984] 2 CMLR 502. The case concerned an application for judicial review of a system set up by the Minister limiting the entry of milk and cream into the UK, and the required health inspections, to authorised ports, to be designated by the Minister. In designating these ports none of the applicant importers' traditional ports of entry was included. Since the new ports were considerably more inconvenient to the applicant importers the Minister's measures clearly operated as a hindrance to imports, measures of equivalent effect to quantitative restrictions prima facie in breach of Article 30 EC. The question was whether they were permitted under Article 36 EC. Article 36 EC permits restrictions on imports, exports or goods in transit where they are 'justified' on the grounds, inter alia, of the protection of health and life, provided that they do not constitute 'a means of arbitrary discrimination or disguised restriction on trade between member states'. These provisions had been interpreted by the ECJ as representing a test of necessity or proportionality. Forbes J noted that this test had been interpreted by the ECJ as meaning that the measure 'must not go beyond what is strictly necessary' to meet a genuine need. Following an examination of the facts he concluded that the measures in question were not necessary. The designated ports, as traditional meat ports were not, as was argued, more 'experienced' to deal with imports of milk and cream; these products required a quite different treatment and expertise. The obvious choice on the grounds of experience would have been the traditional ports. Thus there were clearly other ways, less harmful to imports, by which the minister's objectives could have been achieved. Like Ackner LJ in *Brind*, Forbes J noted the difference between the *Wednesbury* test and the principle of proportionality and suggested that the measures were 'probably not impugnable on *Wednesbury* principles. It would be difficult to say that the Minister had gone wrong'. Nevertheless he concluded that the system might have been challenged successfully 'even on *Wednesbury* principles'.

R v *Minister of Agriculture, Fisheries and Food ex parte Bell Lines* is an exemplary judgment, but the applicants' case, unlike the defendant's claim in *Stoke-on-Trent* v *B & Q*, was strong, and the challenge was to administrative action. The landmark case for the application by English courts of the proportionality principle (as well as for questions of access and remedies noted above) is the House of Lords' decision in *EOC* v *Secretary of State for Employment* [1994] 1 All ER 910. This action, brought by the EOC, was for a declaration that provisions of the Employment Protection (Consolidation) Act 1978, which provided for a more advantageous threshold of protection as regards unfair dismissal and redundancy for full-time workers than for part-time workers, was indirectly discriminatory on the grounds of sex. The Court of Justice had established in *Bilka-Kaufhaus* (case 170/84) that where, because of the gender composition of the work force, the disadvantage suffered by part-time employees falls predominantly on one sex (in this case women) a difference in treatment between part-time and full-time workers will constitute indirect sexual discrimination in breach of EC law (Article 119 (equal pay); Directive 76/207 (equal treatment)). It will only be permissible if the difference in treatment is 'objectively justified'. In order to be objectively justified the measures in question must

(a) correspond to a genuine need of the undertaking,
(b) be suitable for obtaining the objective pursued by the enterprise, and
(c) be necessary for that purpose.

The burden of proof of objective justification falls on the party alleging justification.

Given clear evidence in *EOC* v *Secretary of State for Employment* that the part-time work force in the UK was predominantly female, the impugned threshold provisions of the Employment Protection (Consolidation) Act were found to be indirectly discriminatory. Thus one of the principal questions before the House of Lords was whether they were objectively justified. It had been argued successfully before the Court of Appeal that the different and less advantageous threshold of protection for part-time workers provided under the Employment Protection (Consolidation) Act was justified on social grounds, to reduce costs to employers to encourage them to employ part-time workers and thereby increase the availability of part-time work, which suited the needs of women. Whilst the House of Lords acknowledged that an increase in the availability of part-time work might be regarded as a beneficial social policy, the question was whether the Minister had *proved* that the measures in question were suitable and necessary to achieve this end. Examining the evidence for the Secretary of State, which consisted of an affidavit by an official in the Department of Employment setting out the views of the Department, Lord Keith found that it 'did not contain anything capable of being regarded as factual evidence demonstrating the correctness of these views'. Evidence submitted by the EOC from employers' organisations and trade unions revealed, unsurprisingly, a diversity of views. The experience of other member states indicated that a more equal treatment of part-time and full-time workers did not diminish the availability of part-time work; indeed, in France, which had provided for the same rights for part-time and full-time workers, the supply of part-time work had increased The House concluded (unanimously on this issue) that 'no objective justification for the threshold provisions of the 1978 Act had been made out', and granted a declaration that these provisions were incompatible with Article 119 and Directives 75/117 and 76/207.

This approach, paying scrupulous regard to the evidence, both as to the genuineness of the need and the necessity of the measures designed to meet that need, provides an impeccable example for our courts as to the correct approach to the application of the principle of proportionality.

In the cases considered above national authorities were obliged to apply the proportionality principle in the context of the interpretation and application of specific rules of Community law. Outside this context the extent to which measures designed to implement community law can be construed as 'within the scope of Community law' remains unclear. If, as *Bostock* indicates, measures falling within member states' discretion must be assessed in the light of the appropriate principles of *national* law, it may be hoped that in the interest of uniformity and the protection of individual rights, national rules and principles will be interpreted as far as possible to comply with general principles of Community law, particularly those concerned with the protection of fundamental human rights. It would not be impossible, for example, for the *Wednesbury* rule to be applied in the light of the principle of proportionality. As Sir John Laws has suggested (at (1993) PL 59, at p. 71)

Just as judges have evolved the *Wednesbury* principle, so can they refine it, and build differential principles within it. They may accord a place in our public law to the principle of proportionality.

CONCLUSIONS

The obligation of national courts to provide real and effective protection for individuals' Community rights has not required a major rewriting of the English law of judicial review. Encouraged, and sometimes driven, by the demands of Community law and, indirectly, by the European Convention on Human Rights, as well as by a reforming spirit, judicial review has developed, and protection substantially increased particularly over the last twenty years. Access to review has been extended, as have the range of remedies available. Traditional barriers and immunities, if not abolished, have been re-examined, and limited. Lacunae have been filled. There has been a growing insistence on openness and accountability in decision-making. This progress has been achieved largely by the Courts, incrementally, working within the framework of existing rules, aided where necessary by rulings from the Court of Justice. As Lord Lester observed, 'membership of the Community (has) profoundly (altered) the constitutional role of British judges as law-makers by widening the scope of judicial review of substance and merits as well as of form and procedure' ('English Judges as Law-Makers', (1993) PL 269). Such changes as have occurred, even if required by Community law, have accrued to the benefit of all. Rightly, the courts have sought to avoid a double standard.

However, it cannot be said that the English law of judicial review is yet fully effective to protect individuals' rights under Community law. Whilst it is capable of providing effective protection, such protection cannot be universally guaranteed. Despite the lead provided by the House of Lords in cases such as *Datafin* (1986), *Roy* (1992), *CCSU* (1985), *Factortame* (1991), *M v Home Office* (1993), *EOC v Secretary of State for Employment* (1994) and *R v Chief Constable of West Midlands Police ex parte Wiley* (1994), the caselaw is not consistent. Success depends on choosing the best authority, on following the best practice. In reviewing discretionary acts, even when they involve infringements of fundamental rights, too much still depends on subjective assessments of 'fairness' and 'reasonableness'. We have yet to move to a system of review based on general rights and a general principle of objective justification for actions taken in derogation of those rights, incorporating the principle of proportionality. But we seem to be on the way.

SEVEN

Impact on private law

As well as conferring on individuals rights in public law to challenge acts and omissions of a public nature for breach of EC law, Community law also gives rise to rights in private law. Where such rights arise from directly effective Treaty provisions or Regulations they may be invoked directly against all parties, public or private. Where they arise from Directives they may be invoked directly against 'public' bodies, as defined in *Foster* v *British Gas* (case 188/89), or indirectly, under the principles laid down in *Von Colson* (case 14/83) and *Marleasing* (case C 106/89), against private parties. Directly effective Decisions may be invoked against their addressees. Rights claimed under *Francovich* are by their very nature enforceable only against the state.

As in actions involving public law, the remedies and procedures required to be available in domestic courts for breaches of private rights derived from EC law are not in principle different from those available for similar actions based on domestic law. Thus these rights may be invoked, before the appropriate court or tribunal, both as a cause of action and a defence, in actions for breach of contract, or tort, or restitution, or in claims based on statutory rights, and protected by injunctions or declarations, or a remedy in damages, or specific statutory remedies, in the same way, and according to the same principles, as apply to equivalent claims under national law. The difficulty, arising from the special nature of EC law, lies firstly in ascertaining what is a 'similar' or 'equivalent' action under domestic law, and secondly, whether the remedy provided in respect of such a claim is effective, or sufficiently effective, to protect individuals' Community rights and deter parties from breaching Community law. In actions against public bodies, as was seen in Chapter 6, jurisdictional problems may prove a barrier to effective enforcement. A claim may fail because it falls in the 'twilight' zone between public and private, domestic and Community law. When the appropriate claim and procedure have been identified, access to the courts, or to particular remedies, may be limited or denied. Although in principle public authorities are subject to the same private law obligations as apply to private parties, policy may operate, as it was seen to do in public law, to restrict liability, even to confer immunity.

JURISDICTIONAL PROBLEMS

The *O'Reilly* v *Mackman* Rule

In pursuing a claim in private law, for example for compensation, or restitution, the normal approach would be to proceed by writ. However, where that claim is against a public body or in respect of 'public' acts and is based on the alleged illegality of the defendant's acts or omissions, the question of legality will need to be established as a matter of public law. The *O'Reilly* v *Mackman* [1983] 2 AC 237 rule (see Chapter 6) was designed to ensure that persons should not be allowed to evade the safeguards provided under RSC Order 53 by choosing to proceed in ordinary proceedings where their claim was essentially a claim in public law (see Chapter 6). In the majority of claims based on EC law the plaintiff's private rights will depend on establishing that the defendant's action, although permissible under national law, is unlawful under Community law. Indeed, were this not the case it would be unnecessary to invoke EC law. Thus where a person proceeds by writ against a public body, or in respect of public acts, he risks rejection under the *O'Reilly* v *Mackman* rule.

As was noted in Chapter 6, the *O'Reilly* v *Mackman* rule has been much distinguished and its effect diminished since its introduction in 1982. In *EOC* v *Secretary of State for Employment* [1994] 1 All ER 910, Lords Lowry and Browne-Wilkinson expressed doubts concerning the procedural restrictions of the rule, Lord Lowry suggesting (at p. 926) that one day it might be 'the subject of ... further consideration by the House of Lords'. In *Doyle* v *Northumbria Probation Committee* [1991] 1 WLR 1340, Henry J refused to strike out the plaintiffs' application by writ in a claim for breach of contract, the success of which depended on the resolution of a public law issue, on the grounds that it did not amount to abuse of process. It was a genuine private law claim: 'it was not a public law challenge disguised as a private law action'. Moreover, as he pointed out, were the applicants to be required to bring a free-standing claim for judicial review, their delay had been such that 'it would be difficult to envisage the court granting them leave to apply for judicial review'. Although the claim concerned only domestic law Henry J's reasoning would be admirably suited to a claim based on EC law.

Limitations of Order 53

This is the converse of the problem posed by the *O'Reilly* v *Mackman* rule. In *Doyle* the claims in both public and private law were interdependent and against the same authority; the right claimed arose from the defendant's alleged public wrong. Therefore it would have been appropriate (although it was not necessary) to proceed under Order 53. Where the plaintiff's only possible right against the defendant is in private law, even though his claim may involve a challenge to domestic law, the plaintiff has no choice but to proceed by writ. In

EOC v *Secretary of State for Employment* [1994] 1 All ER 910, Mrs Day, a part-time worker employed by the Hertfordshire County Council, was joined with the EOC in their action against the Secretary of State, under Order 53, for a declaration that the threshold provisions of the Employment Protection (Consolidation) Act 1987, which permitted discrimination against part-time workers, were in breach of Community law. As the House of Lords pointed out, the objective of her claim was to obtain from her employers the same rights in respect of unfair dismissal and redundancy as full-time workers. This was a claim in private law. Since the defendant Secretary of State was not her employer, he was not liable to meet her claim, even if the claim was sound. The appropriate forum for such a claim was before an industrial tribunal, which had been 'entrusted by statute to deal with such claims and was fully competent' to do so (p. 918). It follows that although in an action under Order 53 the High Court may order that the action proceed as if begun by writ, this will only avail the applicant if he has a claim *against the same defendant* in private law.

A Question of National or Community Law?

Where a national authority is responsible for implementing Community law the area of discretion permitted to that authority, and thus the question of whether a particular act is a matter of purely national law or is challengable for breach of Community law, may be unclear. It depends, ultimately, on the Court of Justice's assessment as to whether a particular act or omission falls 'within the scope' of Community law. In these circumstances a claim may fail because it is argued exclusively on the basis of Community law or national law.

In *R* v *Minister of Agriculture, Fisheries and Food ex parte Bostock* ((case C 2/92), see Chapter 6) the Court found that in matters of detailed implementation of the Community's milk quota system, member states were not obliged to comply with general principles of equality, the right to property and unjust enrichment as a matter of Community law. The determination of rights as between tenant and landlord farmers was a matter for national law. Thus if the applicant tenant was to obtain compensation for loss of his valuable 'reference quantities', which accrued as a windfall to his landlord, he could only do so on the basis of principles of domestic law. In these circumstances (with the benefit of hindsight) it would have been advisable to argue, as well as under general principles of EC law, from principles of national law, such as estoppel and unjust enrichment, and the rules based on those principles, and for an interpretation of those rules as far as possible in a manner consistent with general principles of Community law.

In not dissimilar circumstances the plaintiff in *Cato* v *Minister for Agriculture, Fisheries and Food* [1989] 3 CMLR 513 (CA), a fisherman was seeking compensation or a grant to which he claimed he was entitled. The grant was payable on the decommissioning of fishing boats, under a scheme set up by the Minister, pursuant to EC Directive 83/515, the purpose of which was to reduce fishing capacity in the EC. National authorities were responsible for implementing the scheme. Under the Fishing Vessels (Financial Assistance) Scheme 1993 ('the Scheme') set up by the Minister, the Minister was entitled to ('may') approve the application for a grant once he was 'satisfied' that the conditions for the award of the grant were fulfilled. The plaintiff, on the advice of the Minister's official, had sold his boat to H subject to an undertaking from H that it would be used as a houseboat and not for fishing. H changed his mind and sold the boat to B and M, also subject to an undertaking that the boat should not be used for fishing. The Minister's official was involved as adviser in all these proceedings. B and M subsequently re-equipped the boat and re-registered it for fishing on 17 December 1984. The Ministry's decision to reject the grant was made on 25 February 1985, the Minister not being 'satisfied' that the conditions for the award of the grant had been fulfilled. Had the grant been awarded before the date of re-registration it would have been repayable by B and H. The plaintiff (who had proceeded under Order 53, but, being out of time, was allowed to continue as if he had begun by writ) argued his case on the basis of English law, in breach of contract, estoppel, and negligent misstatement. On appeal the claim for negligent misstatement was dropped, and a claim for breach by the Minister of a private right was permitted, exceptionally, to be introduced.

The Court of Appeal, following an extensive survey of the authorities, found that the conditions for the claim in contract and estoppel were not established under English law. Purchas J (Balcombe LJ concurring) acknowledged that, had the Minister been satisfied that the conditions for the grant had been fulfilled, the discretionary function of the Minister would be spent and the plaintiff would have acquired a private right against the Minister. But he found that the plaintiff had never acquired that right, since the Minister had not been satisfied that the requisite conditions had been fulfilled. Stocker J, who came to the same conclusion as to the outcome, although finding it 'a most unfortunate case', thought that the applicant's right lay only in public law. According to his interpretation of the rules 'there was nothing to justify the minister's failure to be satisfied'. However, this was a matter of public law, a case for judicial review. It did not constitute a private law right . Thus it could not be considered in the existing private law proceedings. He regretted that as a result of the court's decision, the purpose of the Directive and the Scheme and the entitlement of the applicant to a grant had not been fulfilled.

Although the claim was undoubtedly a private law claim, to be decided according to the appropriate principles of national law, it is regrettable that the case was argued and focused almost entirely on fine points of domestic law and the literal provisions of the Scheme, with scant regard to the purposes of the Directive, which clearly included the award of compensation for persons such as the plaintiff who opted to participate in the scheme. Purchas LJ held that it was 'not necessary' to adopt a free 'construction' approach to the English regulations, based on *Litster* v *Forth Dry Docks & Engineering Co Ltd* (see Chapter 2), as was argued by counsel for the plaintiff, since the Scheme was 'in sympathy with the Directive'. Stocker J adopted a purposive interpretation, with an eye to the Directive and its objectives, and concluded that the Minister had misapplied the rules but, regrettably, this did not give rise to a private right. Since the matter concerned the implementation by national authorities of policies laid down by the Community, which included a right to compensation, arguably the question of rights under domestic law should have been pleaded, and the law interpreted, not literally, but in the light of the objectives of the Directive, as was done by Stocker LJ, and of general principles of law. This would include the principles of legitimate expectations and unjust enrichment, principles respected and reflected in substantive rules of domestic law. Following this approach it would not have been impossible to have found the plaintiff entitled to a grant, a private right entitling him to a private law remedy.

FINDING THE EQUIVALENT REMEDY

Many of the rights arising from the principles of direct or indirect effects, or on the principles laid down in *Francovich*, expressed by the Court of Justice as rights capable of being invoked by individuals before their national courts, may be construed as private law rights in English law. This does not mean that individuals seeking a remedy for breach of those rights are automatically entitled to the full range of private law remedies available under national law, injunctions, declarations and damages, or specific remedies available under statute or secondary legislation. The principle of national treatment requires that claims based on EC rights obtain the same treatment and have access to the same remedies as are available for 'similar' actions based on domestic law. Thus in order to obtain a remedy in damages the plaintiff must bring his claim within one of the existing categories of cases for which damages are available under domestic law. It is only when national remedies are ineffective, or not sufficiently effective, that existing remedies and procedures may need to be modified or further,' special' remedies provided.

Given the extent and diverse nature of Community rights, many of which are not prima facie of a personal nature, the initial problem is to ascertain what is an equivalent claim under domestic law. Private rights, even rights based on similar principles, for example rights to restitution, or protection against unfair competition are protected in English law in a variety of ways, and to differing degrees, by a patchwork of sometimes overlapping, sometimes contradictory, rules of common law or equity or statute. It may be necessary to dig deep and search wide to find the appropriate rule. However, our law is sufficiently rich that it should be possible in the vast majority of cases to find an 'equivalent' domestic rule. Where there is a choice of remedies or a conflict between them the Community principle of non-discrimination (see Chapter 5) requires that the rule which provides the most effective protection for the individual's Community rights should be applied. In this context, with limited exceptions (e.g., EC competition, public procurement law), reverse discrimination, a lesser degree of protection for claims based solely on domestic law, if undesirable as a matter of policy, is permitted under Community law.

EFFECTIVENESS OF NATIONAL LAW REMEDIES

Once the appropriate 'similar' claim under domestic law has been identified, the second and major problem is to decide whether it is effective, or sufficiently effective, to protect individuals' Community rights and deter breaches of

Community law. If it is not it will need to be modified. Where no 'similar' claim exists a new rule will have to be provided. Since an examination of the effectiveness of judicial protection under domestic private law based on distinctions between the liability of public and private bodies or between different causes of action is likely to confuse rather than clarify, the question will be approached by focusing on the remedies available in English private law. A distinction will, however, be made between the protection of common law rights and statutory rights and remedies. The impact of statute on common law remedies will also be considered.

Injunctions

The Court's jurisdiction to grant injunctive relief stems from the Judicature Acts of 1873 and 1925: the principles on which injunctions, interim or final, are granted derive from the common law. An individual has no general standing in English private law to sue to prevent an unlawful act; he may only sue to protect or prevent an infringement of a private right, that is, to prevent a breach or contract, or a tort, or to protect a property right.

Although there is some dispute as to the precise nature of the private rights in respect of which an injunction may be granted, particularly as to the scope of the concept of 'property' rights, or rights analogous to property rights (see e.g., *Eastham* v *Newcastle United Football Club Ltd* [1963] 3 All ER 139) there is little doubt that EC rights based on directly or indirectly effective provisions of Community law or under *Francovich* are sufficient to support an application for injunctive relief in English law. However, in order to claim such relief in private law it will be necessary to show not only that the rights are capable of being invoked but that in this particular case have been, or are about to be, infringed. An individual cannot sue for a private law injunction simply to prevent unlawful action, for example to prevent environmental damage or unfair trading practices in breach of EC law: he must show that the defendant's acts interfere, or threaten to interfere, with his particular rights. Whilst these rules may be effective to protect individuals' rights, and are no doubt justified in order to avoid a multiplicity of claims, it is doubtful that they serve to further the second purpose of the effectiveness principle, namely to deter parties from breaching Community law. This second objective can only be achieved if there is scope for representative action. This matter will be considered further below.

Interim relief Access to an injunction does not in itself guarantee effective enforcement of EC law. The latter depends on the way in which the court's discretion is exercised, particularly in respect of the granting of interim relief. The principles governing interim relief suggested by the Court of Justice in *Zuckerfabrik Süderdithmarschen* (cases C 143/88 and C 92/89, for details see Chapter 5) are not dissimilar to the *American Cyanamid* v *Ethicon* [1975] AC 396 guidelines applied by the House of Lords in *Factortame (No. 2)* [1991] 1 All ER 70, and should in most cases be effective to protect individuals' rights, particularly if there is mutual provision for cross-undertakings in damages to protect against interim loss, as suggested in Chapter 6. However, where interim relief is the only way in which individuals' rights may be effectively protected, or parties deterred from breaching Community law, as may be the case in matters concerning threatened damage to the environment (see e.g., *Rose Theatre Trust Co., Independent*, 4 July 1989, noted Chapter 6) or breach of EC public procurement rules, the requirement of a 'strong prima facie case' (*American Cyanamid*) or 'serious and irreparable damage' (*Zuckerfabrik*) should be interpreted generously, in the light of the special nature of EC law, and the fact that the existence of a prima facie case of breach of EC law may not always be clear. Moreover, in the case of breach of public procurement rules the difficulties of proving damage or calculating the amount of damage are such that damages, although available in principle, will often not provide an adequate remedy. This will be discussed further below.

If doubts existed before, it is clear following *Factortame (No. 2)* that injunctions and interim injunctions are now available against all bodies, private and public, including the Crown, and that they may be granted to prevent the application of any provision of domestic law, including statutory provisions, to prevent a breach, even a putative breach, of Community law.

Declarations

Under Rules of the Supreme Court Order 15, r. 16 a court may make a 'binding declaration of right whether or not any consequential relief is claimed'. 'Provided that a substantial question is raised which one person has a real interest to raise and the other to oppose, then the court has a discretion to resolve it by a declaration which it will exercise if there is good reason for so doing' (per Lord Denning in *Pyx Granite* v *Ministry of Housing and Local Government* [1958] 1 QB 554 at p. 571). However, some legal right of the plaintiff must be in issue. The court will not 'declare the law generally' or 'give advisory opinions' (per Lord Diplock in *Gouriet* v *Union of Post Office Workers* [1978] AC 435 at p. 501). Thus, in the context of an action based on EC law, the same rules apply as to an injunction. A plaintiff may seek a declaration to establish his legal position when a Community right affecting his particular interests has been, or is in danger of being, infringed. As with injunctions, the opportunity for representative bodies to seek a declaration to protect collective interests would greatly enhance the effective enforcement of Community law, as was demonstrated in *EOC* v *Secretary of State for Employment* [1994] 1 All ER 910.

Damages

Although damages (as understood in the widest sense as meaning the payment of money) may be awarded under Order 53 r. 7, or in private law actions, the right to damages in the form of compensation or restitution is a private law right. For an individual seeking damages, whether against a private or a public body, it is not enough to prove a breach by the defendant of his Community rights. If damages are to be awarded according to the principles applicable to 'similar actions in domestic law', they will only be available (apart from when granted in lieu of an injunction, under Lord Cairn's Act 1858) if the defendant's unlawful act constitutes a tort, or a breach of contract or a breach of a private right entitling the plaintiff to restitution, or a breach of a right equivalent to a statutory right entitling him to damages. Thus, having ascertained which action might be regarded as the appropriate 'equivalent' remedy, the question arises whether that remedy is 'effective' as required by EC law. As in the case of injunctions and declarations, where individual claims are numerous but small, for example in cases involving consumer claims or claims based on breach of EC environmental or competition law, an improved facility for the processing of class claims ('joined cases facility') and an opportunity for interest groups to take representative action would undoubtedly serve both to increase the effective protection of individuals' rights to damages and to deter breaches of Community law.

Tort   An action for damages based on EC law may be brought under a variety of torts. A breach of EC environmental rules may constitute a nuisance or be subject to the rule in *Rylands and Fletcher* (1866) LR 1 Ex 265, the 'strict liability' rule; a breach of EC competition law may involve the economic torts such as passing off, or inducement of breach of contract, or unlawful interference with trade; a breach of any EC right may be actionable in negligence, or for breach of statutory duty. A breach of a public law duty may constitute misfeasance in public office. Where these torts are established, damages, awarded on a compensatory principle, intended to put the plaintiff in the position he would have been in had the tort not occurred, are full. Restitutionary damages may also be granted in an action based on tort (e.g., passing off). The rules of causation (including mitigation) and remoteness, the latter based on a broad test of foreseeability (*Wagon Mound Nos. 1 and 2*) are generous, and normally applied in a manner favourable to the plaintiff. Thus where a substantive tort is established the effectiveness principle is satisfied, provided the plaintiff's common law rights have not been curtailed by statute (see below).

However, not all breaches of Community law will constitute torts. Public authorities are given considerable latitude under the law of negligence by judicial manipulation of the rules, particularly the concept of duty of care. The tort of misfeasance in public office, requiring a deliberate, or at the most knowingly unlawful act on the part of a public body, reflects a similar concern to protect public bodies. Both may be based on sound policy reasons. Breaches of EC economic rules, designed to regulate trade, for example breaches of the free movement of goods provisions, such as Article 30 EC (prohibition of quantitative restrictions on imports and exports or measures of equivalent effect) or Regulations governing the Common Agricultural Policy (CAP), will not necessarily constitute substantive torts. In *Garden Cottage Foods* v *Milk Marketing Board* [1983] 2 All ER 770, the House of Lords was asked to consider whether a breach of Article 86 EEC, which prohibits undertakings from abusing their dominant position in the EC, gave rise to an action in private law, sounding in damages. In fact the plaintiffs, Garden Cottage Foods, were seeking an interim injunction to prevent the alleged abuse, a withdrawal of supplies of bulk butter, which threatened to put them out of business. The Court of Appeal had granted that relief on the ground that it was necessary to provide effective protection for the plaintiff's interests, since it was uncertain whether they would, if successful at trial, be entitled to damages. Lord Diplock, speaking for the majority in the House of Lords, suggested, although he did not consider the point 'unarguable', that

> it would be difficult to see how it [could] . . . be successfully argued . . . that a breach of Article 86 which causes damage to an individual citizen . . . does not give rise to a cause of action . . . for breach of statutory duty.

What he did consider was unarguable was the proposition that if Article 86 gave rise to any form of action in English law, the plaintiff would only be entitled to an injunction, not damages. This he suggested would be 'wholly novel' in English law.

Lord Wilberforce, in a powerful dissenting judgment, did not share his views. He suggested that there were many cases in English law in which an injunction but not damages might be granted. He expressed grave doubts that a breach of Article 86 should give rise to an action for breach of statutory duty. To say that an action which is prohibited under Community law automatically becomes a tort or breach of statutory duty was in his opinion 'a conclusionary statement concealing a vital but unexpressed step'.

No doubt encouraged by the majority view of the House of Lords in *Garden Cottage Foods* v *Milk Marketing Board*, the plaintiffs in *Bourgoin SA* v *Ministry of Agriculture, Fisheries and Food* brought an action against the Ministry for an injunction and damages for losses suffered as a result of the Ministry's alleged breach of Article 30 EC. The alleged breach was a ban on the import of French turkeys, which they argued was contrary to Article 30 and was not justified under Article 36 EC. This proved to be correct when the Court delivered a judgment in Article 169 proceedings shortly after the claim in *Bourgoin* was lodged. The plaintiffs' action was brought under the torts of: breach of statutory duty; an 'innominate' tort; and misfeasance in public office. The question was whether the plaintiff's claim disclosed a cause of action under English law. Mann LJ, following *Garden Cottage Foods*, and unable to distinguish Article 30 from Article 86 EC, concluded that the alleged breach constituted a private law right actionable for breach of statutory duty. In the Court of Appeal (the claim based on an 'innominate' tort having been dropped, having been found not to exist in English law), Parker LJ, in a judgment that was clearly policy driven (based on the potential breadth of public authorities' liability for breach of statutory duty and their difficulties in ascertaining whether a particular act was in fact in breach of EC law), distinguished *Garden Cottage Foods*. He concluded that a breach of Article 30 simpliciter was akin to an ultra vires act in English law; as such it was actionable only in public law, by means of judicial review, or under the tort of misfeasance in public office. Oliver LJ, dissenting, although sympathetic to the policy arguments outlined by Parker J, concluded that directly effective Community law, being expressed as giving rise to rights for individuals which national courts must protect, must give rise to rights in private law, and that an action for damages for breach of statutory duty was the only means whereby the plaintiff's Community rights could be adequately protected. The Court of Appeal was, however, unanimous in agreeing with Mann J that an action could lie in the tort of misfeasance in public office. Malice, in the sense of a deliberate intention to injure the plaintiff, was not an essential ingredient of the tort. It was sufficient if, as the Minister had conceded for the purpose of the appeal, the Minister had acted with knowledge of the illegality of his acts and their effect on the plaintiff.

The applicability of the tort of breach of statutory duty to claims based on EC law was further considered in *An Bord Bainne Co-operative* v *Milk Marketing Board (MMB) and the Dairy Trade Federation (DTF)* [1988] 1 CMLR 605, in the context of a claim for damages suffered as a result of the defendants' discriminatory pricing policy for milk, which the plaintiffs alleged was in breach of EC Regulation 1422/78. The question before the Court of Appeal was whether the DTF could join the Ministry of Agriculture as defendant in the proceedings, so that they might obtain an indemnity for, or a contribution towards, their liability, if proved, in respect of the plaintiff's claim. The DTF's claim, based on the Minister's breach of statutory duty, was that the Ministry had failed to take the necessary measures to ensure that the Regulation was applied, as required by Article 10 of the Regulation. No allegation of negligence or misfeasance was made.

Although the allegation was based on breach of an EC Regulation, not a Treaty provision, and concerned administrative acts as opposed to legislative or quasi-legislative acts, the Court of Appeal felt unable to distinguish *Bourgoin*. 'In the absence of a claim in negligence or misfeasance' said Parker LJ, 'the only remedy for ministerial action or inaction is by way of judicial review. There is no right to damages'.

If this view is correct (and it is submitted that it is), that a simple breach of EC law will not *necessarily* give rise to a right to damages in English law for breach of statutory duty, the question remains whether the principle of effective protection for individuals' Community rights requires that it should do so.

It is submitted that it should not, and that to provide a remedy in damages for breach of statutory duty for *all* infringements of Community law would expose parties, public and private, to an unacceptable degree of liability. A breach of Community law, whether by public or private parties, is akin to an ultra vires act. Such an act may be committed negligently, even innocently. Just as public bodies are protected from liability in negligence in respect of such acts, so there should be some protection for parties, public or private, committing similar breaches of EC law. The tort of breach of statutory duty, although prima facie wide, and strict as regards liability, is rigorously controlled, by reference to the intention (often fictional) of the legislature. As a result it is notoriously unpredictable. Even in the clearest case, for example a breach by an employer of health and safety legislation, success cannot be guaranteed (e.g., *T* v *Surrey CC* [1994] 4 All ER 577). If a simple breach of EC law were sufficient to give rise to liability under this tort it would be uncontrolled. Until it has been interpreted by the Court of Justice the meaning and scope of Community law, as Parker LJ pointed out in *Bourgoin*, is often unclear. Moreover, the damage suffered is often purely economic. Because such losses ('indeterminate in amount, time and class', per Cardozo CJ, *Ultramares Corporation* v *Touche* (1931) 255 NY 170 at p. 179) are hard to contain there are restrictions on their recovery under English law, particularly in tort. Other member states impose similar restrictions, albeit in different ways, for example by stricter rules of causation and remoteness of damage. The non-contractual liability of Community authorities is also confined, and for similar reasons (see Chapter 10).

Thus there is justification for the majority view of the Court of Appeal in *Bourgoin*. Many breaches of Community law will constitute substantive torts entitling the plaintiff to damages. Such remedies as exist should, if necessary to protect a Community right intended to benefit the plaintiff, for example a measure in the field of social protection, be generously construed and lacunae filled. 'Simple' breaches, for example in the field of economic regulation, such as breaches of Articles 30, and, it is submitted Articles 85 and 86, may be protected by injunction or declaration, if necessary by speedy interim relief. As Lord Wilberforce commented in *Garden Cottage Foods* (at p. 738), 'there is nothing illogical or even unusual in a situation in which a person's rights extend to an injunction but not to damages'. As the Court of Appeal had concluded in that case, interim relief would have provided effective protection for the plaintiff's rights. Provision for cross-undertakings, as suggested in Chapter 6, would increase the effectiveness of interim protection for all parties. Such damages, granted in lieu of an injunction under Lord Cairn's Act 1858 would be liquidated and different in kind from damages in tort. Since Lord Diplock's dicta concerning the tort of breach of statutory duty in *Garden Cottage Foods* were qualified and obiter, it is submitted that Lord Wilberforce's and the Court of Appeal's view is to be preferred, and that persons seeking damages for breaches of EC competition (or any other) rules should use and develop existing torts rather than indiscriminately applying the much criticised remedy of breach of statutory duty. Like the 'nominate tort' it should be rejected as a *general* remedy for 'simple' breaches of EC law. It should only be used, as it should be used in English law, sparingly, where the EC rights invoked, and their purpose to benefit the plaintiff, are clear.

Claims under Francovich   Although a claim based on *Francovich* is equivalent to a claim in tort, as a special remedy raising particular problems it merits separate consideration. *Francovich* established a new Community principle according to which 'a state is liable to make good damage to individuals caused by a breach of Community law for which it is responsible' (para. 37). Although the principle was laid down in specific terms, in the context of a failure to implement a Directive (para. 39) it is likely that, as was suggested by Advocate-General Mischo, it would apply to 'every failure to observe Community law in the past, whether that failure is in breach of provisions of the Treaty, Regulations or Directives, whether they have direct effect or not'. It is clear from the case that the provision breached does not have to be directly effective to give rise to liability, since the Directive in question in *Francovich* was not. However, in order to succeed, a number of criteria must be satisfied. The plaintiff must establish

(a)   a breach by the state of a Community obligation;

(b)   that the plaintiff has been deprived of a Community right intended for his benefit;

(c)   that the content of that right is clear ('determined from the provisions of the Directive'); and

(d)   that the breach has caused damage to the plaintiff ('a causal link between the breach of the obligation of the State and the damage suffered by the plaintiff').

Since the Court's ruling under Article 177 was not limited in its temporal effects (see Chapter 4), a claim may be brought under *Francovich* in respect of past failures. It is possible that *Emmott* (case 208/90), concerned like *Francovich* with a failure to implement a Directive, may be invoked to prevent the running of time for limitation purposes until the breach of Community law has been rectified (see Chapter 5). Although in *Francovich* the breach of its obligations by the defendant Italian state had been established by the Court in Article 169 proceedings (*Commission* v *Italy* (case 22/87)), it is thought that a prior finding of 'failure' by a state, whether (express) in Article 169 or (implied) in Article 177 proceedings, is not essential. It remains to be seen whether the criteria of clarity (c) and the question of whether the provision breached is intended to benefit the plaintiff (b) are generously construed (as is the principle of direct effects) or strictly construed. Even if interpreted strictly the scope for states' liability under *Francovich* is potentially very wide.

An important question, yet to be resolved, is whether liability under *Francovich* is strict, or, if 'fault' is required on the part of the State, what degree of fault is required to establish liability. Some answers may be provided when the Court of Justice rules on these questions in *Brasserie du Pêcheur SA* (case 46/93) and *Factortame (No. 3)* (case 48/93) (see Chapters 2 and 5).

Although enunciating a new principle of state liability in *Francovich*, the Court suggested, following traditional principles enunciated in *Rewe-Zentralfinanz* v *Landwirtschaftskammer Saarland* ((case 33/76), see Chapter 5), that a State was 'obliged to make good the consequences of the damage caused within the context of national law on liability'. The question arises, which British law is applicable to claims based on *Francovich*, and, assuming it exists, will it be effective to protect individuals' rights under *Francovich*?

The nearest equivalent cause of action in English law would appear to be the tort of misfeasance in public office. Under this tort public authorities can be liable in damages for unlawful acts (or omissions) committed deliberately or with knowledge of their invalidity (*Bourgoin* (CA)). Depending on the whether there is a fault requirement for liability under *Francovich*, and, if so, the degree of fault which must be proved, the tort of misfeasance might be appropriate, or could be adapted, for example by extending the knowledge requirement to include constructive knowledge, to meet the demands of EC law. Except under the principles of *Rylands and Fletcher* ((1866) LR 1 Ex 265), and breach of statutory duty, and some claims in nuisance, or under specific statutory provisions, there is no strict liability (in the sense of liability without fault in the form of at least negligence) for unlawful acts in English law. To the extent that a finding of breach or failure may involve a finding of *legislative* failure the application of *Francovich* via the tort of misfeasance will clearly break new ground. However, as was suggested in Chapter 6, and as appears to be borne out by *EOC* v *Secretary of State for Employment* (1994), in assessing the question of breach for the purposes of establishing liability under *Francovich* it is not necessary to declare that an act or omission of Parliament has *breached* Community law; a court may simply find that the act or omission is *incompatible* with EC law. Thus, provided that the Court of Justice does not insist on a principle of strict liability, it is within the power of the British courts, operating within existing principles, to provide a remedy which is effective to protect individuals' rights under *Francovich*. If on the other hand the Court decides that liability is strict under *Francovich*, a new remedy, of alarming potential and creating serious problems for national courts, will be required.

Whatever the Court's decision in *Brasserie du Pêcheur* and *Factortame (No. 3)* on the question of fault, there is a strong case for the introduction of uniform Community rules for the application of *Francovich*. Difficulties faced by individuals in enforcing Community rights against 'private' parties based on the principles of direct and particularly indirect effect (see Chapter 2) are likely to result in increasing resort to *Francovich*. Hints to this effect have been dropped by the Court of Appeal in *Doughty* v *Rolls Royce* [1992] 1 CMLR 1045 and the House of Lords in *Kirklees Metropolitan Borough Council* v *Wickes* [1992] 3 All ER 717. The Court of Justice's crucial ruling in *Faccini Dori* (case C 91/92) that Directives cannot be enforced horizontally, which averted to the possibility of an alternative remedy against the state under *Francovich*, will encourage this trend. If this occurs, as is likely, in all member states, it is essential, in the interests of equality, that the rules governing such an important remedy be uniform. Uniformity requires not only similar rules relating to fault, but in relation to all the criteria for liability, as well as in the assessment of damages and the determination of questions of remoteness, all of which differ significantly from state to state. If inequalities are to be avoided these issues must be resolved during the next few years.

Contract   Actions to enforce a contract, or to defend an action for breach of contract, may be based on EC law. A third party may seek to challenge certain conditions in a contract for breach of EC law. A particular clause in a contract, for example an agreement to market particular products in a particular manner, or subject to particular conditions, may involve a breach of Article 30 or Articles 85 or 86 EC (e.g., *Rau* v *de Smedt* (case 261/81), Article 30; *Pronuptia* v *Schigallis* (case 161/84), Article 85). A contract of employment may contain provisions, express or implied, contrary to migrant workers' EC rights, for example the right to equal treatment with national workers under Article 48 EC or Regulation 1612/68 (e.g., *Sotgiu* v *Deutsche Bundespost* (case 152/73)), or rights under EC sex discrimination laws.

Contractual provisions which infringe EC law will be unenforceable. Where the offending parts of an agreement cannot be severed the entire contract may be avoided. Clearly where business partners freely agree to particular terms which are found to breach EC law they cannot recover for losses suffered when the contract is avoided, since they have caused their own loss. However, where one party, for example an employer or trading partner, seeks to impose obligations on another party which are permissible under domestic law but in breach of EC law or in breach of one party's EC rights, resulting in damage to the latter, or unjustly enriching the former, damages may be recoverable.

Since in these circumstances the right breached is not a contractual right the equivalent national law remedy is not an action for breach of contract. Where the damage suffered by the plaintiff results from misrepresentation, or undue influence, or duress, or action in restraint of trade, or an infringement of one party's statutory rights, damages may be compensatory or restitutionary, and will be awarded, and their adequacy assessed, according to the common law or statutory rules applicable to claims based on these principles.

Restitution There are many situations in which national authorities may impose taxes or levies or charges in breach of EC law. Article 12 EC prohibits member states from 'introducing between themselves any new customs duties on imports and exports or any charges of equivalent effect'. Levies may be imposed by member states, pursuant to EC rules, on goods imported from 'third countries' (i.e., countries outside the EC) under the Common Customs Tariff (CCT), or on agricultural production under the Common Agricultural Policy (CAP). These rules may be found to be invalid in Article 173 or Article 177 proceedings (see Chapters 8 and 9). Where a demand for money is made in breach of EC law or under an EC provision found to be invalid it may be resisted. Where it is paid it may be recovered. As was noted in Chapter 5, the principle of effective judicial protection requires that money levied by national authorities in breach of EC law, or pursuant to EC rules found to be invalid, must be recoverable by the party from whom it was levied, unless the latter has passed on the loss (*Amministrazione delle Finanze dello Stato* v *SpA San Giorgio* (case 199/82). In assessing whether the loss has been passed on national procedural rules must not render recovery 'virtually impossible' or excessively difficult'. These rules are based on the wider principle of unjust enrichment, itself a general principle of Community law. This principle also applies to claims against private bodies. Any action in breach of EC law resulting in unjust enrichment may form the basis for a claim in restitution.

English law recognises no general doctrine of unjust enrichment. The right to restitution is based on a complex network of rules of common law (e.g., quasi contract) and equity (e.g., constructive trusts, breach of confidence), in actions based on contract (e.g., mistake, duress) or tort (e.g., passing off, deceit) or statute (e.g., s. 33, Taxes Management Act 1970). These rules sometimes overlap and sometimes contradict each other. As specific rules they are subject to specific limitations, some arising accidentally, from the vagaries of the common law, some, particularly statutory exclusions and restrictions, policy based. Not all these limitations are objectively justified. Thus although a plaintiff seeking to recover money on restitutionary principles for actions in breach of EC law has access to a wide range of remedies, and, where successful is entitled to full and effective restitutionary damages, he may fail to fit or plead his action under accepted restitutionary heads. Alternatively he may fall victim to established restrictions or immunities. As suggested in relation to claims in tort, where there is a choice of remedy, or a conflict of rules, the non-discrimination principle requires that the most effective remedy be available to plaintiffs claiming under EC law.

In recent years the English courts, seeking to fill unwarranted lacunae, have moved towards a more principled approach, overtly recognising that the basis of many restitutionary claims is the principle of unjust enrichment (see *Lipkin Gorman* v *Karpnale Ltd* [1992] 4 All ER 512; Swadling, W. J. (1992) All ER Annual Review 255). In *Woolwich* v *IRC* [1992] 3 All ER 737 a majority of the House of Lords (Lord Goff, Lord Slynn, Lord Browne-Wilkinson) held that money paid to a statutory authority in the form of taxes or other levies pursuant to an ultra vires demand was recoverable even when it resulted from a mistake of law. Prior to that decision recovery had been limited to cases of mistake of fact, or duress, or undue influence, or under the doctrine of *colore officii*; there was no clear decision, and much authority against the proposition, that restitution might be granted for payments made in mistake of law. Although the case did not involve Community law the decision was clearly influenced by EC law. As Lord Goff pointed out (at p. 764), given the principles of Community law laid down in *San Giorgio* ((case 199/82) see Chapter 5), 'it would be strange if the right of the citizen to recover overpaid taxes were to be more restricted under domestic law than European law'.

The decision in *Woolwich* v *IRC*, and the court's approach, filling judicial gaps creatively but according to existing principles, provides an admirable example for future claims for restitution based on EC law, especially if the law is interpreted and developed in the light of the underlying principle of unjust enrichment. Although the decision in *Woolwich* v *IRC* was limited to its particular facts, Beatson J has suggested ((1993) 109 LQR 401) that, as was suggested by the Law Commission in its consultation paper (CP 120 (July 1991)), it should be extended to allow recovery for the payment, in mistake of law, of any levy in breach of public law or EC law. Since a claim for restitution based on EC law, whether against a public or a private party, will normally involve a mistake of law, such an extension would appear to be essential to the effective protection of individuals' Community rights.

A further question is whether the defences to claims for restitutution provided under English law are compatible with Community law. It is submitted that existing defences of illegality, ministerial receipt, bone fide purchase and change of position would not be acceptable as *general* defences to claims based on EC law. Likewise Beatson J's suggestion of a defence of change of understanding of the law and the Law Commission's suggested defence based on the disruption of public finances would be unlikely to be acceptable as *general* defences. The Court of Justice's free, teleological approach to interpretation has on occasions resulted in a change of understanding of the law. Whilst it has been prepared to limit the effects of its rulings in such cases, in the interests of legal certainty (e.g., *Defrenne* v *Sabena (No. 2)* (case 43/75); *Barber* v *Guardian Royal Exchange Assurance Group* (case C 262/88), see Chapter 4), it has only once suggested (and has since disapproved this position, see *Roquette Frères* (cases 145/79 and C 228/92) noted Chapter 8) that this should be a bar to recovery *in the case in which the ruling is given*. The same reservation would be likely to apply to a defence based on a disruption of public funds. The retrospective effects of a decision could be limited, but recovery by the plaintiff not denied. On the other hand Beatson J's alternative suggested principle, that there should be no recovery if this would unfairly enrich the payer (as in Finance Act 1989, ss. 24, 29), by focusing on the question of unjust enrichment, would allow for the use of existing defences where the enrichment was found to be 'unjust' *in the individual case*.

Statutory Rights and Remedies: Statutory Restrictions

Many private rights under domestic law, for example in the field of sex discrimination, employment protection or social security, are granted under statute. As well as providing for rights, the statute (or secondary legislation) will prescribe the procedures and remedies for the enforcement of these rights, and the appropriate, often specialised, tribunals. Procedures and remedies may also be specialised, according to the nature of the claim, for example the right of industrial tribunals to order reinstatement or re-engagement of employees who are unfairly dismissed (Employment Protection (Consolidation) Act 1978), or the right of the courts to suspend or set aside decisions or actions (but not concluded contracts) taken by a contracting authority in breach of EC Public Procurement rules. But access to remedies, and the remedies themselves, may be limited. Although this is not made explicit, these limitations are designed to secure particular policy ends.

Where individuals are seeking to enforce rights which are analogous to statutory rights based on EC law they will be subject, under the principle of national treatment, to the same procedures and remedies as are provided for similar claims under national law. In rejecting Mrs Day's claim, joined with that of the EOC, for judicial review against the Secretary of State for Employment ([1994] 1 All ER 910), based on a breach of EC sex discrimination rules, the House of Lords rightly directed her to apply to an industrial tribunal. The question which arises in the context of a claim for the enforcement of a Community right is whether the particular statutory procedures and remedies prescribed for the equivalent domestic claim are effective to protect applicants' rights under EC law.

Clearly it is not possible to examine and assess the effectiveness of the many statutory or legislative remedies potentially relevant to claims based on EC law. The question of whether particular remedies and procedures are effective for the purposes of EC law will depend on a detailed examination of the relevant domestic provisions and their appropriateness as a vehicle for the enforcement of the *particular* Community right invoked. This in turn will depend on the purposes, general and particular, of the EC law from which that right derives. For example the UK Regulations (SI 1991/2679, 2680; 1992/3297) implementing the EC Public Supply and Public Works Compliance Directives, which are limited in terms of complainants, and which fail to provide for the setting aside of concluded contracts, even when granted in clear breach of the rules, although within the letter of the Directives, may be open to challenge as insufficiently effective either to protect individuals' (would-be contractors') rights or to deter awarding authorities from breaching public procurement rules (see further below). Any bar, procedural or remedial, on the ability of a judicial body to provide full and effective protection for individuals' Community rights will prima facie be contrary to EC law, unless it can be 'objectively justified' or the plaintiff has access to an effective alternative remedy.

Statutory limits on damages   As was established in *Marshall (No. 2)* (case C 271/91, see Chapter 5) where damages for the breach of Community rights equivalent to statutory rights are designed to be compensatory, damages must be full. The imposition of statutory limits will not be permitted under EC law. Advocate-General van Gerven suggested that the four components of damage 'traditionally taken into account in rules governing liability' and by implication necessary to full compensation, are damages for loss of physical assets, loss of income, 'moral' damage (injury to feelings), and 'damage on account of effluxion of time' (i.e., interest). These heads correspond to the principal heads of compensatory damages under the common law. Although *Marshall (No. 2)* was concerned with compensatory damage there is no reason to believe that similar principles of 'full' compensation, based on the principle of unjust enrichment, will not apply, statutory restrictions notwithstanding, to claims for restitutionary damages based on EC law. It may be noted that a bar on the ability of industrial tribunals to award interest on an award of damages for the period prior to the hearing will breach the principle of full compensation.

A question which arises, but was not addressed in *Marshall*, is whether a statutory limit on the quantum of damages might be permissible if it were 'objectively justified' under Community law. It might be argued that in the context of certain types of claim against public bodies, for example for the repayment of taxes, or social security claims, some statutory restrictions might be justified. Arguments based on the need to protect the public purse, or the interests of good administration, or on the grounds of disruption of public finances, or a change in the understanding of the law, have been invoked as grounds for denying or restricting the liability of public authorities under the common law. They also underlie statutory exemptions and immunities. To what extent will they be permissible under EC law?

Unless the Court can be persuaded to change its position in *Marshall (No. 2)* it appears that any restriction on, a fortiori exclusion of, individuals' rights to compensation for damage suffered as a result of infringements of Community rights, whether 'common law' or 'statutory' in nature, will not be permitted under Community law. Given the existence of a clear EC right, intended to benefit the plaintiff, a curtailment or denial of damages based on the need to protect the public purse, or to prevent the disruption of public finances would be unlikely to be seen in themselves as 'objective' justification for a statutory restriction on damages when that right has been infringed. On the other hand, where the disruption of public finances results from a change in the understanding of the law, breaching the defendant's legitimate expectations, some restriction on recovery might be justified.

The Court has been willing to accept a limit on the retrospective application of its rulings under Article 177 on the basis of legal certainty, grounded, if not expressed as such, in a change of understanding of the law (e.g., *Defrenne* v *Sabena (No. 2)* (case 43/75); *Barber* (case C 262/88), see Chapter 4). In *Steenhorst-Neerings* (case C 338/91) the Court accepted, as compatible with EC law, a statutory twelve-month limit on the retrospective payment of social security (invalidity) benefit, claimed under EC law, on the grounds of the need to 'preserve financial balance' in a scheme in which claims submitted by insured persons in the course of the year must be covered by the contributions collected during that same year. The payment was described by the Commission in a subsequent case raising similar issues (*Johnson* v *Chief Adjudication Officer* (case C 410/92)) as 'unexpected' by the defendant authority. Thus the threat to the financial balance of the social security scheme arose from a change of understanding of the law, itself resulting from a decision of the Court of Justice. Although applied in the context of the protection of public funds, the same principle of change of understanding of the law, may also apply to protect the legitimate expectations of private parties, as it did in *Barber*. However whilst the Court may be prepared to limit the retroactive effect of a ruling, thereby limiting the scope of the defendant's liability, actual or potential, it is not likely to condone a *general* limit on the quantum of damages recoverable based on this principle. In any case, if derogation from the principle of full and retrospective compensation is to be permitted, the need for such derogation must be proved, *at the time when the case is decided*, before the Court. This was done successfully in *Defrenne* v *Sabena (No. 2)*, and *Barber*. It was not attempted in *Marshall (No 2)*. The question of the retroactivity of a particular ruling can only be reopened in a subsequent case if new issues are raised (see e.g., *Blaizot* (case 24/86); compare with *Barra* (case 309/85)).

If statutory exemptions or limitations on damages are not likely to be permitted under EC law, legislative provisions allowing for the exercise of discretion in the granting of damages, whether compensatory or restitutionary, will also be likely to be unacceptable. Thus a provision such as s. 33 of the Taxes Management Act 1970, which allows for the repayment of overpaid income, corporation, capital gains and petroleum revenue taxes where it is 'reasonable and just' would be unlikely to be regarded as constituting 'objective' justification for the purposes of EC law.

Statutory provisions exempting public authorities from common law liability, for example in nuisance or negligence, would also be unlikely to be acceptable in the context of a claim based on EC (e.g., environmental) law unless they could be objectively justified in the individual case. Again arguments may be mounted for limiting the retroactive effect of a ruling from the Court of Justice where that ruling results in a change of understanding of the law.

The Need for Representative Action

Provided that the plaintiff is able to establish the existence of a private law right based on EC law and a threat to that right, whatever the remedy sought there should be few problems in relation to standing. But private action alone will not always be effective, or sufficiently effective, either to protect individuals'

Community rights or to deter breaches of Community law. Some 'private' acts in breach of EC law, for example acts, whether of private or public bodies affecting consumers or the environment, or competition, may need to be challenged in the public interest, by a body representing the public interest. Representative action may also be necessary, or desirable, to protect collective private interests.

As was noted in Chapters 5 and 6, the Commission is concerned to extend the present access to the courts by bodies representing both public and private interests. As it pointed out in its White Paper on Access to Justice in Consumer Affairs (COM (93) 576), even though access to the courts is available to individuals whose rights are affected by breaches of Community law, the damage suffered in individual cases may be too small to justify the cost of litigation. To meet this problem EC Directive 86/450 (1984 OJ L 250/17) on Misleading Advertising and Directive 93/13 (1993 OJ L 95/29) on Unfair Terms in Consumer Contracts require states to provide means whereby 'persons or organisations regarded under national law as having a legitimate interest' may institute proceedings before the courts or competent administrative bodies against suspected infringements of the Directives. States which fail to give effect to these provisions, or which adopt a restrictive view as to the bodies 'regarded as having a legitimate interest' will clearly breach EC law. The Commission has also sought, so far unsuccessfully, to introduce a Directive giving consumer associations a general right to act in courts on behalf of general interests of consumers (COM (87) 210). In the absence of specific Community provision for standing by representative bodies it could be argued that states are in any case obliged, by Article 5 EC and their duty to ensure 'effective judicial protection', to allow such representation by bona fide interest groups in order to protect collective private interests. This would be particularly valuable in areas such as environmental law or consumer law, where individuals might lack personal standing or, even if they did have standing, might not be willing to act.

Akin to the representative claim, and arguably also necessary to the effective enforcement of private rights based on Community law, is the 'joined cases facility', or 'multi-party action', whereby similar claims may be joined and litigated together following the lodging of individual claims, and the 'joint representation action', whereby a representative body may be given power of attorney to sue on behalf of a group of private litigants (see Green Paper on Access of Consumers to Justice (COM (93) 576). Whilst the former is available in the UK, current procedures have been criticised by the Legal Aid Board as cumbersome and costly; the latter is not available under English law. The provision of such facilities, and the improvement of existing 'class' action facilities, would act as a deterrent against breaches of Community (as well as domestic) law and, representing a more efficient use of resources, would be more likely to attract legal aid than individual claims. It would undoubtedly increase the effective enforcement of Community law.

Effectiveness of Damages as provided under English Law

As has been suggested, where damages, whether compensatory or restitutionary, are awarded according to common law principles, without statutory or jurisdictional restrictions, they will be sufficiently effective to protect individuals' Community rights as well as to deter breaches of Community law. In addition to awarding damages under Advocate-General van Gerven's four 'traditional' heads, damages may be awarded under English law for wasted expenditure and even for speculative losses in the form of lost profits and loss of a chance. Exemplary damages, the purpose of which is punitive, may also be available.

Loss of a chance There have been problems in relation to claims for loss of a chance. In order to succeed a plaintiff must prove, according to the civil law standard, on the balance of probabilities, that the defendant's unlawful action deprived him of a quantifiable chance of receiving a benefit, or avoiding a detriment. In *Chaplin v Hicks* [1911] 2 KB 786 (CA), the plaintiff was held entitled to recover for the loss of a chance of winning a beauty competition, when, having been chosen for the final selection, the defendants, in breach of contract, failed to advise her in time for her to appear at the final interview. Since her chances of success had she appeared were estimated at 25% she was awarded a sum representing 25% of what she would have received had she won. However in *Hotson v East Berkshire Health Authority* [1987] 2 All ER 909, in a claim based on the defendant health authority's negligence in failing adequately to treat the plaintiff following a fall, thereby depriving the plaintiff of a 25% chance of a good recovery, the House of Lords refused to grant a remedy for the loss of a chance. They did so, in a somewhat unsatisfactory judgment (see critique by Stapleton (1988) 104 LQR 389) on the basis of causation: since it had been proved that the plaintiff had a 75% chance of the same outcome (i.e., disability) as a result of the fall, the fall must be taken to have been proved as the sole cause of the plaintiff's damage. This ruling, which was no doubt policy driven, does not bode well for claims for loss of a chance in tort.

The claim for loss of a chance will be relevant to some claims under EC law. An EC national or a member of that national's family may have been deprived of an opportunity of employment in breach of the principle of non-discrimination on the grounds of nationality of Article 6 EC or Regulation 1612/68. Under the EC Public Works and Supplies Compliance Directives, persons suffering loss or damage for action in breach of EC public procurement rules are entitled to damages. The assessment and quantification of damages is left to be determined according to the rules of national law. A claim by a would-be contractor, unable to tender or tender successfully, as a result of the contracting authority's failure to observe EC public procurement rules, will often be for loss of a chance. It will be difficult to prove, on a balance of probabilities, that, had he been able effectively to compete, he would have been awarded the contract. To what extent will his rights be effectively protected under existing rules?

To the extent that the contractor has been deprived of a right to compete for an award, the claim would appear to be closer to *Chaplin v Hicks* than to *Hotson*. The fact that the claim is not in contract is, it is submitted, irrelevant. Provided that the claim is appropriate a claimant under EC law is entitled, under the non-discrimination principle, to claim the more effective remedy. Moreover, the House of Lords did not suggest in *Hotson* that there could be no claim in tort for the loss of a chance. On the other hand the loss of a chance to compete is of little value unless you can prove a chance of *being successful*. In *Chaplin* v *Hicks* the plaintiff's chances of success were deemed to be equal to that of the other finalists; it is doubtful whether this can be presumed in the case of an opportunity to tender. Unless a plaintiff contractor can prove that his chances of success are equal to those of other tenderers, or that, on a balance of probability, he would have won the contract, his damages may be limited to wasted expenditure and, perhaps, a small sum for vexation and distress. Thus a remedy in damages is unlikely to be effective either to protect the rights of individual contractors or, since awards are likely to be small, to deter contracting authorities from breaching EC public procurement rules. Ready access to injunctive relief, including interim relief, and provision for the setting aside of concluded contracts entered into in breach of EC law, would be far more effective in achieving both of these objectives. Furthermore, in exercising its discretion to grant injunctive relief or to suspend or set aside decisions or actions taken in the course of the contract award procedure, or (assuming it could claim that power) concluded contracts, a court must balance both the interests of contractors and the public interest in promoting free competition and enforcing EC public procurement rules *against* the public interest in avoiding delay. In most cases the balance will surely lie in favour of the former. If the public procurement rules are effectively enforced they are more likely to be obeyed.

Exemplary damages   Unlike compensatory and restitutionary damages, which are designed primarily to protect the plaintiff's interests, exemplary damages are directed at the defendant, their function being to deter and punish unacceptable behaviour. Of limited application in English law, on the grounds that they blur the distinction between the civil and criminal law, their use has been confined to three situations, laid down in Lord Devlin's classic judgment in *Rookes* v *Barnard* [1964] AC 1129, and subsequently confirmed by the House of Lords in *Cassell* v *Broome* [1972] AC 1027. These are

(a)   oppressive and unconstitutional action by servants of the government;
(b)   where the defendant's conduct has been calculated by him to make a profit for himself which may well exceed the compensation payable to the plaintiff; and
(c)   where use of exemplary damages has been expressly authorised by statute.

Given the need for effective enforcement of Community rules, and that one of the purposes of the effectiveness principle as applied to remedies is to deter parties, public and private, from breaching Community law, exemplary damages could play a limited but useful role in the enforcement by national courts of EC law. Whilst in areas such as competition law the Commission has extensive powers to fine undertakings acting in breach of EC rules, and, in the cases of flagrant breach, does not hesitate to use them, in other areas, for example in the field of environmental protection, or in the enforcement of public procurement rules, where private law claims for damages may be wanting, or awards of damages small, even deliberate and serious infringements of EC law may go unpunished and therefore undeterred.

Whilst politically sensitive, a claim for exemplary damages under (a), of oppressive and unconstitutional action by servants of the government, could lie in respect of public action in flagrant breach of EC rules, where claims for misfeasance would fail to provide an effective deterrent. Category (b), if imaginatively applied, might be available to deter gross breaches of, for example, environmental rules. Additionally, or alternately, provision could be made under (c) for cases in which exemplary damages were deemed to be necessary to ensure observance of Community rules. If national courts are to be required, increasingly, to apply EC competition rules (see Commission's Notice on co-operation between national courts and the Commission (1993 OJ C 39.6), see further Chapter 11) there is a case for the use of exemplary damages. They have been used effectively in this context in the USA. In view of our courts' resistance to an extension of the use of exemplary damages, and the strong pull of precedent (see e.g., *Gibbons* v *South West Water Services Ltd* [1993] QB 507), it may be argued that the issue of exemplary damages should be addressed, and the rules developed, through action at the Community level, with a view to ensuring equality of application in all member states. The question of exemplary damages in the context of a claim based on *Francovich* (cases 6 and 9/90) will be considered by the Court when it gives its ruling in *Factortame (No. 3)*.

Strict liability   There is no *general* principle of strict liability in English private law. Apart from the limited torts of the *Rylands* v *Fletcher* rule, and nuisance, and breach of statutory duty, or under particular statutes (e.g., Nuclear Installations Act 1965), liability depends on proof of fault, requiring, at the least, negligence. Whilst there may be a case for extending strict liability in the context of EC law, as with exemplary damages this would be better achieved by action by the Community. This has been done in the field of product liability with Directive 85/374 (implemented by the Consumer Protection Act 1987), and proposed by the Commission in respect of civil liability for damage caused by waste.

Time Limits

Prima facie the time limits imposed by the common law in respect of private law actions based on tort, or contract, or for restitution, that is, six years from the date on which the cause of action accrued (or three years for personal injury claims, twelve years for actions for the recovery of land), are effective to meet the demands of EC law. Time limits for claims based on statutory rights, although short, often no more than three months, normally provide for discretion for their extension where it is 'just and equitable' (s. 76(5), Sex Discrimination Act 1975) or where a tribunal considers it 'reasonable'

(s. 67(2), Employment Protection (Consolidation) Act 1988). Most courts and tribunals are willing to exercise this discretion generously, particularly in claims involving EC law. However, as the Court of Justice pointed out in *Emmott* v *Minister for Social Welfare* ((case 208/90), see Chapters 2 and 5) where a state has failed to implement its obligations under Community law persons seeking to rely on Community law before their national courts may be in a state of uncertainty: they may be unaware of the full extent of their rights. Therefore, in an action based on EC Directives, although the time limits prescribed for similar actions based on domestic law will continue to apply, time will not begin to run until the Directive has been fully and correctly implemented.

Although the judgment was expressed to apply 'particularly' to actions based on (directly effective) provisions of EC Directives, because of the 'special nature' of Directives, which are required under Article 189(3) to be implemented by member states, the principle will not necessarily be limited to such actions. The reasoning on which the decision was based, the 'state of uncertainty' of individuals seeking to rely on EC law in the face of conflicting provisions of national law could be extended to claims based on Treaty provisions, and (perhaps with greater justification) to claims based on *Francovich*. It is likely that it will not apply to claims based on the indirect effect of Directives, since to allow this would surely breach the legitimate expectations of private parties. These matters have yet to be tested before the Court.

Even if the principle laid down in *Emmott* is confined to claims under directly effective Directives, it has the potential hugely to increase the scope for claims in private law based on these provisions. Many years may elapse between the deadline for implementation and the date on which a Directive is fully and correctly implemented. Where a state fails deliberately or knowingly (or *quaere* with constructive knowledge) to implement the Directive, action may appropriately be brought, or indemnity sought, under *Francovich*. But where a Directive is implemented, it is thought correctly, and it proves, following a ruling from the Court of Justice, that it was not, 'public' bodies will be highly vulnerable under this principle, especially if the Court's ruling, as was the case in *Marshall (No. 2)*, although unexpected, is not limited in its effects in time. Whilst it would not seem unfair to hold government bodies liable in these circumstances, or the state under *Francovich* (depending on culpability), it would surely run contrary to the principles of fairness and certainty to hold all public bodies, as broadly defined in *Foster* v *British Gas* ((case C 188/89), see Chapter 2), liable retrospectively, without limitation as to time.

Because of these problems it is possible that the Court will encourage parties seeking to rely on directly effective Directives in these circumstances to claim under *Francovich*, as it did when faced with the problems of horizontal effects in *Faccini Dori* (case C 91/92). Alternatively parties sued on the basis of directly effective provisions may seek indemnity against the state, also under *Francovich*. This would require some relaxations of the conditions for liability under *Francovich* (see Chapters 2 and 5). The case of *Steenhorst-Neerings* indicates that the Court may be prepared to limit the effect of *Emmott* by distinguishing it and accepting, at least in the case of statutory benefits, that a limit on the retrospective payment of awards based on directly effective provisions of

Directives (as opposed to a limitation on the time within which such proceedings must be brought), may be objectively justified.

CONCLUSIONS

As in the case of public law it has not been necessary radically to alter the English system of private law remedies to meet the demands of EC law. Applied with determination and imagination there is sufficient wealth of authority in the common law, and sufficient principle, to ensure access to the courts, both by individuals and representative bodies, and to enable the courts to provide protection which is effective to meet most claims based on EC law. The need to bridge the gap between domestic and Community law has provided the incentive and the opportunity for a re-examination of the rules in the light of principle, with a view to overcoming entrenched deficiencies in national law. In this way the House of Lords in *Woolwich* v *IRC* [1992] 3 All ER 737, working within the framework of existing rules, was able to fill a lacuna for the benefit of all plaintiffs, whether or not they seek to rely on EC law. The case demonstrated, as Beatson pointed out (1993 LQR 401) that 'there is a continuing role for the common law as an instrument for legal change'. It is to be hoped that the example set by *Woolwich* will be followed.

Where EC law is clearly intended to confer rights on individuals in private law the remedies provided in tort or under the laws of contract or restitution are capable, in most cases with minimal modification, of providing effective protection for those rights. It is submitted that although the principles of direct and indirect effect are expressed as 'rights granted to individuals enforceable before their national courts', not all of those rights are intended, as Oliver LJ suggested in *Bourgoin*, to confer on individuals a private right to damages. Just as individuals with a 'sufficient' or 'real' interest or a right such as to merit judicial protection are entitled to seek judicial review or apply for an injunction or a declaration, so may individuals assert their directly effective and even indirectly effective Community rights in pursuit of these remedies in private law. In neither case does this entitle them automatically to a remedy in damages. A remedy in damages can only be claimed when a private right has been infringed in circumstances in which the law has conferred a right to damages. Those circumstances have been provided, in most cases where appropriate, under the laws of tort and contract and the laws governing restitution. Only *Francovich*, the full implications of which are still unknown, will require a significant adaptation of the rules.

A more potent threat to the effective protection of individuals' Community rights are the statutory restrictions and immunities, and national measures purporting to implement Community law, particularly Directives. National implementing measures may comply with the letter of Community law in terms of the remedies required to be provided, but, in disregarding the purpose of the Community measures, may fail to guarantee their full force and effect. Such measures should never be applied without regard to the 'parent' measure: they should always be examined for their effectiveness in achieving its general and particular purposes.

The greatest problems, in implementation and enforcement, arise where the Community rights claimed are inchoate or unclear. Although the Court of Justice requires *in principle* that Community law should be sufficiently clear and precise to be directly effective (and this must also by implication apply to indirectly effective provisions), or to give rise to a claim under *Francovich, in practice* the precise nature of such rights found to be capable of being invoked can be far from clear. A ruling from the Court of Justice may give rise to rights, and financial obligations, which were not, prior to that ruling, foreseeable. National courts may be reluctant to give effect to these rights restrospectively, particularly if they are to be applied on the principles of *Emmott*, without limitation of time. Such an application may result in a serious disruption of public funds, or the financial equilibrium of undertakings, public or private. Community law has not so far admitted a *general* defence to, or limitation on, liability based on these principles. If Community law is to be developed by the Court, as it must, and the legitimate interests and expectations of public authorities and public and private undertakings protected, the effects of such rulings should be limited. This is permissible under Community law. But the Court of Justice will only limit the effects of its rulings where the need for such a limit is proved. Thus it is for member states, and 'interested parties', public and private, to intervene in Article 177 proceedings, as they are entitled to do (Article 37, Protocol on the Statute of the Court of Justice) to ensure that whilst private Community rights are protected, defendants, actual and potential, are not exposed to excessive liability.

PART THREE

Challenging Community obligations

EIGHT

The basis for challenge: the role of Article 177 and preliminary rulings on the validity of Community legislation

INTRODUCTION

Most of the preceding chapters were concerned with the rules, and the adequacy of national remedies, for the enforcement of Community rights. But the principles of direct effects, and indirect effects, and state liability under *Francovich*, are a two-edged sword; as well as creating rights they also give rise to obligations. Individuals as well as member states and public bodies are vulnerable under Treaty Articles, or Regulations, or Decisions, whether addressed to themselves or to other persons. The obligations contained in Directives will be binding on public parties, and may inform the interpretation of domestic law to the detriment of private parties. States are exposed to liability under *Francovich*. Since the obligations of Community law must take precedence over conflicting provisions of domestic law, the only way in which they may be avoided is by challenging their legality. The law-making institutions of the Community, like member states under Article 5, are obliged to act within the law ('within the limits of the powers conferred upon [them]' Article 4 EC). A coherent system of legal protection requires that acts and omissions of Community institutions can be challenged for their legality by those persons on whom Community obligations or detriments are imposed.

The EC treaty provides a direct route to judicial review before the European Courts under Article 173 (action for annulment, supplemented by Article 184) and Article 175 (action for failure to act). Community acts may also be challenged indirectly under Article 177 in a reference from national courts for a ruling on the validity of Community law.

Any binding Community act, that is any act in the nature of a Regulation, or a Directive or a Decision, may be challenged on the grounds of

(a)   lack of competence;
(b)   infringement of an essential procedural requirement;
(c)   infringement of the Treaty or any rule of law relating to its application; or
(d)   misuse of powers (Article 173(2)).

Similarly any failure to act 'in infringement of (the) Treaty' will be open to challenge under Article 175. It is submitted that the term 'infringement of the Treaty' is wide enough to encompass all four grounds for annulment listed in Article 173. Since these grounds form the basis for any claim for judicial review of Community law, as well as for a finding of an unlawful act such as to give rise to a claim in damages under Articles 178 and 215(2), they will be considered as a preliminary issue here.

THE GROUNDS FOR ANNULMENT

(a)   Lack of Competence

This is a version of the English doctrine of substantive ultra vires. The EC institution responsible for the adoption of an act must have legal authority under the Treaty or secondary legislation to adopt the particular act in question. The legal basis or bases for the act will be documented in the preamble to legislation (see Table 3 in the Appendix). Since there may be some substantive overlap between different Treaty provisions, with different procedural (for example voting, consultation) requirements (e.g., compare Article 118 (health and safety of workers) with Article 100 (rights of workers affecting the functioning of the internal market), the Commission's choice of legal base can be crucial, and is not infrequently challenged. However, since areas of Community competence and the scope of the Commission's powers cannot be precisely defined, and the Court is prepared to allow the Commission some leeway in these matters, such challenges are rarely successful (but see *Germany & Others* v *Commission* (cases 281, 283–5, 287/85); *Parliament* v *Council* (case C 295/90)).

(b)   Infringement of an Essential Procedural Requirement

This is equivalent to procedural ultra vires in English law. The procedures to be adopted in the process of enactment of a particular measure, for example for consultation or co-operation or co-decision with Parliament, or consultation with the Economic and Social Committee or the Committee of the Regions, will depend on its legal base in the Treaty and/or secondary legislation enacted under the Treaty. The procedures followed will also be recorded in the preamble to the legislation. In addition the Treaty contains a general requirement that legislation must state the reasons on which it is based and refer to proposals and opinions which were required to be obtained (Article 190). The

Court has held that reasons must not be too vague or inconsistent; they must be coherent, and mention figures and essential facts on which they rely; they must be adequate to indicate the conscientiousness of the decision and detailed enough to be scrutinised by the Court (*Germany* v *Commission* (case 24/62)). Where consultation is required the body consulted must be given a reasonable time in which to express an opinion. In *Roquette Frères SA* v *Council* (case 138/79) a Council Regulation was annulled on the grounds that although Parliament had been consulted, it had not been given sufficient time to comment on the proposal. A requirement to consult does not mean that the opinion obtained must be followed.

(c) Infringement of the Treaty or any Rule of Law relating to its Application

Any act falling under grounds (a) and (b) would also fall within this provision. Arguably this category is wide enough to embrace all four grounds for annulment, as was suggested in respect of Article 175. However as well as providing grounds for annulment for breach of *any* Treaty provision, for example the duty of confidentiality under Article 214 (see *Adams* v *Commission (No. 1)* (case 145/83)) or any provision contained in secondary legislation it also permits annulment for breach of *any rule of law relating to the Treaty's application*. It is principally in this context that the Court has invoked general principles of law arising from 'constitutional traditions common to the member states' or 'international treaties for the protection of human rights on which member states had collaborated or of which they are signatories' (*J. Nold KG* v *Commission* (case 4/73)). These principles, and their significance, have been discussed at length in Chapters 1 and 6. Although the Court allows Community institutions considerable latitude in the exercise of discretionary powers, particularly as regards the implementation of economic policy in areas such as the CAP, even measures of this nature have been annulled for breach of the principles of legal certainty (*August Töpfer & Co GmbH* v *Commission* (case 112/77)) and equality (*Royal Scholten-Honig (Holdings) Ltd* v *Intervention Board for Agricultural Produce* (case 103 and 145/77)) and proportionality (*R* v *Intervention Board ex parte Man (Sugar) Ltd* (case 181/84)). These principles, particularly the last, are more rigorous as a means of control of administrative action than the *Wednesbury* test of reasonableness. Nevertheless, businessmen are expected to anticipate and guard against foreseeable developments, within the bounds of normal economic risks. (*Mulder* v *Council and Commission* (cases C 104/89 and 37/90)). As was the case with national implementing measures challenged for breach of EC law (see Chapter 6) general principles in the form of procedural rights, which are often prescribed expressly in secondary legislation (e.g., Regulation 17/62, competition law) are strictly enforced.

(d) Misuse of Powers

A misuse of power is not necessarily an abuse of power; nor does it require an improper motive. It is simply a use of power for purposes other than those for which it was granted. These purposes may be ascertained from the Treaty; more often they will be found in specific provisions of secondary legislation. This ground is rarely relied on by the Court, perhaps because in many cases it may be subsumed under ground (a) or (c). It did, however, provide the ground for annulment in *Simmenthal SpA* v *Commission* (case 92/78) when the Court found that a power granted to assist one group of economic agents (producers), was being used to help another (distributors) (see Chapter 9 and Article 184).

There is an extensive overlap between these grounds. For example a challenge based on a breach of natural justice, the right to be heard, such as was sufficient to form the basis for annulment of a Commission decision in *Transocean Marine Paint Association* v *Commission* (case 17/74), could fall under ground (b) or (c). Thus it is not surprising that the Court is often vague as to the precise ground on which its decision is based. Nevertheless, in seeking annulment it is advisable to plead all possible applicable grounds.

ARTICLE 177 AND RULINGS ON VALIDITY

As was noted in Chapter 1, whilst member states and Community institutions have, with a minor exception in the case of Parliament, general standing as 'privileged' applicants to act under Articles 173 and 175, and can challenge any binding act (subject to a strict two-month time limit in the case of Article 173), the standing of individuals, defined as 'natural or legal persons' is limited. Subject to exceptions, they may only challenge Decisions addressed to themselves or Decisions addressed to 'another person' in which they can show 'direct and individual concern'. Similarly they can only challenge the failure of a Community institution to address a decision to them, or to another person, *which they are entitled to demand*. It is for this reason that they may need to turn to Article 177. Clearly if they are seeking a remedy in national law, whether to challenge national measures or to obtain damages against national authorities, even though their claim may depend on a challenge to (an underlying) Community law, they must proceed via national courts and Article 177.

As well as providing for rulings on the interpretation of Community law (see Chapter 4), Article 177 provides for preliminary rulings from the Court of Justice on 'the validity ... of acts of the institutions and of the European Central Bank' (Article 177(1)(b)) on request from national courts and tribunals. Any binding Community act (clearly Treaty provisions cannot be challenged) may be challenged on any of the grounds provided under Article 173. Provided the individual has a genuine claim, and standing to bring an action under domestic law, for example to challenge a national measure implementing Community law, or to recover levies demanded by national authorities pursuant to obligations of Community law, and proceedings are brought within the limitation period appropriate to the domestic action, he may challenge the validity of the Community law on which the domestic action is based *whatever its nature*, and regardless of its date of promulgation. It is thus wider in its scope for individuals than Article 173, and has come to their help when action under Article 173 has failed (e.g., *Royal Scholten-Honig (Holdings) Ltd* v *Intervention Board for Agricultural Produce* (cases 103 and 145/77), Article

177; compare with *Koninklijke Scholten-Honig NV* v *Council and Commission* (case 101/76), Article 173).

The principles governing Article 177 were considered in detail in Chapter 4. Apart from the fact that the Court has jurisdiction to interpret the Treaty, but no power to challenge its validity, its provisions apply equally to rulings on interpretation and rulings on validity. Hence they will not be repeated here. However the different nature and purpose of rulings on validity may, arguably should, affect the way in which national courts and the Court of Justice approach and exercise their powers under Article 177.

A domestic court may interpret Community law, and it may find a provision of Community law to be valid, but it has no power to declare its invalidity (*Zuckerfabrik Süderdithmarschen AG* v *Hauptzollamt Itzehoe* (cases C 143/88 and 92/89)). Thus the doctrine of acte clair, which must be applied in the strictest sense, can only be applied to establish that a Community measure is *valid*. Provided that the applicant can show a prima facie case of invalidity and it is relevant to his case, a decision on the question will be 'necessary', therefore access to the Court of Justice should not be denied. Where a claim turns on the validity of Community law and there is no appeal from a domestic tribunal, *whatever its nature*, it should be permitted to refer. A refusal of jurisdiction by the Court of Justice, as in *Nordsee* (case 102/81) on the grounds that it does not constitute a 'court or tribunal' within Article 177(1) could deprive the plaintiff of the only effective protection available under Community law. Similarly, although national courts and tribunals with 'permissive' jurisdiction under Article 177(2) have a discretion to refer, where a decision on the validity of a Community measure is necessary to enable such a court to give judgment, there is nothing to be gained, and much to be lost, by a refusal to refer. Clearly, any court whose decision is final *in the particular case*, must refer. There is no room here for 'abstract' theories concerning mandatory jurisdiction under Article 177(3) (see Chapter 4). In seeking a ruling on the validity of a Community measure the national court is required to set out the reasons for which it is alleged that the measure is invalid (*Zuckerfabrik Süderdithmarschen* (cases C 143/88 and C92/89)).

Until the case of *TWD Textilwerke* (case C 188/92) the Court of Justice had given national courts and individual applicants every encouragement to refer. In refusing to admit claims for annulment under Article 173 it often adverted to the possibility of an alternative challenge under Article 177 (e.g., *Spijker Kwasten* v *Commission* (case 231/82)). However in *TWD Textilwerke* the Court refused its jurisdiction to rule, in Article 177 proceedings, on the validity of a Commission Decision addressed to the German government, requiring the government to recover state aid granted to the applicant in breach of EC rules, on the grounds that the applicant should have challenged the Decision under Article 173. Although TWD Textilwerke had been informed by the German government of the Decision, and their right to challenge it under Article 173, they had failed to act in time. Whilst it appeared that under existing case law the applicants did have standing to challenge the Decision under Article 173, being directly and individually concerned, (see Chapter 9) the matter was not unequivocally clear. Certainly they could reasonably have supposed that they would have been entitled to challenge the Decision at a later date, under Article 177, when the government sought to recover the aid. Whilst a refusal of jurisdiction under Article 177 may perhaps be justified where the measure which the applicant seeks to challenge is addressed to himself, there is less justification for denying him access when it is addressed to another person, and his standing to challenge that measure under Article 173 is uncertain. In these circumstances mere advice that he has a right to act under Article 173, whether from national or Community authorities, should not deprive him of the opportunity of a ruling under Article 177.

The full implications of *TWD Textilwerke* remain uncertain. It is to be hoped that access to a ruling on the validity of a particular measure under Article 177 will not be denied in every case in which the plaintiff might have had standing to challenge that measure under Article 173. Nevertheless given the present uncertainty a party who appears to have standing to challenge a Community act under Article 173 would be wise to proceed under that article, and to do so in time. Only if it is clear that he would not be entitled to act under Article 173 should he rely exclusively on Article 177.

Effects of a Ruling of Invalidity

The effect of a ruling of invalidity may also be different from that of a ruling on interpretation. Although the Court of Justice has no express power to limit the effect of its rulings under Article 177, as it does under Article 174 following the annulment of a Regulation, or part of a Regulation, under Article 173 (see Chapter 9), the Court has invoked Article 174 in order to limit the retrospective effect of a ruling of invalidity in the case of Regulations. Because Regulations are normative, and may be challenged under Article 177 long after their date of entry into force, a declaration of invalidity which was retrospective in effect could seriously affect past transactions entered into on the basis that the provision in question was valid. This would clearly breach the principle of legal certainty. Thus the Court is more ready to limit the retrospective effects of a ruling of invalidity than of a ruling on interpretation. When it does so, it normally limits its effects along the lines of *Defrenne* v *Sabena (No. 2)* (case 43/75), to the case in question and claims already lodged, and claims arising subsequent to judgment (e.g., *Pinna* (case 41/84)). On rare occasions it has declared its rulings purely prospective, denying even the plaintiff a remedy (*Roquette Frères* v *French State* (case 145/79)). It has since disapproved this practice, at least in Article 177 proceedings, on the grounds that such a limitation would deprive the plaintiff of his right to effective judicial protection (*Roquette Frères SA* v *Hauptzollamt Geldern* (case C 228/92) decision of 26 April 1994).

Although a ruling on invalidity would not prima facie be appropriate to establish a failure to act to complement the shortcomings of Article 175, certain failures, for example a failure to provide for the award of a grant, payable to one group of farmers but not to another comparable group, in breach of the principle of equality, could be challenged by an attack on the legality of the Community measure setting up such a system. Whilst this cannot result in the payment to the plaintiff of the grant, it may if successful result in the withdrawal or revision of the disputed measure. A failure to act on the part of a Community institution could also be established, with the same limited effects, in a ruling on the interpretation of Community law. As will be seen in Chapter 9, the scope for individuals to demand action from the Community institutions under Article 175 is in any case limited.

Following a ruling from the Court of Justice the national court will grant the appropriate remedy on the principles outlined in Chapters 5 to 8.

Interim Relief

As established in *Zuckerfabrik Süderdithmarschen* (cases C 143/88 and 92/89), national courts may be required to grant interim relief pending a ruling from the Court of Justice under Article 177 on the validity of Community law, and where this is necessary to provide effective judicial protection for individuals, they are obliged to do so. The principles on which relief should be granted were outlined in Chapter 5.

NINE

Action before the Court of Justice: action for annulment (Article 173); indirect challenge (Article 184); action for failure to act (Article 175)

INTRODUCTION

The direct route to judicial review of Community acts and omissions before the Court of Justice is provided under Article 173 (action for annulment), Article 184 (the indirect challenge), and Article 175 (action for failure to act) EC. Article 177, as discussed in Chapter 8, provides for *indirect* access to judicial review via the courts of member states. This will only avail the applicant if he has a claim under national law to which the question of the validity of Community acts or omissions may be attached. As *TWD Textilwerke* (case C 188/92) now demonstrates, where an individual has locus standi to challenge a particular act under Article 173 he may not be permitted to challenge it under Article 177.

Although Articles 173, 184 and 175 are interrelated they will be considered separately. Also, although these Articles are of primary importance to member states and Community institutions, the main focus of this chapter will be on the role and effectiveness of these remedies as regards 'natural or legal persons', as seems appropriate in a book concerned primarily with the enforcement of Community law by individuals. Competence to apply all claims by 'natural or legal persons' under these Articles has now been transferred to the Court of First Instance, subject to appeal on points of law to the Court of Justice.

ARTICLE 173: THE ACTION FOR ANNULMENT

Under Article 173 the Court of Justice has power to

... review the legality of acts adopted jointly by the European Parliament and the Council, of acts of the Council, of the Commission, and of the European Central Bank, other than recommendations and opinions, and of acts of the European Parliament intended to produce legal effects vis-à-vis third parties.

It shall for this purpose have jurisdiction in actions brought by a Member State, the Council or the Commission on grounds of lack of competence, infringement of an essential procedural requirement, infringement of this Treaty or of any rule of law relating to its application, or misuse of powers.

The Court shall have jurisdiction under the same conditions in actions brought by the European Parliament and the European Central Bank for the purposes of protecting their prerogatives.

Any natural or legal person may, under the same conditions, institute proceedings against a decision addressed to that person or against a decision which, although in the form of a regulation or a decision addressed to another person, is of direct and individual concern to the former.

The proceedings provided for in this Article shall be instituted within two months of the publication of the measure, or of its notification to the plaintiff, or, in the absence thereof, of the day on which it came to the knowledge of the latter, as the case may be.

Acts Capable of Annulment

It is clear from the exclusion from Article 173 of recommendations and opinions and the emphasis on acts 'intended to produce legal effects' that only binding acts of the institutions in question are capable of annulment. This includes not only Regulations, Directives and Decisions but any measures, whatever their nature or form, which are intended to have similar 'binding' effects. In *Commission* v *Council (Re European Road Transport Agreement)* (case 22/70) the measure challenged by the Commission was a Council 'resolution' which settled the negotiating procedure to be adopted in the preparation of the agreement, a matter which the Commission argued was outside the Council's powers. Although the Commission did not succeed in its claim the measure, as a legally binding act, albeit *sui generis*, was held to be open to challenge.

Similarly, in *Re Noordwijks Cement Accord* (cases 8–11/66) a registered letter, sent by the Commission to the applicants, informing them that their immunity from fines for breaches of EC competition law was at an end, was held to be susceptible to annulment under Article 173. Although not defined as a Decision the letter in question was in the nature of a Decision, since it produced legal effects for the applicants and brought about a change in their legal position. This principle, that it is the nature and effect of the act and not its form which determines whether it may be challenged, is important, since if an act is not recognised as capable of annulment it may not be challenged in time. Preliminary measures on the other hand, intended simply to pave the way for a final decision but not in themselves producing binding effects, are not reviewable (*Nashua Corporation* v *and Commission and Council* (cases C 133 and 150/87)).

Standing to Sue

Article 173 provides the principal means of review of Community acts for member states, the Council and the Commission, and, to a more limited extent ('for the purpose of protecting their prerogatives'), the European Parliament and the European Central Bank. As 'privileged' applicants they have a right to challenge any binding act under Article 173, subject only to limitation as to time. On the other hand the standing of individuals, described as 'natural or legal persons', is limited. They can only challenge Decisions addressed to themselves or decisions or Regulations in the form of Decisions addressed to another person which are of direct and individual concern to themselves (Article 173(4)).

There is no problem for individuals where the decision is addressed to themselves (with one exception relating to a refusal to act under Article 175, to be considered below). Many decisions addressed to individuals, for example Decisions of the Commission under Regulation 17/62 in the field of competition law, have been successfully challenged under Article 173. Fines have been reduced following proceedings for annulment under the Court's 'unlimited' jurisdiction in regard to penalties in this sphere (Article 172). The difficulties arise when the decision or decision 'in the form of a Regulation' is addressed to 'another person'. The applicant must then prove

(a)   that the measure is in substance a Decision;
(b)   it is of direct concern to the applicant: and
(c)   it is of individual concern to the applicant.

These requirements are cumulative. Because they must all be fulfilled the Court may approach the question of admissibility, and reject the application, on any one ground. It proceeds in no particular order. Although the case law has not been entirely consistent, the criteria, (particularly the criterion of individual concern), have been strictly interpreted. However, in declaring an action under Article 173 inadmissible the Court has often pointed to the possibility of an alternative challenge under Article 177. This advice must now be read in the light of the Court's decision in *TWD Textilwerke* (case C 188/92).

Decisions addressed to 'another person': the three criteria

(a)   The measure must be in substance a Decision   There are many cases in which an individual may seek to challenge a Regulation. Many of the Commission's policies, for example in the highly regulated field of the CAP, or the CCT, are implemented by Regulation. As a result of these Regulations benefits, for example subsidies, may be withdrawn or detriments, such as levies, imposed, adversely affecting individuals. The Court has insisted that an individual applicant cannot challenge a 'true' Regulation in Article 173 proceedings (e.g., *Koninklijke Scholten-Honig NV v Commission* (case 101/76)). This is probably necessary, to avoid a multiplicity of actions. In most legal systems there are restrictions on individuals' right to challenge normative

measures. However, in deciding whether a particular act is in substance a Regulation the Court has held that it is necessary to examine its nature and content rather than its form (*Confédération Nationale des Producteurs de Fruits et Légumes* v *Council* (cases 16,17/62)). A 'true' Regulation is a measure of general application; it is normative; it applies to objectively determined situations and produces legal effects on categories of persons viewed abstractly and in their entirety. A Decision on the other hand, defined in Article 189 EC as 'binding on the persons to whom it is addressed' is an individual act, addressing designated persons individually. Thus in *International Fruit Co.* v *Commission* (cases 41–44/70) the Court found that a 'Regulation' laying down the quantity of import licences to be issued to fruit importers, calculated on the basis of applications received from importers during the preceding week, in fact comprised a 'bundle of decisions' addressed to each applicant importer.

The Court has also held measures to be 'hybrid' in nature: part of a 'Regulation' may be in the nature of a decision to a particular party, identified by name or by implication, part, normally the rest, may be normative. Thus in the Japanese ball-bearings cases (*NTN Toyo Bearing Co.* v *Council* (cases 113, 118–121/77)), four major Japanese producers of ball-bearings were held entitled to challenge certain provisions of an EC anti-dumping Regulation. Although the measure was of general application some of its provisions specifically referred to the applicants.

In recent years, principally in the context of anti-dumping measures, which are normally enacted by Regulation, the Court has relaxed the requirement that the measure challenged must be in the nature of a decision as regards the applicant and allowed individuals to challenge 'true' Regulations , *provided they can establish direct and individual concern*. In *Extramet* v *EC Council* (case C 358/89), an individual importer was permitted to challenge a 'true' anti-dumping Regulation on this basis. As Advocate-General Jacobs pointed out in his submissions in the case, the principal of 'effective judicial protection', which applied to Community institutions as well as to member states, required that persons such as the applicants, who were seriously affected by the measure, and might have *no other opportunity to challenge the Regulation* (having no claim before a national court) should not be denied an opportunity to challenge its legality under Article 173. Similarly in *Sofrimport* v *Commission* (case C 152/88), which was not an anti-dumping case, an importer was permitted to challenge a Regulation suspending imports into the EC of apples from third countries solely on the basis of direct and individual concern. Since, as will be seen, the test for individual concern involves much the same enquiry as the question of whether the measure is in the nature of a decision vis-à-vis the applicant, the Court may have concluded that the requirements of direct and individual concern are sufficient in themselves to stem the tide of applications by individuals seeking to challenge Regulations under Article 173.

The Court has held that a decision addressed to a member state is a decision addressed to 'another person' for the purposes of Article 173(4) (*Plaumann* v *Commission* (case 25/62)). It also appears to presume that, even though a decision addressed to a member state may lay down normative rules, it is nevertheless a Decision which can be challenged by individuals, provided they can establish direct and individual concern. In *Government of Gibraltar* v *Council & Commission* (case C 298/89) the Court refused to admit a challenge to a Directive by the government of Gibraltar (treated as a natural or legal person) on the grounds that Directives, being normally a 'form of indirect regulatory or legislative measure', were not open to challenge by such persons. However in this case the government was unable to show individual concern. It is thus an open question whether a Directive could be challenged by individuals who are able to establish direct and individual concern.

(b)   Direct concern   A measure will be of direct concern to the applicant if it leaves the state no real discretion in implementation. Many Community measures affect individuals as a result of implementing action taken by national authorities. For example national authorities may refuse a grant or a licence to import goods from third countries pursuant to rules laid down by EC Regulations or Decisions. They may need Community permission or authorisation to act in a certain way. Provided that the measure affecting the applicant is not a matter lying within the state's discretion it will be of direct concern to the applicant. Thus in cases such as *Alfred Toepfer KG* v *Commission* (cases 106 and 107/63) and *Werner Bock KG* v *Commission* (case 62/70), decisions of the Commission confirming (*Toepfer*) or authorising (*Bock*) action by national authorities were held to be of direct concern to the applicants. Without such confirmation or authorisation the national authority could not have acted as it did. Conversely in *Società Eridania* v *Commission* (cases 10 and 18/68) an attempt by rival producers to challenge a Commission decision, addressed to the Italian state, confirming the award of grants to certain (named) sugar producers, was held not to be of direct concern to the applicants. Although the system of aid was laid down by the Community, the decision concerning the allocation (i.e., the amount) of aid was left to the states' discretion. The appropriate challenge in such a case would be to the national action, based on national law.

(c)   Individual concern   The concept of individual concern has been construed very restrictively by the Court. In order to establish individual concern the applicant must prove that the Decision challenged affects him 'because of certain circumstances peculiarly relevant to him, or by reason of circumstances in which he is differentiated from all other persons, and not merely by the mere fact that he belongs to a class of persons who are affected' (*Plaumann* v *Commission* (case 25/62)). Thus Plaumann, an importer of clementines, was unable to challenge a Commission Decision, addressed to the German government, refusing the government permission to reduce its customs duties on clementines imported from outside the EC, since he was only affected by the decision as a member of a class. There was nothing to differentiate his position from that of any other importer of clementines.

The difficulty lies in determining what characteristics will be regarded as 'peculiarly relevant' to the applicant, 'differentiating him from all other persons'. The Court has held that it is not enough that his business interests are adversely affected (*Società Eridania* v *Commission* (cases 10 and 18/68)); or that they are affected differently from, or to a greater degree than, other persons (*Calpak* (cases 789 and 790/79)); or that the identity of the person affected is known to the responsible Community institution when a particular measure is passed (*UNICME* v *Council* (case 123/77)); or that there is a causal connection between the enactment of the measure and the applicant's particular case (*Spijker Kwasten* v *Commission* (case 231/82)); or even that he is the only person likely to be affected (*Glucoseries Réunies* v *Commission* (case 1/64)). Whilst these factors may be necessary, they are not sufficient in themselves to constitute individual concern.

Whilst there is no single satisfactory test for individual concern it is possible to detect some common features in the cases which have succeeded in establishing individual concern. In almost all of these cases the Decision (whatever its name), although addressed to another person, is referable, expressly or impliedly, specifically to the applicant's situation, either alone, or as a member of a fixed and *closed* class. For example a Decision, addressed to a state, may have been issued in response to a licence or tender application by the applicant (*International Fruit Company* v *Commission* (cases 41–44/70); *Alfred Toepfer KG* v *Commission* (cases 106 and 107/63); *Werner Bock KG* v *Commission* (case 62/70) (licences); *Simmenthal SpA* v *Commission* (case 92/78) (tender)), or in connection with the granting of state aid to the applicant (*Philip Morris Holland BV* v *Commission* (case 730/79); *TWD Textilwerke* (case C 188/92)), or anti-dumping duties imposed on the applicant (Japanese ball-bearings cases (cases 113 and 118–121/77)). Nor is it necessary that the applicant should have been named or identified personally in the impugned measure. In *Sofrimport SARL* v *Commission* (case 152/88) the applicant fruit importers were held entitled to challenge certain EC anti-dumping Regulations suspending the issue of import licences for, and limiting imports of, apples from third countries. Because the Commission was required under one of the Regulations to take into account the 'special position of products in transit' the applicants, who had products in transit at the time when the offending Regulation took effect, were held to be individually concerned. 'Such persons', the Court pointed out, 'constituted a restricted group which could not be extended after the contested measure took effect'. On the other hand where a Community measure applies *generally*, to future as well as past situations, affected individuals will not be deemed to be 'individually' concerned, even if they are the only persons likely to be affected (*Spijker Kwasten* v *Commission* (case 231/82)).

A similar situation in which the necessary link may be proved to establish individual concern is where the measure in question, if not directed at the applicant, is issued as a result of proceedings in which he played a legitimate part. For example persons with a 'legitimate interest' are entitled to complain to the Commission seeking action against suspected breaches of EC competition laws (Regulation 17/62, art. 3(2)). Similar rights are granted to individuals under EC anti-dumping rules. Complainants may be given further rights to be involved in proceedings arising as a result of their complaint. Where the Commission issues a Decision to an undertaking ('another person') as a result of such complaints complainants and parties involved in the proceedings are deemed to be 'individually concerned' to challenge that Decision. Since they have a right to complain or to be involved they are entitled to institute Article 173 proceedings in order to protect that right (*Metro-Grossmärkte GmbH* v *Commission* (case 26/76) (competition); *Timex Corporation* v *Council and Commission* (case 264/82) (anti-dumping)).

As noted above, the Court has been more lenient in its approach to anti-dumping rules. An individual seeking to challenge a Decision addressed to another person under the anti-dumping rules may be individually concerned on the principles outlined above. He may be a complainant, as in *Timex*, or in the position of addressee, express or implied, of the Decision, as in the Japanese ball-bearings cases (see also *Allied Corporation* v *Commission* (cases 239 and 275/82)), or singled out for special treatment under Community legislation, as in *Sofrimport*. But the Court has found individual concern in less restricted circumstances. In *Extramet* v *Council* (case C 358/89) it was prepared to find that an independent importer, not singled out in the Regulation in question nor involved in the relevant anti-dumping proceedings, and whose particular situation had not been taken into account in establishing the existence of dumping, nevertheless possessed individual concern to challenge an EC Regulation imposing anti-dumping duties on imports of calcium metal from the People's Republic of China and the Soviet Union. The particular characteristics giving rise to individual concern in Extramet were

(a)   they were the largest importer of the product forming the subject matter of the anti-dumping measure and were the end users of the product;

(b)   their business activities depended to a very large extent on the imports in question and were seriously affected by the contested Regulation;

(c)   there was a limited number of manufacturers of the product concerned and the importers had difficulty in obtaining supplies from the sole Community producer, who was the applicant's main competitor for the processed product.

It remains to be seen whether *Extramet* is a case decided on its own special facts, or whether it signals a trend towards a more liberal approach to the question of individual concern where the number of potential applicants is limited and the effect of the measure on their interests is severe. The principles expressed were not confined to anti-dumping cases.

Outside these categories of cases there are special cases when individual concern has been established on particular facts, seemingly on policy grounds. In *AE Piraiki-Patraiki* v *Commission* (case 11/82) a number of Greek manufacturers and importers of cotton yarn who had entered into contracts prior to a Commission Decision to the Greek government imposing a quota system on the import of such yarn, although affected as members of a class (of similar manufacturers and importers) were held to be entitled to challenge that Decision. In this case the Greek Act of Accession (Article 13(3)) had imposed a duty on the Commission, when laying down rules during the transitional period following Greece's entry into the Community, to consider those whose contracts might be affected by such rules; this was sufficient to establish individual concern. The case does not lay down a *general* rule that persons whose existing contracts may be affected by a Community rule will be deemed to be individually concerned in that rule.

More exceptional is the case of *Parti Ecologiste 'Les Verts' v European Parliament* (case 294/83). Here the Green Party was held entitled to challenge a decision of Parliament allocating funds for the European election campaign of 1984, even though the Decision affected all political parties and the Green Party was simply affected as a member of a class. The decision is thought to have been influenced by political considerations and is not likely to be of relevance to the majority of claims for individual concern by natural or legal persons.

Time Limits

Admissibility is not the only hurdle for applicants. They must bring their case within the prescribed time. The limit for bringing an action under Article 173 is short. Proceedings must be instituted within two months of

(a)   the publication of the measure, or
(b)   its notification to the plaintiff, or
(c)   in the absence of notification, the date on which it came to the knowledge of the plaintiff, as the case may be (Article 173(3)).

Where the measure is published time runs from the fifteenth day after the date of publication in the Official Journal (for publication requirements see Article 191 EC and Chapter 1). Where notified it runs from the day following the receipt by the person concerned of notification of the measure (Rules of Procedure of the Court (1991), Article 81). The 'date of knowledge' is the date on which the applicant became aware of the measure, not of the fact that it was capable of challenge. Limitation periods may take into account the distance of the applicant from the Court (Article 81). In reckoning time limits 'only the date of judgment at the Court of Justice shall be taken into account' (Article 37(3), Rules of Procedure).

The time limits are strictly observed. Once they have expired the applicant cannot seek to challenge a measure by the 'back door', either by illegitimate use of Article 184 (*Commission v Belgium* (case 156/77)), or by alleging failure to act under Article 175 when the responsible institution refuses, by means of a Decision, to amend or withdraw a disputed measure (*Società Eridania v Commission* (cases 10 and 18/68)), or to take the requested action (*Irish Cement v Commission* (cases 166 and 220/86), see further below). This stance, in these circumstances, when the plaintiff is simply seeking to circumvent the time limits of Article 173, is understandable. Short time limits are justified, in the interests of legal certainty, in the context of actions for judicial review: they cannot be allowed to be evaded. However, to deny the plaintiff a right to challenge a Decision, not addressed to himself, under Article 177, on the grounds that he should have proceeded under Article 173, as the Court did in *TWD Textilwerke* (case C 188/92), is open to question. Where a Community act is addressed to a particular person, he should perhaps be required to challenge it subject to limits of time under Article 173. But where it is addressed to another person, and the plaintiff seeks to challenge it in a genuine claim, a fortiori by means of defence, before his national courts, should he be denied access to the Court of Justice in Article 177 proceedings simply because he could have taken action under Article 173? The Community, as well as member states, is required to provide 'effective judicial protection' for individuals' rights. Such protection will be undermined if *TWD Textilwerke* develops into a Community version of the *O'Reilly* v *Mackman* rule.

Having established locus standi, and brought his action in time, the applicant must prove his case for annulment. This will be decided on the grounds provided under Article 173(2), discussed at length in Chapter 8.

Effects of a Successful Action under Article 173

Under Article 174

> If the action is well founded, the Court of Justice shall declare the act concerned to be void.
>
> In the case of a regulation, however, the Court of Justice shall, if it considers this necessary, state which of the effects of the regulation which it has declared void shall be considered as definitive.

The Court may declare only part of a measure to be void (*Etablissements Consten and Grundig* v *Commission* (cases 56 and 58/64)).

Under Article 176

> The institution or institutions whose act has been declared void ... shall be required to take the necessary measures to comply with the judgment of the Court of Justice.

As was noted in Chapter 8, in annulling a Regulation or parts of a Regulation under Article 174, or declaring it invalid under Article 177, the Court has invoked Article 174(2) in order to limit the effects of its ruling where this is necessary in the interest of legal certainty, normally on the principles laid down in *Defrenne* v *Sabena (No. 2)* (case 43/75). However, it interprets its powers under Article 174(2) flexibly. It has declared its ruling to be wholly prospective (*Roquette Frères* v *French State* (case 145/79), principle doubted in *Roquette Frères SA* v *Hauptzollamt Geldern* (case C 228/92)), and has even decreed that articles of a Regulation, although 'annulled', should remain in place pending the introduction of a replacement measure, also in the interests of legal certainty (e.g., *Commission* v *Council* (case 59/81)). On the same reasoning it has preserved the effects of an annulled decision for all persons except the applicant (*Simmenthal* v *Commission* (case 92/78)).

Interim Relief

The Court's power to grant interim relief is governed by Articles 185 and 186 of the EC Treaty and Articles 83–90 of the Court's Rules of Procedure (OJ L

176 4 July 1991, p. 7). These rules are also binding on the Court of First Instance (Rules of Procedure of the CFI, OJ L 136 30 May 1991 p. 1, Articles 104–110).

Under Article 185 EC

Actions brought before the Court of Justice shall not have suspensory effect. The Court of Justice may, however, if it considers that circumstances so require, order that application of the contested act be suspended.

Under Article 186 EC

The Court of Justice may in any cases before it prescribe any necessary interim measures.

Action under Article 185 is only admissible if the applicant is challenging that measure 'in proceedings before the Court'. Similarly action under Article 186 will be admitted only if it is made by 'a party to the case before the court and relates to that case' (Article 83(1) of the Rules of Procedure). Thus the relief sought must fall within the scope of the principal action (see e.g., *Ford of Europe Inc* v *Commission* (cases 228 and 229/82)). Normally in acting under Articles 185 or 186 the Court will not consider whether the main action is inadmissible, unless a prima facie case is made out or it is manifestly so.

An application under Articles 185 and 186 must

state the subject matter of the proceedings, the circumstances giving rise to urgency and the pleas of fact and law establishing a prima facie case for the interim measures applied for' (Article 83(2) of the Rules of Procedure).

The decision, normally made by the President of the Court 'shall take the form of a reasoned order, from which no appeal shall lie' (Article 86(1) of the Rules of Procedure).

The enforcement of the order may be made conditional on the lodging by the applicant of a security, or an amount to be fixed in the light of the circumstances' (Article 86(2) of the Rules of Procedure).

These provisions apply to all proceedings before the Court, except, it is thought, proceedings under Article 177. Since these proceedings originate in national courts, interim relief will normally be granted in these courts, on the principles laid down in *Zuckerfabrik Süderdithmarschen* (cases C 143/88 and 92/89), see Chapter 5).

The Court has insisted that the purpose of interim relief is to maintain the status quo. It will not grant relief if its decision could prejudice the results of the main application.

The Court's approach to the question of 'prima facie case' is variable, but generally not strict. In *Publishers' Association* v *Commission* (case 56/89R) a claim for the suspension of a Commission decision refusing exemption under Article 85(3) for the publishers' Net Book Agreement was accepted as 'not devoid of all foundation'. Claims may be admitted because they are 'arguable' or 'strongly arguable', or 'prima facie sound'. Having established a prima facie case interim measures will only be granted in cases of urgency. The question of urgency is assessed in relation to the *necessity* for granting interim relief in order *to prevent serious and irreparable damage* to the party seeking relief (*Cargill* v *Commission* (case 229/88R)). Purely financial damage is not regarded as irreparable unless, in the event of the applicant's success in the main proceedings, it could not be wholly recouped.

The Court is flexible in its approach to these criteria. As Schermers has pointed out

> these factors are mutually related. When suspension causes little damage, the Court requires less urgency than in a case where grave practical problems will arise as a result of the suspension' (Schermers and Waelbroeck, 'Judicial Protection in the European Community', (1992)).

As the Court noted in *Publishers' Association* v *Commission* (case 56/89R), a balance must be struck between the risk to the applicant and the public and Community's interest in ensuring that Community law is observed. For this reason, and for reasons of legal certainty, the Court is reluctant to suspend Regulations and Directives. Applications for interim relief have, however, not infrequently been successful against Decisions, particularly in the field of competition law.

Whether or not interim relief is granted, interim losses may be suffered by a party who succeeds at trial. In the context of actions under Article 173 a denial of relief can result in interim damage to individual applicants. Conversely, the granting of such relief, resulting in the non-enforcement of Community law, may damage the Community interest. An effective system of protection requires that compensation should be paid to a party (who is ultimately successful) not only for interim losses suffered by individuals but also for damage to the Community interest. In the latter case such provision would also serve to deter unjustified claims. Although the Court has power under Article 86(2) of the Rules of Procedure to order the lodging by the applicant of a security, this has so far been of limited use, to secure the payment of money owing or owed to the Community. In *Zuckerfabrik Süderdithmarschen* (cases C 142/88 and 92/89) the Court suggested, in Article 177 proceedings, that *national* courts should also be in a position to require adequate guarantees, such as the deposit of money, where the suspension of enforcement of Community law would be likely to lead to financial risk to the Community. Arguably Article 86(2) of the Rules of Procedure and the Court's dicta in *Zuckerfabrik* could provide the basis for a demand for the lodging of a security in order to protect the Community interest in enforcing the law.

Where interim relief is denied in Article 173 proceedings there appears to be no interim protection for individuals. In *Commission* v *Germany* (case 195/90R) the Court decided that the Commission was not obliged to lodge a deposit when it was taking action (in this case under Article 169) simply to enforce the law. This reflects the position in English law taken by the House of Lords in *Hoffman La Roche* [1975] AC 295 and *Kirklees Metropolitan Borough Council* v

Wickes [1991] 4 All ER 240 (cases noted and criticised in Chapter 6). If this is the case an individual who succeeds at trial in an action under Article 173 may receive no compensation for damage suffered prior to trial. Although the Court has suggested that interim losses suffered by individuals may be recouped by an action for compensation under Articles 178 and 215(2) EC (see *Cargill* v *Commission* (case 229/88R)), such compensation cannot be guaranteed. As in English law there is in Community law no automatic right to damages for losses resulting from the application of unlawful acts (see further Chapter 10). This lack of provision even for liquidated damages in respect of interim loss represents a significant gap in the judicial protection of individuals.

ARTICLE 184: THE INDIRECT CHALLENGE

Article 184 provides that

> Notwithstanding the expiry of the period laid down in the fifth paragraph of Article 173, any party may, in proceedings in which ... a regulation of the Council, of the Commission or of the ECB is at issue, plead the grounds specified in the second paragraph of Article 173 in order to invoke before the Court of Justice the inapplicability of that regulation.

The purpose of Article 184 is not to evade the limitations of Article 173 by allowing individuals to challenge Regulations or applicants generally to avoid the time limits laid down in that Article, but to achieve the setting aside of an act, prima facie lawful, by *indirect* challenge to the legislative measure on which it is based. By establishing the 'inapplicability' of the Regulation, on the grounds prescribed for annulment under Article 173, the measure based on that Regulation itself becomes unlawful.

Thus Article 184, which can only be invoked before the Court of Justice, is essentially a complementary remedy. The Regulation of which the legality is called into question must be applicable, directly or indirectly, to the issue with which the main application is concerned (compare *Italy* v *Council and Commission* (case 32/65); no direct judicial link). Article 184 will be invoked principally in conjunction with an action for the annulment of the Regulation's 'offspring' measure under Article 173.

Although 'privileged' applicants are entitled to challenge Regulations under Article 173, it is thought that since they fall within the definition of 'any party' under Article 184 they are not barred from action under that Article. Since the legality of the Regulation may not be 'in issue' until the enactment of some subsequent act based on that Regulation, even privileged applicants would be likely to be out of time to bring proceedings for its annulment under Article 173. A member state was not denied the right to act under Article 184 in *Italy* v *Council and Commission* (case 32/65).

Article 184 is expressed only to apply to Regulations. However, in keeping with its view that it is the substance and effect and not the form of a measure which determines its true nature, the Court has held that Article 184 may be invoked to challenge any *general* act having binding force. In *Simmenthal SpA* v

Commission (case 92/78), the plaintiff meat-processing company was seeking to annul, under Article 173, a Decision addressed to the Italian government, in which it was directly and individually concerned. The basis of its claim was that the 'parent' measure, a general notice of invitation to tender, on which the Decision was based, was invalid. The Court held that since the notice was a general act which, if not in the form of a Regulation, produced similar effects, it could be challenged under Article 184. It was found to be inapplicable on the ground of misuse of powers. The power under which the notice was passed (under an earlier Regulation) to set minimum purchase prices for beef had been granted to help processors; it had been exercised to help importers in general.

Attempts have been made to invoke Article 184 illegitimately, to challenge a Regulation simpliciter, or to challenge a measure which the applicant could have challenged under Article 173, but failed to challenge in time. They have always failed. In *Commission* v *Belgium* (case 156/77) Article 184 was raised as a defence to an enforcement action against Belgium under Article 95(2), for infringement of Community law in respect of state aids. The Belgians had failed to comply with a Commission Decision of May 1976, addressed to the Belgian government, requiring the government to abolish cerain state aids within a three-month period; nor had they challenged that Decision. In proceedings brought by the Commission in December 1977 for non-compliance with the Decision, the Belgian government, invoking Article 184, argued that the Decision was invalid. The Court found that the claim was in essence a claim for the annulment of the Decision of May 1976. The Belgian government had been free to contest this Decision but had failed to do so within the time limit. It could not allow the time to elapse and then question the legality of the decision under Article 184.

The effect of a successful action under Article 184 speaks for itself. The Regulation is simply 'inapplicable'. As a result any measure based on that Regulation is automatically void. The Regulation will not necessarily be withdrawn or amended, for reasons of legal certainty, but any subsequent measure based on that Regulation can also be challenged under Article 173, together with Article 184.

ARTICLE 175: ACTION FOR FAILURE TO ACT

Article 175 EC is complementary to Article 173. Together they ensure not only that EC institutions act within their powers but also that they take action when they are legally obliged to do so. Because Articles 173 and 175 represent different aspects of the same legal remedy their provisions are based on similar principles, known as the 'unity' principle. They are also closely interrelated. Because of the way in which the Court has interpreted Article 175, an action begun under Article 175 may be concluded by a challenge to the defendant institution's 'definition of position' (its response to the demand for action) under Article 173 (e.g., *Star Fruit Co. SA* v *Commission* (case 247/87)).

Under Article 175

Should the European Parliament, the Council or the Commission, in infringement of this Treaty, fail to act, the Member States and the other institutions of the Community may bring an action before the Court of Justice to have the infringement established.

The action shall be admissible only if the institution concerned has first been called upon to act. If, within two months of being so called upon, the institution concerned has not defined its position, the action may be brought within a further period of two months.

Any natural or legal person may, under the conditions laid down in the preceding paragraphs, complain to the Court of Justice that an institution of the Community has failed to address to that person any act other than a recommendation or opinion.

The Court of Justice shall have jurisdiction, under the same conditions, in actions or proceedings brought by the ECB in the areas falling within the latter's field of competence and in actions or proceedings brought against the latter.

Like Article 173, Article 175 is of primary importance to 'privileged' applicants, who are defined more widely here to provide *general* standing to 'the other institutions' (i.e., Parliament) of the Community. Privileged applicants have a right to challenge any failure on the part of the Community institution, provided that the failure is 'in infringement of the Treaty'. An infringement of the Treaty would include any failure to act pursuant to obligations in the EC Treaty or secondary legislation arising under the Treaty. Natural or legal persons, as under Article 173, have limited locus standi. Since natural or legal persons can only challenge a failure to 'address to that person any act other than a recommendation or an opinion' under Article 175, this appears to limit their standing to a right to demand a decision addressed to themselves. There is no express equivalent to the provision for challenge to decisions addressed to another person based on direct and individual concern. This has now been rectified by the Court. In *Nordgetreide v Commission* (case 42/71) Advocate-General Roemer suggested that since Articles 173 and 175 formed part of one coherent system an individual should have the right to demand a Decision vis-à-vis a third party in which he was directly and individually concerned. This suggestion was impliedly accepted, albeit expressed in negative terms in *Bethell v Commission* (case 246/81). Here an attempt by Lord Bethell to force the Commission to take action against certain European airlines for alleged anti-competitive practices in breach of EC competition laws was rejected on the grounds that he had failed to show that the Commission had failed to adopt, in relation to him, a measure which he was legally entitled to claim. Thus a failure to address a decision to another person may only be challenged by a third party if the latter is *legally entitled to demand that action*. This is the Article 175 equivalent of direct and individual concern. Since an individual will rarely be entitled to demand such action it is not surprising that all attempts to force the Commission to act against a third party have so far failed.

Where an individual seeks to compel an institution to address a decision, whether to himself or to another person, which he is not entitled to demand, he will not be permitted to challenge a decision refusing to act *even though it is addressed to him*. This has been tried on occasions, as a 'back door' attempt to compel the institution to act. It has always failed (see *Alfons Lütticke GmbH* v *Commission* (case 48/65); *Star Fruit Company SA* v *Commission* (case 247/87); *Bethell* v *Commission* (case 246/81)). A 'negative' decision, a refusal to act, will only be open to attack under Article 173 if the positive decision sought were also open to attack, that is, if it would have been addressed to the applicant or if the applicant could have established direct and individual concern (*Nordgetreide* v *Commission* (case 42/71)).

The Procedure

The institution concerned must first be called upon to act. The institution concerned may then either act or 'define its position' (Article 175(2)). Although it has no obligation to define its position if it is not obliged to take the action requested, it will normally do so. If it is so obliged, and fails to define its position, the applicant has two months in which to bring his case before the Court.

In a consistent if unsatisfactory line of cases, beginning with *Alfons Lütticke GmbH* v *Commission* (case 48/65) the Court has held that a definition of position under Article 175(2) ends a failure to act. This means that once the defendant institution has defined its position, Article 175 becomes superfluous. However, this need not be the end of the road for the applicant. Provided that he was *entitled to demand* the action requested, he can then attack that definition of position, as a Decision addressed to himself, under Article 173. The applicant in *(FEDIOL EC Seed Crushers' and Oil Producers' Association* v *Commission* (case 191/82) was successful in this attempt. Having complained to the Commission of suspected dumping practices on the part of Brazil, as the applicant company was entitled to do under EC Regulation 3017/79, and having subsequently received a letter from the Commission to the effect that, having undertaken investigations it intended to take no further action, the applicant sought to annul the letter under Article 173. The action was held admissible. Although the applicant could not compel the Commission to act against the (alleged) offending Brazilian companies, that being a matter within the Commission's discretion, it was entitled to a judicial review of the Commission's letter to ensure that its procedural rights had been respected.

The reason why actions by individuals based on Article 175, backed up by Article 173, have routinely failed to be admitted is either that a 'definition of position' has not been recognised as capable of challenge, and challenged in time (*Deutscher Komponistenverbande eV* v *Commission* (case 8/71); *GEMA* v *Commission* (case 125/78)), or because the applicant was seeking action from an EC institution which it was not entitled to demand (*Alfons Lütticke GmbH* v *Commission* (case 48/65); *Star Fruit Co.* v *Commission* (case 247/87) (not entitled to demand that Commission takes Article 169 action); *Bethell* v *Commission* (case 246/81) (not entitled to demand action by Commission in respect of breaches of EC competition laws)).

Not surprisingly natural or legal persons have few rights under EC law to demand a particular action on the part of EC institutions. Their rights are principally of a procedural nature, in the form of a right to complain, or to be consulted, or to submit observations, principally in the field of competition law. Therefore Article 175 will inevitably be of limited use to them. Its primary value is to privileged applicants, to member states and EC institutions, who, being entitled to challenge any failure, may use Article 175 to prod an EC institution into action. This was done successfully in *European Parliament* v *Council* (case 13/83), when Parliament obtained a ruling from the Court that the Commission had failed to introduce measures to secure freedom to provide transport services, as required by Articles 75, 59, 60 and 61. In this case the Commission's definition of position was found to be inadequate; thus Parliament was able to proceed before the Court under Article 175. This was fortunate, since at the time Parliament had no locus standi to bring an action under Article 173. It does now (following the Treaty on European Union) have limited standing, to protect its own prerogative powers (for example to be consulted or involved in the co-operation or co-decision procedures). However, faced with a definition of position under Article 175 which it does not have standing to challenge under Article 173, it may call in aid the Court's suggestion that a 'refusal to act under Article 175 could be brought before the Court on the basis of Article 175 where it did not put an end to the failure to act' (*Parliament* v *Council (Comitology)* (case 302/87)).

Consequences of a Successful Action

Following a successful action under Article 175

> The institution or institutions whose ... failure to act has been declared contrary to this Treaty shall be required to take the necessary measures to comply with the judgment of the Court of Justice (Article 176(1)).

The necessary measures following a successful action under Article 175 will not necessarily be the action required by the applicant. Should he wish to challenge the institution's action in implementing the Court's ruling he could do so under Article 173.

Unlike the position with regard to member states which fail to comply with a judgment against them under Article 169 (see Chapters 1 and 10), no sanctions have been provided against Community institutions which fail to comply with a ruling of the Court under Article 176(1). However, Article 176(2) provides that the obligation imposed by Article 176(1) 'shall not affect any obligation which may result from the application of the second paragraph of Article 215' (governing the Community's non-contractual liability). Thus any EC institution which fails to comply with a judgment under Article 176(1) would be vulnerable to a claim in damages under Article 215(2).

TEN

Community liability in damages: Articles 178 and 215(2)

Although individuals may obtain effective protection against unlawful acts or omissions of the EC institutions by an action for judicial review under Articles 173, 184 or 175, or by a ruling on validity under Article 177, particularly if adequate interim relief is available, there are occasions when the only effective protection lies in the award of damages. The EC Treaty provides for the award of damages under Articles 178 and 215(2). Under Article 178

> The Court of Justice shall have jurisdiction in disputes relating to compensation for damage provided for in the second paragraph of Article 215.

Article 215(2) states that

> In the case of non-contractual liability, the Community shall, in accordance with the general principles common to the laws of the Member States, make good any damage caused by its institutions or by its servants in the performance of their duties.

As with actions for annulment and failure to act, claims by 'natural or legal persons' have now been transferred to the Court of First Instance, subject to appeal on matters of law to the Court of Justice.

The reference in both articles to 'compensation' for 'damage' suggests that these Articles are concerned with the award of tortious damages. They do not prima facie appear to provide for a claim for restitution from the Community. Given the Court's endorsement, as general principles of law, of the principles of unjust enrichment and effective judicial control in the context of domestic actions based on EC law (see Chapter 5), it is likely that it could be persuaded to admit a claim for restitution against the Community based on these Articles.

However, since money paid into or from Community funds is normally channelled through national authorities, the normal route for the recovery of such money, preferred by the Court of Justice, is through an action for restitution against the appropriate national authority, before domestic courts (see e.g., *Haegeman* v *Commission* (case 96/71); *Merkur* v *Commission* (case 43/72), see further below). Only if restitution cannot be obtained through such an action will it be necessary to seek a remedy before the European Court.

Liability under Article 215(2) is to be determined 'in accordance with the general principles common to the laws of the member states'. There are three basic requirements for liability:

(a) a wrongful act (or omission) on the part of the institution (*faute de service*) or its servants (*faute personelle*);
(b) damage to the plaintiff; and
(c) a causative link between the two.

Although these basic elements are common to the laws of the member states, there are significant differences between member states in the scope and content of these rules. Thus the Court has drawn on the general principles underlying these rules in order to develop its own Community principles of non-contractual liability.

LOCUS STANDI

Unlike the position in relation to actions before the Court for judicial review there are no limitations on individuals' standing under Article 215(2) and there is a generous time limitation period of five years, running from the occurrence of the event giving rise to liability (Article 43, Protocol on the Statute of the Court 1988). The Court has held that the limitation period cannot begin to run until all the requirements for liability, particularly damage, have materialized (*Birra Wührer SpA* v *Council & Commission* (cases 256, 257, 265 and 267/80 and 5/81). The extended time limitation period is important, since although an action under Article 215(2) may be in respect of damage caused by a wrongful (i.e., invalid) act or omission on the part of the Community it is not necessary to have taken prior action to establish that illegality under Articles 173 or 175. Despite an earlier, more restrictive view, (*Plaumann* v *Commission* (case 25/62)) the Court has held consistently that an action under Article 215(2) was an 'independent action with a particular purpose to fulfil'. Therefore the expiry of the time limit for challenging the relevant act or omission will not render an action under Article 215(2) inadmissible (*Alfons Lütticke* v *Commission* (case 4/69); *Aktien-Zuckerfabrik Schöppenstedt* v *Council* (case 5/71)). Indeed, an action for damages may be effective in obtaining a declaration of invalidity or unlawful failure to act even though the applicant would have had no standing to challenge that act or omission under Article 173 or Article 175. Furthermore, where damage to the applicant is imminent, or likely with a high degree of certainty to occur, proceedings may be brought under Article 215(2) *before* the damage has occurred (*Kurt Kampffmeyer Mühlenvereinigung KG* v *Council* (cases 56-60/74)). Although the applicant may not be found entitled to damages in principle, he may obtain a declaration of invalidity and a suspension of the offending measure (under Article 185) in time to prevent damage occurring. In all these cases the claim for damages must be genuine. It is unlikely that the Court would allow Article 215(2) to be used simply as a back door route to challenge a Community measure which the applicant had failed to challenge within the time prescribed under Article 173.

As an independent action, designed to provide compensation for (or to prevent) damage, Article 215(2) cannot bring about the annulment of the wrongful act causing the damage. Nor does the Court have the power, as it has under Article 176 following a successful action for judicial review, to order any other 'necessary measures' such as the withdrawal or amendment of the offending act (*Les Assurances du Crédit SA* v *Commission* (case C 63/89)). However, once the unlawful nature of a particular act is established it is likely to be withdrawn, if only to avoid the risk of further claims for damages.

WRONGFUL ACTS OR OMISSIONS

The Community, in the form of the responsible institutions, may be liable for wrongful acts or omissions on the part of the administration (fautes de service) or its servants (fautes personelles). The former enables action to be brought against the system for maladministration, without the need to identify particular responsible defendants. The latter corresponds to the principle of vicarious liability in English law, albeit interpreted in a more restrictive manner. In *Sayag* v *Leduc* (case 9/69), in proceedings brought under Article 188(2) of the Euratom Treaty the Court held that the Community was only liable for those acts of its servants which, by virtue of an internal relationship, were the *necessary* extension of the tasks entrusted to the institutions.

Liability for both *fautes de service* and *fautes personnelles* corresponds loosely with liability for 'operational' failures in English law. Although liability does not require proof of negligence in the English sense, some 'fault' appears to be required. As in the case of negligence, advice given need not be right if it is adopted according to the correct procedures and the conclusions reached are reasonable in the light of the circumstances. 'The nature of the wrongful act or omission is not to be found in a mistaken evaluation of the facts but in the institution's general conduct', such as where provisions 'of a crucial nature' are ignored (*Firma E Kampffmeyer* v *Commission* (cases 5, 7 and 13–24/66)). However an 'excusable' error, once discovered, may become a *faute de service* if it is not quickly rectified.

The Community may also be liable for damage caused by wrongful acts, or a wrongful failure to adopt a binding act when under a duty to do so. Thus liability may flow from the application of an invalid or illegal act in the form or nature of a Regulation, Directive or Decision. However, whilst liability may arise from a 'simple' fault in the case of an individual act such as a Decision addressed to a particular person, the burden on individuals seeking compensation for damage resulting from unlawful normative acts is heavy. Where the damage is caused by a 'legislative act involving choices or economic policy' the plaintiff must prove that a 'sufficiently serious breach of a superior rule of law for the protection of individuals "has occurred"'. This formula, known as the *Schöppenstedt* formula, from the case of *Aktien-Zuckerfabrik Schöppenstedt* v *Council* (case 5/71), applies not only to Regulations but to all binding acts which seek to lay down general rules. In *Government of Gibraltar* v *Council and Commission* (case C 298/89) the Court suggested, in the context of a claim under Article 173, that Directives normally constitute 'a form of indirect regulatory measure'. In *Les Assurances du Crédit SA* v *Commission* (case C 63/89), in a claim for damages based on the alleged invalidity of Insurance Directive 73/239, the Court applied the *Schöppenstedt* formula, pointing out that Community institutions enjoyed considerable discretion in the enactment of harmonisation Directives under Article 57(2) EC (to promote freedom to provide services, freedom of establishment). It is likely that a claim for damages based on a Decision addressed to a member state, requiring the state to lay down general rules, for example the Decision in *Firma E Kampffmeyer* v *Commission)* (cases 5, 7 and 13–24/66) addressed to the German government and authorising it to withhold import licences for maize during a certain period, would also need to satisfy the *Schöppenstedt* formula.

The *Schöppenstedt* Formula

(a) Legislative measures involving choices of economic policy As suggested above, Regulations, Directives and even Decisions addressed to member states laying down general rules will constitute 'legislative' measures for the purposes of Article 215(2). Whilst these measures *must* be enacted under the correct legal base and according to the appropriate procedures, Community institutions enjoy a wide discretion in the framing of the substance of Community legislation. Since the goals of the EC treaty, even following Maastricht, are primarily economic many of its measures, arguably even those involving people, at least as workers, will involve choices of economic policy. Only purely social or political rights such as the rights of European citizenship in Article 8 EC, introduced by the TEU, are likely to fall outside the *Schöppenstedt* formula.

(b) Breach of a superior rule of law for the protection of individuals This element too is extremely wide. Any general principle of law such as the principle of equality or legal certainty or proportionality respected under Community law (see Chapters 1 and 6) is likely to constitute a 'superior rule of law for the protection of individuals', as will any fundamental Community right intended to benefit individuals, whether stemming from the Treaty, such as the right to freedom of movement for workers under Article 48, or to equal pay for men and women under Article 119, or from secondary legislation. In *Firma E Kampffmeyer* v *Commission* (cases 5, 7 and 13-24/66), a provision in an EC Regulation directed at ensuring 'appropriate support for agricultural markets' was construed as intended to benefit, inter alia, the interest of individual undertakings such as importers. Similar economic provisions under the ECSC are, it seems, less likely to be so construed (e.g., *Société Commerciale Antoine Vloeberghs SA* v *High Authority* (cases 9 and 12/60)). It is open to question

whether the free movement of goods provisions of the EC Treaty (Articles 12–16 and 30–34) would be construed as intended to benefit individuals.

(c)   A sufficiently serious breach   A breach of a superior rule of law, even a fundamental rule, clearly designed for the protection of individuals, is not in itself sufficient to give rise to liability under Article 215(2). The plaintiff must prove that the breach is 'sufficiently serious'. This principle has been construed very restrictively by the Court. In *Bayerische HNL Vermehrungsbetriebe GmbH* v *Council & Commission* (cases 83 and 94/76; 4, 15 and 40/77) the Court suggested that in a legislative field in which one of the chief features is the exercise of a wide discretion, the Community does not incur liability unless the institution concerned has 'gravely and manifestly disregarded the limits on the exercise of its powers'.

The question of whether the breach is 'sufficiently serious' to incur liability under Article 215(2) involves a two-fold enquiry. First the Court considers the effect of the measure on the applicant, to ascertain the nature and extent of the harm to his interests. Secondly it looks to the nature of the breach, at the culpability of the institution concerned. For liability to arise the breach must be serious as regards its effects on the applicant *and* inexcusable.

The Effect of the Measure on the Plaintiff

In *Bayerische HNL* v *Council and Commission* (cases 83 and 94/76; 4, 15 and 40/77) the plaintiffs, who were animal feed producers, fell victim to the Community's attempts to reduce milk surpluses. They were seeking damages for losses suffered as a result of an EC Regulation under which they were required to buy skimmed milk powder instead of the cheaper and more effective soya. This Regulation had already been found invalid for breach of the general principles of non-discrimination and proportionality (*Bela-Mühle Bergmann KG* v *Grows-Farm GmbH* (case 114/76); *Granaria BV* v *Hoofd-produktschap voor Akkerbouwprodukten (No. 1)* (case 116/76), Article 177 proceedings). The Court looked at the effect of the breach on the applicants. It found that the measure had affected a wide group of persons, all buyers of protein for the production of animal feed; the difference in price between the skimmed milk and soya had only a limited effect on production costs, insignificant beside other factors such as world prices, and the effect of the Regulation on their profits did not exceed the normal level of risk inherent in such activities. Thus the breach was not sufficiently serious.

By contrast the applicants in *P Dumortier Frères SA* v *Council* (cases 64 and 113/76, 167 and 239/78, 27, 28 and 45/79) succeeded. Again the plaintiffs, a number of gritz and quellmehl producers were seeking damages for losses resulting from an EC Regulation withdrawing subsidies for gritz and quellmehl but retaining them for starch. Since these products were in competition with each other, the Regulation had been annulled for breach of the principle of equality (*Firma Albert Ruckdeschel & Co.* (case 117/76), Article 177 proceedings). The subsidies had been restored following that judgment, but not retrospectively. The plaintiffs claimed for losses suffered prior to judgment.

The Court found that they were a small, clearly defined group and the losses went beyond the risks normally inherent in their business. Therefore they were entitled in principle to damages. Under the same principle the plaintiff milk producers in *Mulder* (case C 104/89) succeeded in obtaining damages for losses resulting from the application of an illegal Regulation as a result of which they received no milk quota. The quota or 'reference quantity' set by the Regulation had been calculated according to output in one particular year (the 'reference year') in which the applicants had not been engaged in production. The Court found that the 'total exclusion' of the producers under this (the original) scheme set up by the Regulation 'could not be regarded as foreseeable or as falling within the economic risks inherent in producing milk'. On the other hand the losses suffered under the scheme introduced by the replacement Regulation, also found invalid, under which they were entitled to a quota representing 60% of their production during a normal 'reference year', in respect of which the applicants also claimed damages, were found to be foreseeable and within the economic risks inherent in their business. Thus this breach was not 'sufficiently serious'.

The Nature of the Breach

This aspect of the enquiry was crucial in the 'Isoglucose' cases (*Koninklijke Scholten-Honig NV* v *Council & Commission* (case 143/77); *GR Amylum NV* v *Council & Commission* (cases 116 and 124/77)). Here the applicants were seeking damages for losses suffered as a result of a Community Regulation which imposed levies on glucose production in order to increase the consumption of Community sugar. Since these products were to some extent in competition with each other the Regulation had been annulled for breach of the principle of equality (*Royal Scholten-Honig* v *Intervention Board for Agricultural Produce* (cases 103 and 145/77), see Chapter 9). Although the applicants comprised a small and closed group, and the damage they had suffered as a result of the system set up by the Regulation was described as 'catastrophic', the breach was found not to be 'sufficiently serious'. The Commission's error in setting up such a system was 'not of such gravity that their conduct could be regarded as verging on the arbitrary'.

Similarly in *Roquette Frères* v *Commission* (case 20/88) the applicants failed to obtain compensation for losses suffered as a result of the Commission's calculations of monetary compensation amounts (MCAs). The MCAs, which were laid down by Regulation, determined the levies payable on the import of certain agricultural products into France. The applicants, who had paid the levies, challenged the validity of the Regulation before the French courts, seeking reimbursement of the sums (allegedly) unlawfully paid. The Regulation was found invalid in Article 177 proceedings. However, because the ruling was held to be wholly prospective Roquette failed to obtain reimbursement from the French courts. Their claim in *Roquette Frères* v *Commission* (case 20/88) for damages from the Commission in respect of these losses also failed. The Commission's fault in calculating the MCAs was found to be a purely 'technical error': it could not be regarded as amounting to a 'serious infringement of a superior rule of law or manifest and grave disregard by the Commission of the limits on the exercise of its powers'. By contrast, in the successful action in *Mulder* (C 104/89), in respect of the original Regulation, the Court found that the Council, in totally excluding the applicant producers from the allocation of a 'reference quantity', had 'failed completely, without invoking any higher interest', to take account of the applicants' specific situation. In doing so they had 'gravely and manifestly exceeded the limits of their discretionary power'. In the second, failed claim, in respect of the replacement Regulation, the institutions on the other hand were engaged in 'necessary economic choices' taking into account the 'higher public interest'.

Thus where the institution's action, although technically 'wrongful', is reasonable, and justified in order to promote a higher Community interest, it appears that it will not give rise to a claim in damages, regardless of the size of the class affected and its impact on their interests.

The above cases all concern damage resulting from normative acts involving the exercise of discretion by the Community institutions concerned. The policy reasons for protecting administrative bodies from liability in damages in respect of such acts, even if they are found 'unlawful' are clear, and admitted in most member states. Public authorities must be free to make difficult policy choices in the wider public interest without fear of incurring financial liability, especially to a large and indeterminate class. The 'looking over the shoulder argument' is a familiar one in English tort law (e.g., *Rowling* v *Takaro* [1988] AC 473 (PC)). However where these acts inflict *special* or *disproportionate* damage on *particular* parties there is a strong case for awarding compensation. Many member states impose strict liability in such situations, on the principle of the equal apportionment of public burdens (*'égalité devant les charges publics'*). The few who suffer exceptional damage should not be expected to pay the price of measures enacted for the benefit of the many. The Court of Justice has not yet endorsed this principle in the context of the Community's non-contractual liability, but it has not ruled out that possibility (see *Compagnie d'Approvisionnement* v *Commission* (cases 9 and 11/71; *Biovilac* v *EEC* (case 59/83)). If there is a case for strict liability in the circumstances there should a fortiori be liability when fault has been proved.

Where a measure, albeit a normative measure, does not involve the exercise of discretion ('choices of economic policy'), the applicant should not be required to satisfy the *Schöppenstedt* rules. This point was not acknowledged in *Sofrimport SARL* v *Commission* (case C 152/88). Here the applicant fruit importers were seeking compensation for losses suffered following the introduction of an EC Regulation suspending imports into the EC of apples from Chile. The Regulation authorising the Commission to enact the offending Regulation required the Commission to take into account the interests of those with 'goods in transit' at the time when the Regulation was made. The applicants had goods in transit at the relevant time. The Court, applying the *Schöppendstedt* formula, found that the Commission had 'failed completely' to take the applicants' interests into account, and held the Commission liable in damages. Whilst the result was no doubt correct it may be doubted whether it was necessary to apply the *Schöppenstedt* formula. Surely the obligation to take into account the interests of those with goods in transit did not involve the exercise of the Commission's discretion; it was a matter in which the Commission had no choice.

DAMAGES

The court is as restrictive in its approach to damages as it is to fault. Although it will award damages in principle in respect of economic losses, such losses must be specific, not speculative. Only actual, certain and concrete damages are recoverable (*Roquette Frères* v *Commission* (case 26/74)). The Court will award damages for lost profits on contracts already concluded when the impugned measure took effect, although even these damages may be reduced on account of the risks involved in such transactions (*Firma E Kampffmeyer* v *Commission* (cases 5, 7 and 13–24/66); 10% reduction on contracts already concluded; no damages on anticipated contracts). In *Comptoire National Technique Agricole (CNTA) SA* v *Commission* (case 74/74) the applicants established that the Commission was liable in principle when it introduced a Regulation, suddenly and without warning, in breach of the applicants' legitimate expectations, but they received no damages. Although CNTA had entered into export contracts on the basis of the situation as it existed prior to the enactment of the Regulation, it was held entitled to recover only for losses actually suffered, not anticipated profits. By contrast *Sofrimport SARL* v *Commission* (case C 152/88) is one of the few examples of a straightforward and wholly successful damages claim based on unlawful provisions of a legislative act. Having been denied the right to import apples from Chile by EC Regulations found, in Article 173 proceedings, to be illegal, the plaintiff company was held entitled to damages on the principles outlined above. Damages were calculated according to the prices actually obtained on the sale of the apples after the original (interim) order of the Court, compared with the prices they would have obtained immediately after the arrival of the goods at the port of destination. They were thus clear and certain.

Where the loss has been passed on to third parties, or could have been passed on in higher prices, no damages will be recoverable (*Interquell Stärke-Chemie GmbH* v *Council and Commission* (cases 261 and 262/78)), unless the applicant can prove that the losses could not have been passed on without losing valuable markets (*P Dumortier Frères SA* v *Commission* (cases 64 and 113/76, 167 and 239/78, 27, 28 and 45/79). An injured party is expected to show reasonable diligence in limiting the extent of his loss; if he does not he must bear the damage himself (*Mulder* (case C 104/89)). The Court is strict in its approach to the mitigation rules.

Damages are payable in the applicant's national currency at the exchange rate applicable at the date of judgment. Interest on that sum is payable from the date of judgment (*Sofrimport SARL* v *Commission* (case C 152/88)).

CAUSATION

The Court is similarly strict in its approach to causation. It has held that the principles common to the law of the member states cannot be relied upon to deduce an obligation to make good any harmful consequence, even a remote one, of unlawful legislation. The damage must be a *sufficiently direct consequence* of the unlawful conduct of the institution concerned. Thus in *P Dumortier Frères SA v Council* (cases 64 and 113/76 *et al*) the plaintiffs were entitled to recover refunds unlawfully withheld under an invalid Regulation, but not for further alleged losses or for general financial difficulties which resulted in the closing of factories. Even though the Regulation may have contributed to these difficulties they were not a sufficiently direct consequence of the unlawful act such as to render the Community liable. Other factors such as obsolescence and financial stringency were responsible. Likewise, where a party engages in business activities to compensate for business lost as a result of unlawful Community acts, any operating losses incurred as a result of these activities will be deemed too remote a consequence, and thus not recoverable from the Community. Business persons are expected to be prudent in the conduct of their affairs (*Mulder* (cases C 104/89, C 37/90). For example, in a claim based on misleading information damage resulting from the use of that information was held only to be recoverable if it would have caused an error in the mind of a reasonable man (*Compagnie Continentale France v Council* (case 169/73)). Thus where the damage may be deemed to have been caused, at least in part, by the applicant, particularly when the applicant is a commercial undertaking, the causative link will be broken and liability denied. The principle of contributory negligence has so far been little used in EC law.

One of the few cases in which it was invoked was *Adams v Commission (No. 1)* (case 145/83). As an employee of Hoffman La Roche in Switzerland Adams passed on information to the Commission concerning Hoffman La Roche's business practices which he suspected were in breach of EC competition law. The Commission subsequently supplied Hoffman La Roche with information which enabled them to identify Adams as the informant. He was tried for industrial espionage under Swiss law and sent to prison. His wife committed suicide. Although he succeeded in an action for damages against the Commission for breach of its duty of confidentiality under Article 214 EC, his damages were reduced on account of his contributory negligence. In failing to give the Commission his precise address, to warn the Commission that the documents which he had supplied, and which found their way to his employers, might give a clue to his identity, and in returning to Switzerland knowing that in doing so he risked arrest, he was deemed 50% responsible.

ASSESSMENT: COMMUNITY LIABILITY V STATE LIABILITY UNDER *FRANCOVICH*

The Court's rules in respect of compensation for damage suffered as a result of the Community's wrongful acts or omissions should be assessed, as are the remedies provided by national courts, in the light of the effectiveness principle. As Advocate-General Jacobs suggested (at para. 33) in *Extramet v Council* (case 358/89), the obligations of the European Convention on Human Rights (Articles 6 and 13) and the laws of member states support the existence of the right to an effective remedy as a general principle of law. Thus the remedies provided under Community law should be interpreted to give effect to that principle. However, the question of whether the Community's rules on non-contractual liability provide effective judicial protection for individuals cannot be assessed in isolation. It must be considered in the light of the whole network of remedies provided by the treaty against unlawful Community action.

Despite the impact of Community regulation, particularly in the economic field, on individual's lives, it is extremely hard to obtain damages from the Community for losses, even significant losses, resulting from unlawful legislative acts. Even if the applicant succeeds in discharging the heavy *Schöppenstedt* burden damages may be denied or reduced on the grounds of causation, or because the damage alleged was not sufficiently clear and certain. Given that the damage resulting from unlawful legislative acts is normally economic, and 'indeterminate in amount, time and class', the Court's desire to limit the scope of the Community's liability is understandable. Such considerations have influenced the English courts' approach to questions of duty of care in negligence, both in respect of economic losses and the liability of public bodies. Member states such as France, which lack a concept of duty, contain liability by stricter rules of causation and remoteness. These rules have clearly influenced the Court of Justice.

In rejecting a claim for damages under Article 215(2) the Court has often pointed out that the applicant is not without a remedy. In the *Isoglucose* cases (cases 116, 124 and 143/77) it suggested that where a person suffers damage as a result of an unlawful Community act, he can challenge that measure before his national court and seek a ruling on its validity under Article 177: the existence of such an action was in itself sufficient to ensure the effective protection of the individual concerned. Not all would agree. Unless rapid and effective *interim* relief is available, a national court may not provide effective protection, hence the crucial importance of such relief (noted in Chapters 6 and 7). Once damage has occurred compensation becomes the only effective remedy. If that damage is attributable to the Community, unless the claim is for the return of money unlawfully paid, the only available claim is before the Court of Justice.

The Court has also pointed to the existence of effective alternative remedies in the converse situation. In rejecting a claim for judicial review under Article 173, for lack of standing, or withholding interim protection, the Court has averted to the existence of a claim under Article 215(2). But as was demonstrated by *Roquette Frères* v *Commission* (case 20/88) and the *Isoglucose* cases (cases 116, 124 and 143/77), even when a Community act has been found unlawful and caused extensive damage, compensation may not be available. Whilst those engaged in business activities may be expected to foresee and guard against the risks 'normally inherent' in their business, it is questionable whether they should be denied a remedy in damages when they suffer special or exceptional losses as a result of Community acts found to be unlawful. Indeed there is a case here for strict liability. As with claims before national courts, the best shield against claims for damages from the Community is rapid and effective interim relief from the Court of Justice under Articles 173 or 215(2) (noted in Chapter 9).

A question which has been raised, and which will be of growing importance over the next few years, is the relevance of Community rules relating to non-contractual liability to claims against member states under *Francovich* v *Italian State* (cases 6 and 9/90). Although the Court suggested in *Francovich* (at para. 42) that national courts must decide such claims 'within the context of national law on liability' the divergence of national rules, and the novelty of such an action, which includes liability for wrongful statutory measures, cries out for new and uniform Community rules. A start will be made when the Court responds to questions submitted by the Bundesfinanzhof in *Brasserie du Pêcheur* (case C 46/93) and the English High Court in *Factortame (No. 3)* (case 48/93). These cases raised questions concerning the fault and damage requirements appropriate to a claim under *Francovich* (see Chapter 5). To what extent will, or should, these rules be modelled on the principles of Community liability outlined above?

Clearly there are close parallels between the two actions. Both concern the liability of public bodies for legislative or administrative acts. Both concern liability for, in the main, economic loss. In both cases policy favours some restriction on liability. The public purse has to be protected against excessive claims. In *Zuckerfabrik Süderdithmarschen* (cases C 143/88 and C 92/89), the Court, arguing for the provision by national courts of interim relief on the same basis as its own powers under Article 185, spoke (at para. 18) of the need to maintain the 'coherence of the system of legal protection' in matters relating to EC law. Thus there is much to be said for basing states' liability under *Francovich* on similar principles to those applicable to claims against the Community under Article 215(2).

However, this does not mean that states can shelter behind the *Schöppenstedt* formula. Member states' obligation to comply with Community law, whether in the implementation of Directives or simply in their duty to observe Community law, does not concern 'legislative acts involving choices of economic policy'. Their duty to comply with Community law is absolute. Where they have a discretion, for example in the choice of 'form and methods' of implementation, or even in matters of substance, they cannot be liable under *Francovich* unless they act outside that discretion and in a manner contrary to the objectives of Community law. A failure by a member state to implement or even observe Community law is, as Advocate-General Mischo pointed out (at para. 47) in *Francovich* (cases 6 and 9/90) not a legislative act but rather in the nature of an administrative act. Thus the appropriate standard is surely the standard applicable to wrongful administrative acts and omissions, namely the simple 'fault' standard. Although what is meant by fault in this context is unclear it is submitted that liability under Article 215(2) for a wrongful administrative act is not strict. Because Community law, and the precise nature of Community obligations are often not clear, at least until the Court of Justice has ruled on the matter, and because of the sensitive nature of the claim, raising delicate constituional issues for national courts, it may be argued that member states' liability under *Francovich* should likewise not be strict. It remains to be seen whether the Court takes a different view in *Brasserie du Pêcheur* (case C 46/93).

On the questions of damage and causation there is also a strong case for uniform rules. As noted above, there is a clear difference between the English rules on causation and remoteness, which, once the duty problem is overcome, tend to be generous, and the rules of other member states. Given that damage resulting from breaches of EC law will often be economic, clearly some control over states' liability under *Francovich* will be required. This can be achieved, as it is under Article 215(2), by the rules governing damage and causation. The need for such control, and its extent, will depend on the degree (or absence) of fault required for liability. Hopefully all these matters will be addressed and clarified in *Brasserie du Pêcheur* (case C 46/93) and *Factortame (No. 3)* (case 48/93).

JURISDICTIONAL PROBLEMS: NATIONAL COURT OR COMMUNITY COURT?

Since much Community law, particularly in the field of economic regulation, for example under the CAP or CCT, is implemented by national authorities, damage resulting from unlawful Community acts is often inflicted through the acts (or omissions) of those authorities. Levies may be imposed, and benefits in the form of grants or subsidies withheld, in good faith, pursuant to the Community's unlawful acts. Consequential damage may be suffered. When this occurs it may not be clear which authority, national or Community, should be sued.

As was noted at the beginning of this chapter, the Community's non-contractual liability is expressed in Articles 178 and 215(2) in terms of 'compensation' for 'damage'. This implies a remedy in the nature of a claim in tort. But damages, as discussed in Chapter 7, can be compensatory, based on a wrong done to the plaintiff, or restitutionary, founded on the principle of unjust enrichment. Restitutionary and compensatory claims may be mixed. In actions for damages against the Community the court has not explicitly distinguished between the two. But where the claim is in fact restitutionary, for money paid to a national authority, albeit pursuant to an invalid EC measure, the Court of Justice has pressed claimants to take action for the recovery of that money from that national authority before their national courts. Indeed, the Court has rejected claims for restitution under Article 215(2) on the grounds that the applicant has not 'exhausted his rights' before his national court (*Firma E Kampffmeyer* v *Commission* (cases 5, 7 and 13–24/66); *Haegeman* v *Commission* (case 96/71)). Whilst this can be justified on restitutionary principles when the money paid remains in the hands of the *national* authorities, as in *Kampffmeyer*, it is less understandable when the money received has been paid into *Community* funds, as was the case in *Haegeman*, or where a claim against the Community for compensatory damages for losses flowing from the invalid Community measure is attached (see e.g., *Kampffmeyer*). The Court has also on occasions insisted that a claim for money *withheld* by national authorities as a result of an invalid EC measure must be made before the claimant's national court (*IBC* v *Commission* (case 46/75); *Lesieur Costelle* v *Commission* (cases 67–85/75)), although it has admitted some such claims under Article 215(2),

(*Holtz* v *Willemsen GmbH* v *Commission* (case 153/73); *CNTA SA* v *Commission* (case 74/74)). Thus the case law is conflicting and confusing, seemingly driven by the Court's desire to limit the Community's workload and liability where an effective remedy can be obtained before the claimant's national court.

Herein lies the problem. Whilst the Court has declared consistently that it will admit a claim for damages where an effective remedy cannot be obtained from a national court (*Roquette Frères* v *Commission* (case 20/88)), this does not help a claimant when the question of whether he can obtain such a remedy is uncertain. Whilst a claim for restitution for money paid to, and retained by, the national authority is likely to be successful on normal restitutionary principles, where the funds have passed into Community hands a claim for restitution against the relevant national authority could in principle be refused. Likewise a claim for money withheld by national authorities on the basis of an unlawful Community act, unless sums have been received from the Community for that purpose. If national authorites are to be held responsible for the payment of such sums (and national courts would appear to be an appropriate forum for such claims) when the *Community* has been unjustly enriched, arguably the relevant Community institution(s) should be required either to indemnify that authority or be joined in the domestic proceedings. This has not so far occurred. Meanwhile, where the prospects of success before national courts are uncertain, the Court of Justice should be persuaded to admit such claims under Article 215(2), as it has done on occasions, at least in respect of sums unlawfully withheld (*Compagnie d'Approvisionnement* v *Commission* (cases 9 and 11/71); *Merkur-Aussenhandels GmbH* v *Commission* (case 43/72); *Holtz & Willemsen GmbH* v *Council & Commission* (case 153/73)). Where a claim for the return or payment of money held by the Community is attached to a claim for compensation against the Community, the action *must* be admitted under Article 215(2), since a national authority cannot be held responsible for the Community's wrong. Where it is the Community's wrongful act which has caused its own unjust enrichment, or caused damage to the applicant, it should, in logic and in principle, be answerable, even though the damage may have been inflicted by a national authority acting (or failing to act) pursuant to obligations of Community law. Conversely, when the fault lies at the national authority's door, that authority should be liable (*Société des Grands Moulins des Antilles* v *Commission* (case 99/74)).

The case of *Krohn & Co. Import-Export GmbH & Co.* v *Commission* (case 175/84) provides an excellent illustration of the relationship between national and Community remedies and the correct approach to Article 215(2). Krohn was an importer seeking compensation for financial losses suffered as a result of the German authorities' refusal to grant the company licences to import manioc from Thailand. In rejecting Krohn's application the authorities were acting on mandatory instructions from the Commission. Krohn brought an action before the German courts seeking an annulment of the authorities' decision and an injunction requiring it to issue the licences. Krohn also brought an action against the Commission under Article 215(2) for compensation for losses suffered as a result of its action in denying the company the licences. The Commission argued that the action under Article 215(2) was inadmissible on the grounds that

(a)   the refusal of the licence came from the national authority;

(b)   the applicant should have exhausted his remedies before his national courts; and

(c)   to admit liability would be equivalent to nullfying the Commission's decison, which the applicant had failed to challenge in time.

All three arguments were rejected by the Court.

With regard to (a), the Court found that although the refusal emanated from the national authority, the unlawful conduct was to be attributed not to the German authorities but to the Community. The Commission was the 'true author' of the decision.

With regard to (b) the Court held that whilst admissibility may depend on the national remedies available to obtain the annulment of the decision, that would only be the case where national rights of action provide an *effective* means of protection for the individual concerned and are capable of resulting in compensation for the damage alleged. Since the alleged wrong had been been committed by the Community, only the Community could be liable in respect of this damage.

The argument based on (c) was clearly wrong, on the principle that an action under Article 215(2) was an 'independent action with a particular purpose to fulfil'.

Thus, where an individual has suffered damage, and the Community is the 'true author' of the decision causing the damage, the only effective remedy is before the Court of Justice under Article 215(2). But since damages against the Community are awarded rarely, and sparingly, particularly when the damage emanates from a wrongful legislative act, the best policy is to prevent damage occurring, either through action before national courts or through action before the Court of Justice under Articles 173, 184, 175 or 215(2). Both national and Community courts have the power to order interim relief. In both cases relief can be speedy. In *Commission* v *Ireland: Re Dundalk Water Scheme* ((case 45/87R), Article 169 proceedings) an interim injunction was granted by the Court of Justice ex parte within three days of application. The crucial question is whether the courts, national or Community, will be prepared to grant such relief, and if they do, or do not, whether they will provide protection by way of cross-undertakings or a deposit of security to the disappointed party. This may be the only way in which an individual with a genuine and viable claim against the Community may be protected.

PART FOUR

Informal routes to enforcement

ELEVEN

Complaints and interventions

Chapters 1 to 10 have been concerned with the ways in which and the principles on which Community rights may be protected, and obligations challenged, in formal legal proceedings. Whether the action is before a national court, perhaps with reference to the Court of Justice under Article 177, or directly before the Court of Justice, proceedings will be lengthy and expensive for individual litigants. Although legal aid may be available in actions before domestic courts, and where it is it will extend to costs incurred in Article 177 references, legal aid thresholds in all member states are low. Also, although under Article 76 of the Rules of Procedure of the Court of Justice 'a party who is wholly or in part unable to meet the costs of the proceedings may at any time apply for legal aid', a study published in 1988 revealed that out of 6001 cases brought before the Court up to 31 March 1988 less than one per cent of cases had given rise to an application for legal aid. The majority of successful applications concerned disputes between the Community and its servants under Article 179 EC ('Paying the Piper: Legal Aid proceedings before the Court of Justice', Kennedy, T., (1988) 25 CMLRev 559).

It is important, therefore, to consider other, less formal means by which infringements of Community law, whether by member states, Community institutions or even individuals, may be established, so that individuals may be able to enjoy their Community rights and avoid their obligations without the need themselves to institute court proceedings. Depending on the nature of the infringement this may be achieved by complaints to the Commission, or the European Parliament, or the EC Ombudsman (to be appointed by Parliament under Article 138e EC), or the authorities of member states. A complaint to the appropriate institution, if genuine and not devoid of merit, will normally prompt an investigation, which may result in an informal settlement, or action against the offending parties, or even court proceedings by the institution concerned. Where an institution institutes legal proceedings before the Court of Justice as a result of a complaint, interim relief may be granted pursuant to Articles 185 or 186 EC and Articles 83-89 of the Rules of Procedure 1991 (see Chapter 9). In *Commission* v *Ireland: Re Dundalk Water Scheme* (case 45/87R), following a complaint from potential tenderers excluded from tendering under the Dundalk Scheme, some conditions of which were subsequently found in breach of Article 30 EC, an interim injunction was granted ex parte in Article 169 proceedings within three days of application. Although interim relief can only be granted by the Court in the context of 'proceedings before the Court' (Article 83(1), Rules of Procedure), the Court has held that since interim relief may be necessary to ensure the effective enforcement of Community rules, the Commission may also order interim measures, according to the same principles as apply to Articles 185 and 186, when acting under Regulation 17/62 to enforce EC competition law (*Camera Care Ltd* v *Commission* (case 792/79R)). This power could be extended to other areas where the Commission is required to act to enforce Community rules (see comment by A-G Tesauro in *R* v *Secretary of State for Transport ex parte Factortame (No. 2)* (case C 213/89)). Thus, in an appropriate case, the informal complaints mechanism can be extremely effective, both in protecting individuals' Community rights and preventing, or bringing to an end, breaches of Community law. Although complaints by single individuals have been sufficient to trigger effective action by the Commission (as they were in *Commission* v *Ireland: Re Dundalk Water Scheme*), such complaints will be all the more effective if they issue from representative organisations and associations, particularly (in the case of complaints to the EC institutions) where they operate from premises in Brussels or Strasbourg where they have ready access to the EC institutions.

COMPLAINT TO THE COMMISSION

Since it is the Commission's task to monitor the application of Community law, to 'ensure that the provisions of (the EC Treaty) and the measures taken by the EC institutions pursuant thereto are applied' (Article 155 EC), the principal avenue of complaint will be to the Commission, to the Directorate-General (DG) responsible for the area in which the infringement is alleged to occur (see Table 2 in the Appendix).

Infringements by Member States

If the complaint concerns a breach of Community law by a member state, and the Commission, following investigation, considers the allegation well founded, it may institute infringement proceedings against the state under Article 169 EC, for failure 'to fulfil an obligation under (the EC) Treaty'. The concept of 'failure' can embrace any failure on behalf of any agency of the state, central or local, executive, legislative or judicial, in respect of any binding obligation of Community law. This would include obligations arising from the EC Treaty and subsequent amending treaties; from international agreements entered into by the Community and third countries where the obligation lies within the sphere of Community competence; from EC Regulations,

Directives and Decisions and from decisions of the European Courts. It can include any wrongful act or omission, ranging from non-implementation to partial implementation to faulty implementation of Community law, or simply maintaining in force laws and practices which are incompatible with EC law. The responsibility of the state is engaged 'whatever the organ of the state whose action or inaction constitutes a failure, even if it concerns an institution which is constitutionally independent' (*Commission* v *Belgium* (case 77/69)). Although proceedings under Article 169 may result from the Commission's own enquiries, or from complaints from the European Parliament, complaints from the public provide an important source of information concerning breaches of Community law by member states. In 1992 1,185 out of a total of 1,545 suspected infringements came to light as a result of complaints from the public (10th Report on the Monitoring and Application of Community Law (1993) OJ C 233 30 August 1993).

Clearly not all complaints result in proceedings before the Court under Article 169. The Commission may decide that the complaint lacks substance, or is not worth pursuing, or is politically unwise. The dispute may be settled during the preliminary stages, or following the Commission's 'reasoned opinion', when the state concerned has had an opportunity to submit its observations. As the Court made clear in *Alfons Lütticke* v *Commission* (case 48/65) an individual complainant has no power to demand action by the Commission under Article 169, and no right to challenge the Commission's reasoned opinion if it refuses to act. The Commission has a complete discretion in these matters. Nevertheless, an informal settlement or reasoned opinion from the Commission may be sufficient to establish the complainant's rights and, where it establishes past failures, could provide a basis for a claim under *Francovich* (cases 6 and 9/90). Where the state fails to comply with the Commission's reasoned opinion and the Commission proceeds before the Court under Article 169 and obtains a judgment that the state has failed to fulfil its EC obligations, that judgment can clearly be invoked in any subsequent claim, whether by the complainant or others, based on EC law, including (depending on future decisions as to its scope) a claim for damages against the state under *Francovich*. A second judgment under Article 169, for failure to comply with the Court's judgment in earlier Article 169 proceedings, would undoubtedly give rise to a claim under *Francovich* (all other conditions being satisfied). Although the Court of Justice now has power in this second judgment to impose a lump sum or penalty payment on the offending state (Article 171 EC), it has no power to order the payment of compensation to parties suffering loss as a result of the state's unlawful action.

Infringements of EC law by member states may also be established by the Commission in special proceedings under Article 93(2) EC, in the context of the granting of state aids. If the Commission finds that aid granted by a state or through state resources is not compatible with the common market or is being misused, it can decide that the state concerned must abolish that aid. If the state concerned does not comply with its decision within the prescribed time, the Commission, or any other interested state, may refer the matter to the Court of Justice direct. Proceedings by the Commission under Article 93(2) have not infrequently resulted from complaints by interested parties such as rival traders prejudiced by the granting of state aid to their competitors (see *Irish Cement* v *Commission* (case 166/86). Moreover the Court has held that where the Commission issues a Decision concerning state aid, whether condemning or authorising such aid, persons such as complainants, 'whose position in the market is significantly affected' or whose 'legitimate interests' may be 'seriously jeopardised' by the aid which is the subject of the contested decision, were entitled to challenge that Decision under Article 173, it being of direct and individual concern to themselves (*Compagnie Française de l'Azote (COFAZ)* v *Commission* (case 169/84)). This applied even though they had not been given a specific right to complain or to be involved in the proceedings under Article 93(2), as is granted expressly to persons with a legitimate interest under EC competition law (see further below).

Infringements by Natural or Legal Persons

The Commission also has power under secondary legislation to act against breaches of Community law by individuals. It has extensive powers, including the power to fine, under Regulation 17/62, in the field of EC competition law. Its power to order interim measures to prevent breaches of EC competition law, affirmed by the Court in *Camera Care* v *Commission* (case 792/79R), has been noted above. It has powers to enforce EC anti-dumping rules under Regulation 2324/88, which include a power to impose anti-dumping duties, provisional and definitive, on the import of dumped products into the EC. A product is regarded as having been dumped 'if its export price to the Community is less than the normal value of the like product' (Article 2(2), Regulation 2324/88). In economic sectors subject to substantial Community regulation, such as the common organisation of the market under the common agricultural and fisheries policies, specific Regulations may give the Commission power to intervene by taking 'appropriate measures' to prevent 'serious disturbances'. Complaints to the Commission by interested parties may trigger action by the Commission in all these areas. In 1994 the Commission introduced a free 'hotline' service, (0800 963595 (UK); 0800 553295 (Ireland)), open 24 hours a day, to enable individuals to report information concerning suspected fraud.

Complainants are given a particular status and particular rights in EC competition and anti-dumping laws. Under Regulation 17/62, art. 3, individuals with a 'legitimate interest' are entitled to apply to the Commission to act against alleged infringements of Articles 85 and 86 of the EC Treaty. Complainants may be heard in the subsequent proceedings and, where the Commission intends to grant negative clearance or exemption, clearing or approving the impugned agreement, they are entitled to submit their observations (Regulation 17/62, art. 19). Where the Commission issues a Decision to another party as a result of a complaint the complainant is deemed to have individual (as well as direct) concern to challenge that Decision under Article 173 (see Chapter 9 and *Metro-SB-Grossmärkte GmbH & Co.* v *Commission* (case 26/76)). Similarly under Regulation 2324/88 'any natural or legal persons who consider themselves injured or threatened' by alleged practices in breach of EC anti-dumping rules are entitled to complain to the Commission, to obtain information, and, on their request, a hearing. They may also request an opportunity to meet other parties directly concerned in the investigation. If the Commission decides not to pursue a complaint, they must be informed of this decision and provided with a summary of the Commission's reasons. In *FEDIOL* v *Commission* (case 191/82), in proceedings for annulment of the Commission's decision not to institute anti-dumping proceedings following complaints by FEDIOL, the Court held that FEDIOL, as complainants, granted specific rights under the current EC Regulation (3017/79) were individually concerned in, and thus entitled to challenge, the Commission's Decision in Article 173 proceedings, in order to ensure that their procedural rights had been respected. Although a review of the Decision could not achieve the substantive result required by complainants, such action might be worth pursuing if the Commission's failure to observe their procedural rights would be likely to have affected the substance of the Commission's decision.

The effect of the Commission's Notice on Co-operation between National Courts and the Commission in Applying Articles 85 and 86 EC   In the field of competition law the scope for individual complaint under art. 3 of Regulation 17/62 may have been reduced by the Commission's Notice on Co-operation between National Courts and the Commission in Applying Articles 85 and 86 ((1993) OJ C 39/6). Here the Commission announced its intention in the future to concentrate its investigations into suspected breaches of EC competition law on cases of particular political, economic or legal significance for the Community. Complaints under art. 3 of Regulation 17/62 by parties with a 'legitimate interest' would henceforth not be sufficient to trigger an enquiry if the complainant could secure adequate protection for his rights through action before his national courts. Thus national courts were to be required to play an increasing role in the enforcement of EC competition law. Although it had been established unequivocally since 1974, in the case of *BRT* v *SABAM* (case 127/73) that Articles 85 and 86 were directly effective, many complainants had chosen to proceed against infringements of these Articles by complaint to the Commission under Regulation 17/62, leaving the Commission to shoulder the burden (and the cost) of the enquiry, rather than by pursuing an action before their national courts. As well as having extensive expertise in applying EC competition law, having itself developed the rules, the Commission had under Regulation 17/62 the powers and resources to undertake the investigations necessary to establish breaches of Articles 85 and 86, and to obtain information both from governments and competent authorities of member states and from undertakings and associations of undertakings. Moreover only the Commission was able to grant exemption for agreements prima facie in breach of art. 85, under art. 85(3), and only the Commission had the power to fine undertakings found to have acted in breach of Articles 85 and 86.

It remains to be seen what complaints under art. 3 of Regulation 17/62 will be rejected by the Commission as not raising issues of 'particular political, economic or legal significance' to warrant investigation by the Commission, and how it will assess whether the complainant will secure 'adequate protection' for his rights before his national courts in a particular case. It may be argued that any problem involving EC competition law which has not been dealt with by the Commission, or, in actions for annulment of the Commission's decisions on competition law, by the Court, would raise 'significant' issues. Where the issues have been dealt with, and the relevant principles of Community law have been established, national courts would seem to provide the appropriate forum to decide disputes involving EC competition law, a fortiori if damages were required to be obtained. Nevertheless, even if the Commission is not over-restrictive in its attitude to complaints under art. 3 of Regulation 17/62 and national courts are required only to apply established principles, national courts will still face problems in applying EC competition law. National courts, particularly those which are non-specialised and subject to an adversarial system as in the UK, are not well equipped to conduct the extensive fact-finding exercise necessary for an effective analysis of agreements and practices allegedly in breach of Articles 85 and 86, nor to undertake the difficult task of economic assessment involved in applying these articles.

The Commission suggested in its Notice a number of ways in which national courts might obtain assistance in applying EC competiton law. They might apply to the Commission for advice and information; they might be guided by informal decisions of the Commission regarding negative clearance (no breach of Article 85) or exemption (breach of Article 85(1) but agreement justified under Article 85(3)), known as 'comfort letters', and by Notices, spelling out the Commission's policy in respect of certain types of agreement. Such 'co-operation' betwen national courts and the Commission could be justified under their 'mutual duties of sincere co-operation', based, according to the Court in *Zwartveld* ((case C 2-88 Imm), see Chapter 4), on Article 5 EC. But as informal measures, issued outside the framework of Regulation 17/62, none of these forms of communication from the Commission would be strictly speaking legally binding. This was acknowledged by the Court in *SA Lancôme* v *Etos BV* (case 99/79), when it held that 'comfort letters', which are issued without extensive enquiry and without the procedural safeguards provided by Regulation 17/62, as purely 'administrative' letters cannot take away the power of national courts freely to apply Articles 85 and 86. Also, although national courts, in deciding matters of competiton law, are advised, indeed obliged to follow binding Decisions of the Commission and the Court, they are still not entitled in law to grant individual exemptions.

Thus the Commission's Notice on Co-operation between National Courts and the Commission in Applying Articles 85 and 86 has given rise to some uncertainty, both for national courts and for individuals. The procedure provided under art. 3 of Regulation 17/62 has been extremely effective in protecting individuals' rights under EC competition law and in bringing to light, for the benefit of the Community, significant breaches of Articles 85 and 86 EC. Thus it is to be hoped that individuals will not be deterred from complaining to the Commission, and that unless an alleged breach of EC law is clearly covered by established authority in the form of a binding Decision of the Commission or the Court, or binding legislative measures such as the Commission's block exemption Regulations, the Commission will not refuse as a matter of principle to admit a complaint by a person with a legitimate interest under art. 3 of Regulation 17/62. Indeed it may be argued that it is obliged in law not to do so.

COMPLAINTS TO THE EUROPEAN PARLIAMENT

Complaints concerning alleged unlawful action by member states or EC institutions may be channelled through the European Parliament, either via the complainant's MEP or, if the complaint comes from a representative body, to the appropriate Parliamentary Committee. A number of Article 169 actions have originated in complaints from Parliament, in many cases following information provided by the public. Although Parliament has no power to take legal action against member states and only limited power to act against Community institutions (see Chapter 9) it may exert influence on these bodies and publicise important issues by public debate.

In introducing the concept of Citizenship of the Union (Article 8 EC) the Maastricht Treaty gave citizens the right to petition Parliament (Article 8d). Under Article 138d

> any citizen of the Union and any natural or legal person residing or having its registered office in a Member State, shall have the right to address, individually or in association with other citizens or persons, a petition to the European Parliament on a matter which comes within the Community's fields of activity and which affects him, her or it directly.

Although the right to petiton Parliament has been available to individuals since 1977, it had no legal basis in primary Community law prior to 1992. Nevertheless the number of petitions rose from 20 in 1977/8 to 900 in 1992/3. The new Articles 8d and 138d can only accelerate this trend (see Epaminodidas, M., 'The Right to Petition the European Parliament after Maastricht' (1994) 19 EL Rev 169).

The Maastricht Treaty, in Article 138e, also provided for Parliament to appoint an ombudsman

> empowered to receive complaints from any citizen of the Union or any natural or legal person residing or having its registered office in a Member State concerning instances of maladministration in the activities of the Community institutions or bodies, with the exception of the Court of Justice and the Court of First Instance acting in their judicial role.

At the time of going to press no appointment had yet been made. Nevertheless when fully implemented these provisions will further strengthen the extra-judicial protection of individuals under Community law.

COMPLAINTS TO MEMBER STATES

Whether the complaint concerns action by another member state, a Community institution or an individual, a complaint by an individual to the appropriate national authority in the complainant's home state could be effective in establishing infringements of Community law.

Like the Commission under Article 169 a member state has the power under Article 170 to take action before the Court of Justice against another member state where it considers that that state has failed to fulfil an obligation under the EC Treaty (Article 170(1)). The procedure is similar to that of Article 169. The state must first bring the matter before the Commission. The Commission will then deliver a reasoned opinion after each of the states concerned has had an opportunity to submit its own case and its observations on the other party's case both orally or in writing.

If the Commission has not delivered an opinion within three months of the date on which the matter was brought before it, the absence of such opinion shall not prevent the matter from being brought before the Court of Justice' (Article 170(4)).

As with Article 169, if the Court finds that the member state has failed to fulfil an EC obligation, the state 'shall be required to take the necessary measures to comply with the judgment of the Court of Justice' (Article 171(1)). Further proceedings for failing to comply with this judgment can also now result in the imposition of lump sum or penalty payments (Article 171(4)).

Although few cases have reached the Court under Article 170 the procedure is capable of playing a useful part in the enforcement process. The Commission's reasoned opinion may be sufficient to clarify the situation and to establish the existence (or not) of an infringement. Where the Commission considers that a breach of community law by a member state has occurred it may itself proceed against that state under Article 169.

In addition to their powers under Article 170, member states, as 'privileged applicants' under Articles 173 and 175, have a general right to bring proceedings under these Articles. Thus acts or omissions of the EC institutions affecting individuals can be challenged in situations in which individuals would have had no standing to act, for example to challenge Regulations.

Member states also have a general right to intervene in 'cases before the Court' (Article 37, Protocol on the Statute of the Court). They are informed of references to the Court under Article 177 and are entitled to submit written observations to the Court within two months of a case being notified (Article 20, Protocol on the Statute of the Court). Submissions made in an application to intervene must be limited to supporting the submissions of one of the parties (Article 37, Protocol on the Statute of the Court).

States have no power under Community law to act against natural or legal persons. However a complaint by a national authority to the Commission, for example concerning a suspected breach of EC competition law, would clearly carry greater weight than a complaint by individual undertakings.

Although a state is not likely to act on single complaints, or on matters in which it has no interest, it could be persuaded to act where the interest of the state, economic or otherwise, was engaged. Such might be the case where another state's failure to comply with Community law resulted in a competitive advantage to that state, or where a Community measure, of doubtful legality, was seen to operate against national or sectoral interests. Thus it is particularly important for individuals to channel their complaints, whether against states, or Community institutions, or individuals, through representative associations or bodies, and for those bodies to alert national authorities of suspected breaches of Community law and, where appropriate, persuade them of the need for action. Both states and representative organisations should keep a watchful eye on Article 177 proceedings. Where a case is likely to raise important issues of national or sectoral interest the state should be urged to intervene. Intervention may be effective in persuading the court to limit the effects of its rulings, as it was in *Defrenne* v *Sabena (No. 2)* ((case 43/75), see Chapter 4).

INTERVENTION BY NATURAL OR LEGAL PERSONS

Any ... person establishing an interest in the result of any case submitted to the Court, save in cases between member states, between institutions of the Community or between member states and institutions of the Community

is entitled to intervene in cases before the court' (Article 37, Protocol on the Statute of the Court).

This provision could be used to advantage by interested representative groups in proceedings under Article 177 or in challenges to Community acts by natural or legal persons under Article 173.

POSTSCRIPT
A look to the future

There is no doubt that questions of enforcement of Community law by national courts will be a principal concern of legal practitioners as well as academics in the 1990s. As Curtin has said (Curtin, D. and O'Keefe, D., *Constitutional Adjudication in European Community and National Law* (1992))

> It will be surprising, when the extent of the Court's involvement in shaping national remedies and creating a Community remedy filters through to national lawyers and judges, if we do not witness over the coming decade a cascade of challenges to the national laws of remedies and procedures on grounds of incompatibility with Community law.

Whilst the momentum of Community law-making may have slowed following Maastricht in deference to the new principle of subsidiarity, the need for effective enforcement of Community law has not diminished. Community solidarity depends above all on the uniform observance of Community law by all member states, a fortiori in periods of recession and uncertainty, when national rivalries and protectionist instincts threaten to emerge.

Although the fundamental principles of direct effect and supremacy of Community law were laid down in the 1960s and developed in the 1970s they did not prove adequate in themselves to protect individuals' Community rights or to deter member states from breaching Community law. Thus the last decade has seen a determined effort on the part of the Court of Justice to increase the effective enforcement of Community law by extending the scope for its enforcement by individuals before their national courts, culminating in the landmark decision of *Francovich* v *Italian State* (cases C 6 and 9/90). Here the Court finally found a means of overcoming the problem of (non) enforcement of Directives against private parties, or against bodies whose 'public' status, for the purposes of enforcement of Directives, was doubtful, by establishing a remedy in damages directly against the state. Arguably a remedy against the state could be regarded as the more appropriate remedy, since it is only when the state has failed to comply fully with its Community obligations that it is necessary for individuals to resort, directly or indirectly, to Community law. The principles of direct and indirect effect were never more than expedients, designed to enforce Community law and secure legal protection for individuals' Community rights in the individual case. The primary responsibility for ensuring that domestic law was in conformity with EC law always lay with the state.

With a few exceptions the UK courts have responded well to the demands of Community law, as have those of other member states. With the aid and under the shelter of the Article 177 procedure our courts have accommodated the principles of direct effects and supremacy of EC law as well as the newer principles concerning the provision of remedies. Indeed, there are signs that they have positively welcomed the effectiveness principle as providing an opportunity to remedy deficiencies in national law, particularly, but by no means exclusively, in the public law field. Reforms introduced in the Community context will also strengthen the judicial protection of individuals in matters of purely domestic law. The House of Lords has indicated that it will not contemplate a double standard (see comment by Lord Goff in *Woolwich Building Society* v *IRC* [1992] 3 All ER 737 at p. 764, cited in Chapter 7).

Difficulties faced by national courts over the application of the principle of indirect effect will lose their significance now that an alternative, arguably more legitimate, remedy is available under *Francovich* v *Italian State* (cases 6 and 9/90). It is possible that claims under *Francovich* will eventually replace actions based on the principle of indirect effect and even those based on direct effects where the opponent's 'public' status is doubtful. However, the scope of *Francovich* is uncertain, and its application by national courts not yet guaranteed. Until the law is clarified claimants will be wise, except in the clearest case, to pursue their claims under the tried principles of direct and indirect effect as well as under *Francovich*.

The extent of the problems raised by *Francovich* will depend on the Court of Justice's answers to the questions referred in *Brasserie du Pêcheur* (case C 46/93) and *Factortame (No. 3)* (case 48/93) (see Chapters 2 and 5). If the principles of state liability are cautiously defined, and liability is found not to be strict, it should be possible for national courts to adapt existing national remedies to give effect to *Francovich*, as suggested in Chapters 6 and 7. If the Court of Justice attempts to establish a broad basis of liability, not based on fault, it runs the risk of non-compliance, even defiance, by national courts. In most member states the impugning of Acts of Parliament, even if only to establish their incompatibility with Community law, is a serious step. The House of Lords was prepared to take this step in *EOC* v *Secretary of State for Employment* [1994] 1 All ER 910, in the context of a claim for a declaration, when the breach of Community law was relatively clear. It is less certain that our courts, or the courts of other member states, will be willing to hold the state liable in damages, unlimited in time, extent and class, in a situation in which the breach of Community law, whether in the form of primary or secondary legislation, or even administrative act, was not at the relevant time at least reasonably clear.

The Court of Justice has not hesitated to limit the Community's liability in damages under Article 215(2). Both in the interests of good administration, and in order to protect the Community against excessive liability, it has imposed a heavy burden on plaintiffs, requiring proof of a high degree of culpability on the part of the defendant institutions, when claiming for losses suffered as a result of unlawful legislative acts involving choices of economic policy. Its rules on causation and damages, which apply to *all* claims for damages, are equally restrictive. Whilst a claim under *Francovich* is not analogous to a claim subject to the strict *Schöppenstedt* rules, a breach of Community law by a member state not being a matter involving 'choices of economic policy', the remedy raises similar concerns for the administration and is subject to a similar risk of unlimited liability. Given the imprecise nature of much EC law, even secondary legislation, the precise scope of member states' obligations under Community law is often unclear. Whilst states should be liable for knowing breaches of Community law, and even for those of which they should have been aware, to hold them liable, retrospectively, for breaches of Community law which were not at the relevant time reasonably clear, would surely breach the fundamental principle of legal certainty. Arguably they should not be liable unless the breach has been established in Article 169 or Article 177 proceedings, or, borrowing from CILFIT (case 283/81) and the European concept of acte clair, the breach is 'so obvious as to leave no room for reasonable doubt' (see Chapter 4).

Whatever the standard adopted, it is essential that *all* the rules for the application of *Francovich*, a remedy with such a potential impact on member states, are clear and uniformly applied throughout the Community. This will not occur if cases are to be decided, as the Court suggested in *Francovich*, on the basis of national rules on liability, or if Community rules are to be developed haphazardly, under the pressures and subject to the limitations of Article 177 proceedings. Thus it is to be hoped that the threat of liability under *Francovich*, and the disparity in national laws governing state liability will persuade member states, working within the EC institutional framework, to create a coherent, fair and harmonised system of rules for its application. The question of justification for restrictions on liability, admitted in claims against the Community, also needs to be addressed.

The application of *Emmott v Minister for Social Welfare* (case C 208/90) will also raise problems for national courts. The scope of the ruling, particularly after *Steenhorst-Neerings* (case C 338/91), remains unclear. Whilst national courts will have little difficulty in applying *Emmott* and extending the time from which national limitation rules begin to run when the state has clearly and culpably failed to fulfil its obligations, whether in respect of Directives, as in *Emmott*, or otherwise, they may be reluctant to do so where this will result in exposing innocent 'public' parties to extensive retrospective liability. This too could be seen as breaching the principle of legal certainty. In view of the difficulty of ascertaining the precise nature of some Community obligations, arguably a procedure should be provided whereby states, in implementing Community law, could obtain an advisory opinion from the Commission in order to assess, prior to enactment, whether proposed national measures are compatible with EC law. Such a procedure could be justified on the basis of member states and the Commission's 'mutual duties of sincere co-operation' under Article 5 EC (*Zwartveld* (case C 2/88 Imm)). A similar procedure has been advocated in the UK domestic context for matters of public law (Laws, Sir John, 'Judicial Remedies and the Constitution' (1994) 57 MLR 213). Whilst such approval could not prevent the Court from finding, in a subsequent ruling, that the measures were incompatible with Community law, it could serve to protect member states against liability under *Francovich* (and public bodies under *Emmott*), at least until they had time to discover and rectify the breach.

The need to work towards greater harmonisation of national legal systems, particularly in respect of remedies and procedures, is not confined to claims based on *Francovich* or *Emmott*. Nor is it driven solely by the demands of EC law. As Koopmans T has pointed out (Koopmans, T., 'European Public Law, Reality and Prospects (1991) PL 53 at p. 63)

> by looking at what actually happens we can see that a system of European Public law is progressively taking shape. By reflecting on its course we can discover that this system will continue to develop. It should do for the sake of peace among European nations: but also because the growing internationalisation of society must be submitted to the rule of law . . . The evolution of one system of law is a necessity.

These comments need not be confined to matters of public law. Membership of the Community provides the opportunity and the incentive for the judicial authorities of member states to pool their expertise and experience and, drawing on common principles and the best practices in all member states, to devise a system of law tailored to the needs of the twenty-first century. There is provision for such co-operation in the Treaty on European Union 1992 (Article K). Meanwhile the Court of Justice will continue to play its part in creating a 'coherent system of legal protection' in the European Community. Hopefully it will bear in mind, as it has in the past, that such a system calls for similar principles, and similar standards of protection, not only in the national courts of the member states, in respect of infringements of Community law by member states and individuals, but also in claims based on unlawful acts and omissions of the EC institutions, before the European Courts.

APPENDIX

TABLE ONE

Index of Community Activities
Official Journal (L) Series:
Directory of Community legislation
in force

The analytical structure of the register is based on a decimal-type subdivision with the following 20 chapters:

01.	General, financial and institutional matters.
02.	Customs union and free movement of goods.
03.	Agriculture.
04.	Fisheries.
05.	Freedom of movement for workers and social policy.
06.	Right of establishment and freedom to provide services.
07.	Transport policy.
08.	Competition policy.
09.	Taxation.
10.	Economic and monetary policy and free movement of capital.
11.	External relations.
12.	Energy.
13.	Industrial policy and internal market.
14.	Regional policy and co-ordination of structural instruments.
15.	Environment, consumers and health protection.
16.	Science, information, education and culture.
17.	Law relating to undertakings.
18.	Common, foreign and security policy.
19.	Co-operation in the fields of justice and home affairs.
20.	People's Europe.

TABLE TWO

Directorates-General EC Commission

DG I.	External Economic Relations
DG IA.	External Political Relations
TFE.	Enlargement Task Force
DG II.	Economic and Financial Affairs
DG III.	Industry
DG IV.	Competition
DG V.	Employment, Industrial Relations and Social Affairs
DG VI.	Agriculture
	Veterinary and Phytosanitary Office
DG VII.	Transport
DG VIII.	Development
DG IX.	Personnel and Administration
DG X.	Audiovisual Media, Information, Communication and Cultural
DG XI.	Environment, Nuclear Safety and Civil Protection
DG XII.	Science, Research and Development
	Joint Research Centre
DG XIII.	Telecommuications, Information Market and Exploitation of Research
DG XIV.	Fisheries
DG XV.	Internal Market and Financial Services
DG XVI.	Regional Policies
DG XVII.	Energy
DG XVIII.	Credit and Investment
DG XIX.	Budgets
DG XX.	Financial Control
DG XXI.	Customs and Indirect Taxation
DG XXIII.	Enterprise Policy, Distributive Trades, Tourism and Co-operatives

TABLE THREE

Preamble to Directive 76/207

COUNCIL DIRECTIVE

of 9 February 1976

on the implementation of the principle of equal treatment for men and women as regards access to employment, vocational training and promotion, and working conditions

(76/207/EEC)

THE COUNCIL OF THE EUROPEAN COMMUNITIES,

Having regard to the Treaty establishing the European Economic Community, and in particular Article 235 thereof,

Having regard to the proposal from the Commission,

Having regard to the opinion of the European Parliament([1]),

Having regard to the opinion of the Economic and Social Committee([2]),

Whereas the Council, in its resolution of 21 January 1974 concerning a social action programme([3]), included among the priorities action for the purpose of achieving equality between men and women as regards access to employment and vocational training and promotion and as regards working conditions, including pay;

Whereas, with regard to pay, the Council adopted on 10 February 1975 Directive 75/117/EEC on the approximation of the laws of the Member States relating to the application of the principle of equal pay for men and women([4]);

Whereas Community action to achieve the principle of equal treatment for men and women in respect of access to employment and vocational training and promotion and in respect of other working conditions also appears to be necessary; whereas, equal treatment for male and female workers constitutes one of the objectives of the Community, in so far as the harmonization of living and working conditions while maintaining their improvement are *inter alia* to be furthered; whereas the Treaty does not confer the necessary specific powers for this purpose;

Whereas the definition and progressive implementation of the principle of equal treatment in matters of social security should be ensured by means of subsequent instruments . . .

(¹) OJ No C 111, 20. 5. 1975, p. 14.
(²) OJ No C 286, 15. 12. 1975, p. 8.
(³) OJ No C 13, 12. 2. 1974, p. 1.
(⁴) OJ No. L 45, 19. 2. 1975, p. 19.

TABLE FOUR

European Communities Act 1972

SCHEDULE 1

'Community instrument' means any instrument issued by a Community institution.

'Community obligation' means any obligation created or arising by or under the Treaties, whether an enforceable Community obligation or not.

'Enforceable Community right' and similar expressions shall be construed in accordance with section 2(1) of this Act.

'Entry date' means the date on which the United Kingdom becomes a member of the Communities.

'European Court' means the Court of Justice of the European Communities.

'Member', in the expression "member State", refers to membership of the Communities

Section 2   SCHEDULE 2

PROVISION AS TO SUBORDINATE LEGISLATION

1.—(1)   The powers conferred by section 2(2) of this Act to make provision for the purposes mentioned in section 2(2)(a) and (b) shall not include power—

  (a)   to make any provision imposing or increasing taxation; or

  (b)   to make any provision taking effect from a date earlier than that of the making of the instrument containing the provision; or

  (c)   to confer any power to legislate by means of orders, rules, regulations or other subordinate instrument, other than rules of procedure for any court or tribunal; or

(d)   to create any new criminal offence punishable with imprisonment for more than two years or punishable on summary conviction with imprisonment for more than three months or with a fine of more than £400 (if not calculated on a daily basis) or with a fine of more than £5 a day.

(2)   Sub-paragraph (1)(c) above shall not be taken to preclude the modification of a power to legislate conferred otherwise than under section 2(2), or the extension of any such power to purposes of the like nature as those for which it was conferred; and a power to give directions as to matters of administration is not to be regarded as a power to legislate within the meaning of sub-paragraph (1)(c).

2.—(1)   Subject to paragraph 3 below, where a provision contained in any section of this Act confers power to make regulations (otherwise than by modification or extension of an existing power), the power shall be exercisable by statutory instrument.

(2)   Any statutory instrument containing an Order in Council or regulations made in the exercise of a power so conferred, if made without a draft having been approved by resolution of each House of Parliament, shall be subject to annulment in pursuance of a resolution of either House.

3.   Nothing in paragraph 2 above shall apply to any Order in Council made by the Governor of Northern Ireland or to any regulations made by a Minister or department of the Government of Northern Ireland; but where a provision contained in any section of this Act confers power to make such an Order in Council or regulations, then any Order in Council or regulations made in the exercise of that power, if made without a draft having been approved by resolution of each House of the Parliament of Northern Ireland, shall be subject to negative resolution within the meaning of section 41(6) of the Interpretation Act (Northern Ireland) 1954 as if the Order or regulations were a statutory instrument within the meaning of that Act.

Selected bibliography

GENERAL TEXTS

Arrowsmith, S., *Remedies for Enforcing the Public Procurement Rules* (Earlsgate Press, 1993).

Birks, P., *Restitution. The Future* (Sydney: Federation Press, 1992).

Brown, N. & Jacobs, F., *The Court of Justice of the European Community*, 4th edn (London: Sweet & Maxwell, 1994).

Burrows, A., *The Law of Restitution* (London: Butterworths, 1993).

Collins, L., *European Community Law in the United Kingdom*, 4th edn (London: Butterworths, 1990).

Goff & Jones, *Law of Restitution*, 4th ed. (London: Sweet & Maxwell, 1993).

Hartley, T., *The Foundations of European Community Law*, 3rd edn (Oxford: Clarendon Press, 1994).

Lasok, D. & Bridge, J., *Law and Institutions of the European Communities* (London: Butterworths, 1989).

Lewis, C., *Remedies in Judicial Review* (London: Sweet & Maxwell, 1992).

Markesinis, B. S., (ed.) *The Gradual Convergence* (Oxford: Oxford University Press).

Rasmussen, H., *On Law and Policy in the European Court of Justice* (Dordrecht: Martinus Nijhoff, 1986).

Schermers, H. G. & Waelbroek, D., *Judicial Protection in the European Communities*, 5th ed. (London: Kluwer Law & Taxation Publishers, 1992).

Schwartze, J., *European Administrative Law* (London: Sweet & Maxwell, 1992).

Sharpston, E., *Interim and Substantive Relief in Claims under Community Law* (London: Butterworths, 1993).

Steiner, J., *Textbook on EC Law*, 4th ed. (London: Blackstone Press, 1994).

Supperstone & Goudie, *Judicial Review* (London: Butterworths, 1992).

Weatherill, S. & Beaumont, P., *EC Law* (London: Penguin, 1993).

ARTICLES, REPORTS, NOTES

Alder, J., 'Hunting the Chimera — the end of *O'Reilly* v *Mackman*' (1993) 13 *Legal Studies* 183.

Arrowsmith, S., 'Enforcing the EC Public Procurement Rules: the Remedies System in England and Wales' [1992] PPLR 92.

Barav, A. & Green, N., 'Damages in the Natonal Courts for Breach of Community Law' [1986] YEL 55.

Barav, A., 'Damages in the Domestic Courts for Breaches of Community Law by Public Authorities', Chapter 11 'Non-Contractual Liability of the European Communities' Ed Schermers, Heukel & Mead, Martinus Nijhoff Publications, 1988.

Barav, A., 'Enforcement of Community Rights in the National Courts: the Case for Jurisdiction to grant an Interim Relief' (1989) 26 CML Rev 369.

Beatson, J., 'Public and Private in English Administrative Law' (1987) 103 LQR 34.

Beatson, J., 'Restitution of Taxes, Levies and other Imposts: Defining the Extent of the Woolwich Principle' (1993) 109 LQR 401.

Bebr on *Francovich* v *Italian State* (1992) 29 CML Rev 557.

Bingham, Sir T., 'There is a World Elsewhere': The Changing Perspectives of English Law' (1992) 41 ICLQ 513.

Boyron, 'Proportionality in English Administrative Law: A Faulty Transition' (1992) OXJLS 237.

Bridge, D., 'Procedural Aspects of the Enforcement of EC Law through the Legal Systems of the Member States' (1984) 9 EL Rev 28.

Bridges, L., 'The Reform of Judicial Review' (1993) December, *Legal Action Bulletin*, 7.

Bronckers, M., 'Private Enforcement of 1992' (1989) 26 CML Rev 513.

Browne Wilkinson, Sir N., 'The Infiltration of Bill of Rights' [1992] PL 397.

Carty, H., 'Intentional Violation of Economic Interests: the Limits of Common Law Liability' (1988) 104 LQR 258.

Coppell & O'Neill, 'The European Court of Justice: Taking Rights Seriously?' (1992) 29 CML Rev 669.

Curtin, D., 'The Province of Government; Delimiting the Direct Effect of Directives' (1990) 15 EL Rev 195.

Curtin, D., 'The Effectiveness of Judicial Protection of Individuals' Community Rights' (1990) 27 CML Rev 709.

Curtin, D., 'The Decentralised Enforcement of Community Law Rights. Judicial Snakes and Ladders', Chapter 5 'Constitutional Adjudication in European Community and National Law' Ed Curtin & O'Keefe, Butterworths, 1992.

Curtin, D., 'State Liability under Community Law: a New Remedy for Private Parties' (1992) 21 ILJ 74.

Curtin, D., on *Marshall* v *Southampton AHA (No. 2)* [1994] 31 CML Rev 631.

Davidson, J., 'Actions for Damages in the English Courts for Breach of EC Competition Law' (1985) 34 ICLQ 178.

De Burca, G., 'Giving Effect to European Community Directives' (1992) 55 MLR 215.

Epamonidas, M., 'The Right to Petition the European Parliament after Maastricht' (1994) 19 EL Rev 169.

Fitzpatrick, B., & Szyszczak, E., 'Remedies and Effective Judicial Protection in Community Law' (1994) 57 MLR 434.

Fredman, S., and Morris, G., 'The Costs of Exclusivity: Public and Private Re-examined [1994] PL 69.

Ganz, 'Compensaton for Negligent Administrative Action' [1973] PL 84.

Green, N. & Barav, A., 'Damages in the Natonal Courts for Breaches of Community Law' [1986] YEL 55.

Harlow, C., 'Public and Private Law: Definition without Distinction' (1980) 43 MLR 24.

Hepple, R. & Byre, A., 'EEC Labour Law in the United Kingdom: a New Approach' (1989) 18 ILJ 129.

Jacobs, F., 'Damages for Breach of Articles 85 and 86' Note on *Garden Cottage Foods* v *Milk Marketing Board* (1983) 8 EL Rev 353.

Jowell and Lester, A., 'Beyond Wednesbury; Substantive Principles of Administrative Law' [1987] PL 368.

Justice/All Souls Report 'Administrative Justice: Some Necessary Reforms' (1988).

Koopmans, T., 'European Public Law: Reality and Prospects' [1991] PL 53.

Koopmans, T., 'The Birth of European Law at the Crossroads of Legal Tradition (1991) AJCL 493.

Lang, J. Temple, 'Community anti-trust law; compliance and enforcement' (1981) 18 CML Rev 235.

Lang, J. Temple, 'The Powers of the Commission to order Interim Measures in Competition Cases' (1981) 18 CML Rev 49.

Lang, J. Temple, 'Community Constitutional Law: Article 5 EEC Treaty' (1990) 27 CML Rev 645.

Lang, J. Temple, 'The Duties of National Courts under the Constitutional Law of the European Community' Dominic Lasok lecture, 1987.

Lasok, P., '*Francovich* overrules *Bourgoin*: State Liability for Breach of Community Law' [1992] ICCLR 186.

Laws, The Hon Sir J., 'Judicial Remedies and the Constitution' (1994) 57 MLR 213.

Laws, Sir J., 'Is the High Court the Guardian of Fundamental Constitutional Rights'? [1993] PL 59.

Lester, A., 'Fundamental Human Rights: the UK Isolated' [1984] PL 46.

Lester, A., 'English Judges as Law-Makers' [1993] PL 269.

Lewis, C. & Moore, S., 'Duties Directives and Damages in European Community Law' [1993] PL 151.

MacCormick, N., 'Beyond the Sovereign State' (1993) 56 MLR 1.

Mackenzie Stuart, 'The European Communities and the Rule of Law' (Hamlyn Lecture) London, Stevens, 1977.

Mancini, G., 'The Making of a Constitution for Europe' (1989) 26 CML Rev 594.

Mancini, G. & Keeling, D., 'From *CILFIT* to *ERT*: The Constitutional Challenge facing the European Court' (1992) 12 YEL.

Mancini, G. & Keeling, D., 'Democracy and the European Court of Justice' (1994) 57 MLR 175.

Oliver, P., 'Enforcing Community Rights in the English Courts' (1987) 50 MLR 881.

Oliver, P., 'Interim Measures: some Recent Developments' (1992) 29 CML Rev 7.

Pipe, G., 'Exemplary Damages after *Camelford*' (1994) 57 MLR 91.

Plaza, Martin, 'Furthering the Effectiveness of EC Directives and the Judicial Protection of Individual Rights Thereunder' [1994] ICLQ 26.

Public Law Project 'Judicial Review in Perspective: the Future of Judicial Review' 1993.

Robertson, A., 'Effective Remedies in EEC Law before the House of Lords?' (1993) 109 LQR 27.

Ross, M., 'Beyond *Francovich*' (1993) 56 MLR 55.

Schermers, H., 'The European Community Bound by Fundamental Human Rights' (1990) 27 CML Rev 249.

Schockweiler, 'Le Régime de la Responsabilité Extra-Contractuelle du fait d'Actes Juridiques dans la Communauté Européenne [1990] RTDE 26.

Schwartze, J., 'The Administrative Law of the Community and the Protection of Human Rights' (1986) 23 CML Rev 401.

Schwartze, J., 'Tendencies Towards a Common Administrative Law of Europe' (1991) 16 EL Rev 3.

Schwehr, B. & Brown, P., 'Legitimate Expectations snuffed out?' [1991] PL 163.

Shaw, J., 'European Community Judicial Method: its Application to Sex Discrimination Law (1990) 19 ILJ 228.

Steiner, J., 'How to Make the Action Fit the Case: Domestic Remedies for Breach of EEC Law' (1987) 12 EL Rev 102.

Steiner, J., 'From Direct Effects to *Francovich*: Shifting Means of Enforcement of Community Law (1993) 18 EL Rev 3.

Slynn, Lord, 'The Court of Justice of the European Communities' (1984) 33 ICLQ 409.

Swadling, W., Administrative Law [1992] *All ER Annual Review* 255.

Szyszczak, E., on *Emmott v Minister for Social Welfare* (1992) 29 CML Rev 604.

Tanney, A., 'Procedural Exclusivity in Administrative Law' [1994] PL 51.

Tatham, A., 'The Effect of Community Directives in France' [1991] ICLQ 907.

Toth, A., 'Non-contractual Liability of the European Community', Chapter 1 'Non-contractual Liability in the European Communities' Ed Schermers, Heukel and Mead, Nijhoff, 1988.

Usher, J., 'The Imposition of Sanctions for Breaches of Community Law' 1992 RIDE Report.

Van Gerven, W., 'Non-contractual Liability of Member States, Community Institutions and Individuals for Breaches of Community Law with a view to a Common Law for Europe' (1994) 1 *Maastricht J of Eur and Comp Law* 6.

Vesterdorf, B., 'Complaints concerning Infringements of Competition Law within the Context of the European Community' (1994) 31 CMLRev 77.

Wade, Sir W., 'The Crown — old Platitudes and new Heresies' [1992] NLJ 1275.

Weatherill, S., 'National Remedies and Equal Access to Public Procurement' (1990) 10 YEL 244,

Weiler, J., 'Eurocracy and Distrust: Some Questions concerning the Role of the European Court of Justice in the Protection of Fundamental Human Rights within the Legal Order of the European Communities' (1986) 61 *Washington Law Review* 1103.

Weiler, J., 'Journey to an Unknown Destination: a Retrospective and Prospective of the European Court of Justice in the Area of Political Integration' (1993) 31 JCMS 417.

Wilmars, Mertens de J., 'The Caselaw of the Court of Justice in relation to the Review of the Legality of Economic Policy in Mixed-Economy Systems' [1982] LIEI 1.

Wils, W., 'Concurrent Liability of the Community and a Member State' (1992) 17 EL Rev 191.

Woolf, Rt Hon LJ, 'Public Law — Private Law: Why the Divide? A Personal View' [1986] PL 220.

Woolf, Rt Hon LJ, 'Judicial Review: a possible Programme for Reform?' [1992] PL 221.

Woolf, Rt Hon LJ, 'Protection of the Public: a New Challenge' Hamlyn Lecture Series (1990).

Wyatt, D., 'European Community Law and Public Law in the United Kingdom' in Markesinis (ed) *The Gradual Convergence* (OUP, 1994).

Index